Whatever you say I am

Whatever y

ANTHONY BOZZA

ou say I am

THE LIFE AND TIMES OF EMINEM

CORGI BOOKS

WHATEVER YOU SAY I AM
A CORGI BOOK: 0 552 15095 9

Originally published in Great Britain by Bantam Press,
a division of Transworld Publishers

PRINTING HISTORY
Bantam edition published 2003
Corgi edition published 2004

13 5 7 9 10 8 6 4 2

Photo research: Lindsay Goldenberg with Tara Canova

Set in 11/16pt Berling by
Falcon Oast Graphic Art Ltd.

Corgi Books are published by Transworld Publishers,
61–63 Uxbridge Road, London W5 5SA,
a division of The Random House Group Ltd,
in Australia by Random House Australia (Pty) Ltd,
20 Alfred Street, Milsons Point, Sydney, NSW 2061, Australia,
in New Zealand by Random House New Zealand Ltd,
18 Poland Road, Glenfield, Auckland 10, New Zealand
and in South Africa by Random House (Pty) Ltd,
Endulini, 5a Jubilee Road, Parktown 2193, South Africa.

Printed and bound in Great Britain by
Cox & Wyman Ltd, Reading, Berkshire.

Papers used by Transworld Publishers are natural, recyclable products made from wood
grown in sustainable forests. The manufacturing processes conform to the
environmental regulations of the country of origin.

To Marshall Bruce Mathers III. For his life as he's lived it and as he's told it, and everything that he's changed on the way.

Contents

Acknowledgments

Without the aid, encouragement, conversation, work, and inspiration of these people, this book would not be. Thanks to my editor, Carrie Thornton, for the Jedi mind tricks she employed to understand me and to keep me on track and as on time as she could. To Trisha Howell and Patty Bozza (no relation) for their calm and patience with me. Jim Fitzgerald for his sage edit adages, and everyone at the Carol Mann Agency for their assistance and representation. My circle of friends, peers and sounding boards were essential to my process, particularly Joseph Patel, Tanya Selvaratnam, Jon Caramanica and Matt Diehl—thank you many times for your insight and empathy. I thank Lindsay Goldenberg for her tireless support, research assistance, observations, patience, love, and for believing in me. To my mother and step-father for the pep talks and advice, respectively, and for collectively keeping me in touch with the tastes of "the aged." Unbeknownst to my editor, my father and stepmother provided several necessary work breaks; I thank you, she doesn't. Thanks to the J. Baker family, nuclear and extended, of Minneapolis, for their prayers and votes of confidence. They are an invaluable asset to that fine city. I would like to thank Eli 5Stone for transforming my stream-of-consciousness ramblings on the polarity of good and evil, shadow and light, and Eminem and Marshall Mathers into the arresting (no pun intended) illustration at the start of this book. I also thank André from OutKast for music as intelligent as his opinions, Dave Marsh for being as cool as I'd hoped he'd be, and everyone interviewed in these pages, artist, critic, or other. I am indebted to Eminem for sharing his passion, conviction, and vision, and to him and Paul Rosenberg for the preference they've shown me over the years, a proximity without which this book would not be possible. Thank you, too, to Jann Wenner for founding *Rolling Stone* and to former managing editor Bob Love for promoting me—two undeniable stepping-stones in the creation of this work.

I'd like to welcome y'all to the eminem show

Introduction

I saw *8 Mile* the day it came out, on November 11, 2002, among a crowd of my fellow New Yorkers, all of us dropping our ten bucks into a pot that by Monday added up to nearly $55 million, the second biggest opening weekend for an R-rated film in history (the title-holder in that category, for now, remains *Hannibal*, a film that played in more theaters than *8 Mile*). The audience that evening was a true cross-section of New York City: black, white, Hispanic, Asian, young, and middle-aged. Some were heavy into hip-hop; some were hooked on pop and MTV; some were drawn by the media buzz; and others—two Goths, a group of metal heads, and a gray-haired couple with a whiff of academia to them—just looked curious. There was a tangible anticipation in the air. I felt as if I were not in line to see a Hollywood feature, but among the cultish generation-spanning devotees of Kiss, Neil Diamond, Tom Jones or James Brown, waiting at a convention or outside of a record store, hoping to get an autograph.

I like to show up early for a film, but even arriving an hour ahead of schedule I was far back in the line. Whether it was to get a jump on Monday's water-cooler talk, to decide if the controversial rapper deserved the Oscar nod the press had speculated, to see what hipsters called the best hip-hop movie since *Wild Style*, or to find the key that would decipher fact from fiction in the canon of Marshall Mathers, we had all lined up to see what we'd see. I had my own ideas, too. I saw the film as an evolution, not so much for Eminem as it was for the cult of celebrity. To me, the film wasn't an indication that he was trying to launch a J. Lo-like "all-media" career (music, film, plain old fame), contrary to a claim I'd hear from people who really hadn't looked that closely, and I was sure that no matter how great Eminem was in *8 Mile* and how many scripts were stuffed in his mailbox at the moment, this might be his only acting credit. What occupied my mind that day was whether or not he knew how he had turned America on its ass, whether he realized how he had our culture—the parts he liked and the parts he didn't—by the balls, and whether he let himself, when he was alone, with no one to see, be happy about it. I wondered if it scared him that everything he rapped about came true.

I took my place behind three girls who looked like they'd take home the prize in any *Sex in the City* trivia contest. I wasn't surprised that they'd see *8 Mile*, but I was surprised that they'd brave the hubbub of opening night. I listened to them debate about Marshall's sexiness and how his celebrated acting ability affected that coefficient. "I used to hate Eminem," one said. "I just thought he was disgusting." I wondered if she'd heard any of his songs before she had decided that she hated him or had heard any of them now that she had changed her mind. One of the other girls voiced my thoughts: "Do you guys have any of his CDs?" They all replied in the negative, though they planned to stop at Virgin Records for the *8 Mile* soundtrack after the show. "I love that 'Lose Yourself' song," one said. "It's like hearing the *Rocky* theme or something—you just want to kick ass!"

Behind me a group of teenage boys bustled in place and hooted when the line started moving into the theater. They discussed where on the Internet to best get a free MP3 copy of the *8 Mile* soundtrack and where they had downloaded "Lose Yourself." They debated whether Brittany Murphy was hot or not and whether her character was a caricature of Eminem's on-again, off-again love, Kim. "Nah," one of them said, "she's supposed to be Christina Aguilera." I had to laugh with them, as they evoked one of Eminem's enemies.

I was as eager as anyone there to see how closely the real life of the rapper wove its way into the script and how a persona swathed in rumor and controversy was defined against a Hollywood re-creation. Everyone around me knew that Eminem's story occupied the center of the film—just like he inhabited the core of our collective American thought at that moment. Like them, I'd come to see how much of his life he bled onto the celluloid. Unlike them, I had an unfair advantage.

I had been in a trailer with Eminem, not on-set in Detroit or at a video shoot in L.A., but in a suburban trailer park forty minutes outside of his hometown back in 1999. It was at the end of a long day shadowed by the looming gray clouds that roam Midwestern skies from September through May. We had spent the afternoon and evening on a driving tour of Detroit, Eminem acting as tour guide, showing me the places that formed and malformed him: his high school, the home where he grew up—the one that two years later was reproduced for *The Marshall Mathers LP stage show*. We passed the stretch of 8 Mile Road in front of the Bel-Air Shopping Center where he was chased by a carload of black guys he'd flipped off. He was beaten right out of his clothes. He had thought it was for his LL-Cool-J-Troop sneakers at the time, which were one of the most expensive models on the market. His mother told me later how he was dropped off, bruised and bleed-ing, in his underwear by a trucker who had intervened. We ate at Gilbert's Lodge, the restaurant where he'd worked as a dish-washer and cook for five years. Rolling through the byways of his past, Eminem was the calmest I'd seen him in the days we'd spent together. He told me the stories of the scenery around us—tales more sad than happy—in heartfelt, heart-broken, matter-of-fact tones. He relived his life for my benefit as a tourist in his own past, as engaged in the telling as I was in the learning.

I was there with him to write my first cover story for *Rolling Stone*. It became the first national glossy coverage on Eminem and remains the most thorough chronicle of his upbringing, until (and if) Eminem decides to tell us all the secrets he's kept to him-self. That first *Rolling Stone* cover, which was meant to feature a naked Eminem holding a lit stick of dynamite over his manhood, made history for us both: it increased my profile as a writer and helped Eminem reach a new dimension of success—whether he was ready for it or not. Our journey in 1999 ended in a snowy trailer park, but it began in New York in the bathroom at his manager's office, where I met Eminem by accident just after he'd finished throwing up a fifth of Bacardi and a slice of pizza. It was all he'd eaten that day but was only an appetizer for what was to follow: three club appearances spiced with four ecstasy caps, chased with ginger ale.

Cruising from Staten Island back to Manhattan that night, Eminem was a different kind of tour guide. Riding a high that would floor most people, he was a lyrical Tasmanian devil, spitting couplets at all of us—his manager (Paul Rosenberg), DJ Stretch Armstrong, collaborator Royce Da 5'9", and a few others—that caused combustive laughter, jaw-gaping awe, or, often, red-faced embarrassment for the subject of his well-aimed darts. He was a living, breathing, drinking, falling, and reeling Slim Shady that night. His energy was almost tangible, as if you could see his synapses firing. The bits of stimuli before him flooded into his dilated pupils, coursed over his brain, and were spit back out at us, redefined in rhymes, jibes and insults impossible to rebut. He commanded the room, the limo, the after-party, wherever we were, not because we, his entourage, were a doting audience—in fact, there were many wits in the bunch—it was because no one could touch him.

At that time, "My Name Is" got more airtime on MTV than Carson Daly, but Eminem was still fairly strapped for cash. His New York appearances had been booked months before, when the rapper was still a broke, underground phenom—the White Shadow of the vinyl and mixtape world. That's where I'd first heard him on "Five Star Generals," the B-Side to Shabaam

Sahdeeq's twelve-inch "Sound Clash," and I was far more impressed than I'd been when I heard his debut LP, 1996's *Infinite*. He was an able rhymer in '96, but he wasn't angry, fed up, or at his wits' end. He was just trying to fit in; just rhyming intricate words because he could. The recordings of his freestyles on Sway and Tech's *Wake Up Show* (where he was named freestyler of the year in 1997), as well as the first version of "Just Don't Give a Fuck," made their way around—so far around as to reach me at *Rolling Stone*—and were something else. Eminem sounded like a drug-fiending Clive Barker creation covering the Beastie Boys' *Licensed to Ill*.

That night in New York, Eminem played an all-ages show on Staten Island, won over a black hip-hop crowd in Manhattan, and at four in the morning entertained a club of models, wannabe models, and all those they attracted. Eminem was as fucked up as anyone I've seen with a microphone outside of a wedding, and he killed 'em across the board.

That New York trip was scenes from a life not quite his; it was still like a life on TV, the life Eminem was about to own. He'd soon be under the scrutiny of the music industry, America, and the world; but back home in Detroit, it was business as usual, which meant that Eminem didn't even have a home. He'd been staying with his friends, or his mother, until she moved away temporarily. When he signed his record deal, he'd bought his mother's trailer from her, out in what he called "hickville bumfuck," because his daughter, Hailie Jade, liked it. His mother left Detroit for her native St. Joseph, Missouri, because of some trouble with the state of Michigan. Apparently she'd allowed Eminem's half brother,

Nathan, then about ten years old, to skip too many days of school (the legal limit in Michigan is one hundred). According to Debbie, she kept him at home for his own good because of bias and bullying. She'd lost custody of him but, after months of appeals and fighting through red tape, had won him back and promptly left town.

After the night of shows and after we'd missed a few planes, I spent the flight talking to Eminem while everyone around us slept. We broke down his broken home, his mother, his grandmother, and the family history that is now the stuff of lyrics. He was very different during that quiet time, as he was on the driving tour of his hometown and as he always is one-on-one. He expressed himself thoughtfully, without boasts or poses. He's nothing if not kinetic, but it's a quick, often subtle switch from Shady to Eminem, from Eminem to Marshall, and back again. It seems to happen as soon as you (or he, maybe) think he's settled into one of them too long. The real Marshall Mathers, the one I met before the fame and have seen less of since, is the most interesting side of him—he's angry and sensitive, shy and curious. The real Marshall is who America is really consumed with. He's a whole new paradigm of the white male: talented, humble, proud, mad, frustrated, hateful, and capable of compassion. At his best and worst, Eminem embraces the contradictions at the heart of our society.

It might have been his hangover, or it might have been my empathy and enthusiasm, but Eminem was relieved that he could relate to me, and he told me as much as he'd told any journalist, at first—to the healthy dismay of his eavesdropping manager. I can

17

only guess, but I think it was somewhere in the air between New York and Detroit that Eminem decided to let me be the one journalist he'd arrange to have interview his mother. It was a coup, the Holy Grail found before the search began. The honor did not come without responsibility. For several months after the story was published, Eminem's mom, then called Debbie Mathers-Briggs, would phone me. Those talks were long, strange, and upsetting, some of the saddest speeches I've heard from anyone. We'd chat about Marshall as a child; and, from my vantage point on the outside, her recollections sounded like tales of a family making do with what they had and finding happiness in their shared struggle. She would ask me why Marshall hated her now and why he was doing what he was doing to her. She stopped calling after she filed her legendary lawsuit against her son and, I assume, heard that the tape of my initial interview with her would be filed by the defense as evidence, should the case come to trial.

By the time we had wrapped that first session up in Detroit, it was late and Eminem, Hailie Jade, Kim, Paul, Larry Solters (Eminem's first publicist) and I were in a van humming along the frozen highway to hickville bumfuck. Well past the townships of Warren and St. Claire Shores, where Marshall spent plenty of time earning the minimum wage and miming Tupac and the Beastie Boys in his bedroom mirror, everyone began to nod off, Hailie first, Paul second. I was tired, too, and the low din of the engine and road, which drowned out the third or fourth go-round of *The Slim Shady LP*, did little to help me stay conscious. I had been a sponge all day, absorbing the experience out of an interest well past professional obligation. Eminem sat on the bench seat in front of me. He had barely slept for three days. He sat erect, staring at the passing road, blinking, thinking, and flicking his hand to the beat. He seemed very far away. Looking back, I see that moment and that night as the final calm before the storm to come for him. As I've followed his career since 1999, spent time with him personally, and interviewed him again and again, I've seen the effect that that storm has had on him.

This book is not so much a biography as it is snapshots and bill-boards: captured moments I've experienced amidst the changing backdrop of Eminem's life and career. The narrative tales I've selected to start each chapter tell the story of a time and place and of a man, Marshall Mathers, that I've come to know from our first meeting in 1999 to the present day. The chapters that follow are an analysis, as much of America as they are of Eminem; as much a portrait of a society as they are of the undercurrents of one man's character. Eminem's life has forked since I first met him; much of it is no longer his, as he is no longer a person but a symbol to so many. Expectations, responsibilities, and the tumult of his life's last four years have made being Eminem more complex, but underneath it all, at his core, he is the same in my opinion and his desires are simple: he lives for hip-hop and his daughter, nothing more.

I've always felt that to understand anyone you must forget yourself and meet them, as much as you possibly can, on their own terms. Go to where they're most comfortable; show them, if you do, that you see what they see, and there's a chance that they'll reveal their true selves. For Eminem, the superstar rapper, the toast of Hollywood circa 2003, his preferred turf is still as humble as the white T-shirts he wears. He relies on what works for him: bending words to his will, honing double-rhymed structures to convey what life has dealt him, ultimately to undo it, at least for the length of a song. His lyrics bite, cut, jab, and burn with an urgency that few artists harness. He uses rap music but he speaks a universal language, the same language of experience, hardship, and humor heard in the blues, jazz, country, and folk, in literature and in stand-up comedy, anywhere a story, through passion, becomes real in the retelling. Marshall Bruce Mathers III, born in Kansas City, raised in Detroit, elevates his life to art. Art is many things, but when it is true, anyone, from anywhere, at any time, can see it and feel it and understand the emotion beneath it, even if they don't speak the language. If the feeling is pure, art can lead the whole world down the artist's rabbit hole, at least for a minute. If that art is a song, everyone hears the message, even if they don't like the words.

This looks like a job for me

1. The evolution of eminem

It is March 1999, and it is cold in Detroit, the kind of cold that freeze-dries sound. Snow piled in banks frames the sides of the road and grows higher the farther the avenues ripple out from the center of the city. The roads here are small highways, just two lanes each way. Far from downtown, off the interstate, the roads narrow. The lights are fewer and the trees are taller. Standing not far from one of these byways, ankle deep in snow, I hear the woosh of a lone passing car. Behind me, the trailer park is silent and as still as a morgue. It is two in the morning. In front of me, a blond guy in baggy clothes trudges up the stairs of a trailer and reads the eviction notice on his front door.

"We took care of that one," Paul Rosenberg says. "Don't worry about it."

The blond guy doesn't answer, he just rips it down and opens the unlocked door.

"He doesn't lock it?" I ask.

"No," Paul says. "They've had so much shit stolen over the years, he doesn't give a fuck anymore."

The double-wide trailer is warm, and I sit on the couch. Before me, on the floor in front of the TV, is a much smaller couch. A groggy, swirly-haired little girl curls up on it while her mother readies her bed. Above her on the wall are glossy photos in black frames: two of Eminem and Dr. Dre dressed as patient and analyst for the "My Name Is" video shoot, the other a solo shot of Dr. Dre with a scrawled note that reads, "Dear Marshall, Thanks for the support, asshole" (mimicking Slim Shady's autograph to a fan working at White Castle in "My Name Is"). The CD rack holds Tupac Shakur, Snoop Dogg, Mase, Babyface, Luther Vandross, and Esthero. On a wall by the kitchen hangs a photocopied list titled "Commitments for Parents." The first line reads, "I will give my child space to grow, dream, succeed, and sometimes fail."

"My mother moved back to Kansas City, so I bought this trailer from her," Eminem says, sitting on the couch. "Hailie feels really comfortable here, so I took over the payments. I'm paying rent for no reason because I'm never here anymore. But when I am, I need a place to stay."

Kim Scott lifts their daughter from her nest and takes her into the second bedroom. Hailie's bed is dwarfed by a mountain of toys, clothes, and boxes. Kim soothes her in hushed tones. It has been a long day that began tonight; a driving tour not sanctioned by the city's board of tourism, through the Detroit streets and neighborhoods where Marshall Mathers spent the better part of the past twenty-six years.

"Man, driving through town tonight brought back a lot of

memories," Marshall says, lowering his voice. "I've been through a lot of shit, man. If I sit and think back on it, it's really fucked up. I mean, all my life has been fucked up."

"Now that you're out of that life, how much does the past bother you? Do you feel sorry that you grew up that way or just unlucky?" I ask.

"No, man," he says. "It's just my life, that's it. When you're living in some fucked-up shit, it doesn't really seem that fucked up to you when you're in it. All you think is 'What am I gonna do now?' Day to day, I'd have to think about what I was gonna do. Even though I had a job for three years, I wasn't making enough money to pay any bills. Me and my girl would get a house with my daughter; we could never stay more than three months. I would try to pay rent, always get behind, and we'd get evicted."

He walks to the kitchen to throw the eviction notice, still crumpled in his hand, into the trash. "The only houses I was able to afford were in the gutter slums of Detroit," he says. "I lived on Fairport on this shitty block and we had this crackhead that kept breaking in. Me and Kim and Hailie caught him one time. Just after Hailie was born, we walked in the house and there was a crackhead in there and all of our shit was gone. We had got robbed at the house we had been in before this one—cleaned out. So when we walked in and I see the TV gone and I'm like, 'What the fuck!' I start screaming, I set Hailie down, and then I hear all these footsteps coming down the stairs. Oh fuck! So I grab Hailie and run outside and Kim runs out. I shut the door and we're out on the lawn, wondering what to do. It was only one dude, but he was coming so fast he sounded like a bunch of people."

He rubs his eyes at the memory. "The guy walks out the back door holding a wrench or something and he sees us out there and he's like, 'I seen 'em! They went that way.' So I didn't run after him directly, I ran through the house and grabbed the first thing I could find, a frying pan off the stove, and I came through the back door after him. He ran, and I tell you, man, this motherfucker was so cracked out he hopped over this fucking fence that was huge. He just hopped right over it, and I couldn't get up anywhere near the top. That whole time was fucked."

Kim closes Hailie's bedroom door and sits beside her boyfriend on the couch. He looks at her sidelong. "Remember the crack-head?" he says through a smirk at the recollection.

"He left ashes all over the fucking floor, had lunch, and left," she says with the kind of annoyance reserved for inefficient salesclerks.

"Yo, this guy felt so comfortable stealing there," he says, shaking his head. "He broke in three times, and the last time he did, he made a sandwich and left the fucking peanut butter and bread on the counter. And he left his coat there."

"Marshall pissed on it and I took one of Hailie's shitty diapers and wiped it all over it and left it on the porch," she says.

"And he fucking came back," he says. "We could never catch that guy. By the time he was done, he'd taken every fucking thing we had except the couches and the beds. This motherfucker took the pillows, pillowcases, clothes, everything you can imagine. He even cleaned out our silverware."

I look around at the brand-new television, the VCR, and the couch we are sitting on, all obviously bought in the past six months, and I realize that Marshall already lives the entertainer's life. He won't feel afloat existing in hotels and out of suitcases from now on. He has known only flux for the past twenty years, moving from home to home, living in different cities, changing schools, and working more than he didn't, at one job or another, since he was fifteen. His anchors in this world are here in his mother's double-wide: his daughter, Detroit, Kim, and the pen and pad on the counter. There are no mementos of Marshall's childhood here; they exist in his mind, caught in the chaos he churns into words. Those mental pictures have sold 500,000 albums in just two weeks.

It is later than late now and time for me to go. Kim gets up drowsily and Marshall puts his arm around her. I look around the trailer once more, knowing I'll never see it again. Soon enough, neither will they. A few weeks later, they will move in with Kim's mother; some of her neighbors, excited to see Eminem on their block, won't realize he is actually Marshall, Kim's boyfriend, the one who has been stopping by off and on since he was sixteen. Just two weeks after the release of a debut that will go on to sell three million copies in one year, garner two Grammys, and inspire a call to censorship by the editor in chief of *Billboard*, that Marshall, the one who cooked and cleaned at Gilbert's Lodge for his minimum wage, is already gone.

The cold air wakes me as I crunch through the snow on the stairs. Marshall stands in the doorway, Kim at his side, one of Hailie's blankets in his hand. He nods a good-bye. Standing there, the next rap superstar doesn't look dazzling. He looks weary, wary, and content. He's as home as he can be.

IN 1996, MARSHALL BRUCE MATHERS III HAD ALREADY CHANGED HIS

stage name from his initials, M & M, to their phonetic synonym, Eminem, for obvious legal reasons. If M&M/Mars had sued him, it would have been hilarious: he was barely getting by on the five-bucks-and-change minimum wage he received hourly for washing dishes and cooking at Gilbert's Lodge in St. Claire Shores, a suburb of Detroit. At the time, he took home in a month what a top corporate lawyer makes in half an hour. That amount wasn't even enough to cover the costs of pressing *Infinite*, his first independent release. Yet his rap career was under way. Mathers had been signed to an outfit called FBT Productions for four years. He still is, more out of kinship than contract—and, as of 2003, FBT claims production credits on thirty of the fifty-eight songs on Eminem's three major-label albums; his mentor Dr. Dre's count is twelve. FBT is the Detroit production duo Mark and Jeff Bass, two brothers from Oak Park, one of Detroit's more racially integrated areas. The Basses had been playing music and writing songs together since they were kids, their first paid gig coming when they were only seven (Mark) and eleven (Jeff), recording a Greyhound Lines jingle. The Basses grew up tough white kids who felt more at home in black social circles. They've seen their share of street fights—one of which claimed Mark's right eye, necessitating a glass one. As they tried to establish a name for themselves as producers, the pair worked as inexpensive remixers for hire in the late eighties and early nineties, on cuts like the B-52s' "Love Shack" and Red Hot Chili Peppers' "Give It Away." By this time, Mark was well into hip-hop, but his brother remained skeptical. His opinion didn't change when he met the fifteen-year-old white kid his brother was eager to work with. Mark had found this new muse while in his car listening to a group of teens rapping on the radio, on an open-mike show hosted by a DJ called Lisa Lisa. One of them was Marshall Mathers, the one Mark ended up speaking to when he later phoned the studio. Bass invited Mathers down to the brothers' modest basement studio that night. When Mathers arrived at 4:00 A.M., he freestyled with a pair of friends. It was the first time he'd ever seen a studio. The Basses then started cutting tracks with Mathers, watching him experiment with rhyme styles, from laid back to rapid-fire, until he found himself.

Mathers lived with his mother on the East Side of Detroit at the time and spent his nights after work writing rhymes until the early morning. He honed an even-flowing style laced with a gift of rhythm and a preference for intricate vocabulary inspired more by the joy of rhyming words than by weaving a narrative. He began writing songs for an album called *Infinite*, one of the first recorded in the Bass brothers' new studio, the Bassment, in 1996. The Bass brothers borrowed $1,500 from their mom to press 500 copies of the album, signing Mathers to the label they had created, WEB Entertainment. The record landed in local Detroit stores and in the hands of hip-hop radio programmers—and was unanimously ignored.

Infinite chronicles Eminem's early days, his dreams of rap superstardom that flourished while he tried to pay the bills. While he was writing his first record, Mathers's longtime girl-friend, Kim Scott, became pregnant and gave birth to Hailie Jade Scott at Christmas in 1995. The album is laced, in skits and lyrics, with his anxiety about raising his daughter on limited funds, his hope to leave her with half a million dollars, and a fantasy future full of national tours and airplay. Though prophetic, *Infinite* yielded finite results.

"There was a year after *Infinite* where every rhyme I started writing got angrier and angrier," Eminem recalls. "That was from the feedback I got off that album. Motherfuckers was like, 'You sound like Nas and AZ,' 'You're a white boy, what the fuck are you rapping for? Why don't you go into rock and roll?' All types of shit like that started pissing me off." Eminem's frustration at being taken for a poser enraged him. He'd become a staple at open-mike nights at local institutions like designer Maurice Malone's Hip-Hop Shop, a weekly scene in Detroit where MCs battled or just passed the mike. With nothing left to lose, Eminem's battle riffs grew darker, grittier, more nihilistic. His rhymes grew crazed, drug obsessed, and more belligerent than ever. He began to win competitions consistently and became a fixture, someone to beat, as local MCs started coming to the open-mike nights to battle the white boy and make a name for themselves, whether they won or lost to him.

In 1996, just before Christmas and Hailie's first birthday, Eminem was fired from his job at Gilbert's Lodge. He was rehired six months later, this time for a few months, and then fired again, almost exactly to the year. In those interims, he worked where he could, mostly at a Little Caesars Pizza chain. It became so tough to make ends meet while raising Hailie that Eminem stopped rapping and writing for a time. Kim and Marshall fought bitterly, breaking up and making up with schizophrenic regularity.

Eventually Kim moved back in with her family, who had long dis-
approved of Marshall and made it difficult for him to see his
daughter. It was his lowest point, a time when Marshall Mathers
saw suicide as a viable option, nearly ending his journey before it
began.

By this time, Eminem had already met Paul Rosenberg, an
attorney and onetime rapper he met at the Hip-Hop Shop.
Rosenberg had rapped in the early nineties under the name Paul
Bunyan, with a group called Rhythm Cartel. Rhythm Cartel
performed at Detroit spots like the Rhythm Kitchen, another
Maurice Malone-backed party. It took place for a time in Stanley's
Mania Café, a Chinese restaurant that cleared out the tables but
left the takeout counter open while rappers passed the mike,
ciphering impromptu jams on a sound system carted in each
week by a group of dreadlocked promoters. The party, which
Rosenberg says is the best hip-hop party he's seen anywhere,
lasted for about three years, constantly changing venues. Forty-
ounce Colt 45s, not Cristal champagne, were the toast of the
times. There were more dreads than diamonds, and the competition was kept on the mike and off the street. Rosenberg met
Eminem's longtime partner Proof at one of these parties and
Eminem actually saw Rosenberg perform there before they met.
At the time, Rhythm Cartel, Eminem, a transplanted East Coast
rapper named Bukari, and DJ Houseshooz were the only white
regulars to speak of in the Detroit scene.

Proof introduced Rosenberg to Eminem one night at the Hip-
Hop Shop. "The first time I met him," Rosenberg says, "Proof had
him at the Hip-Hop Shop late in the day, after all the freestylers

had cleared out. He had him sort of audition for me, although I don't think Em knew that's what Proof was doing. He just had Em up there rapping by himself over instrumentals, and not too many people were around. I was just checking him out and I thought he was really good. The day we really met was when he had just started selling his *Infinite* album. All his friends were really excited because he had product, you know, which was a rare thing. And his was fairly professional looking compared to what other people's homemade product was looking like, so he was excited. He was in a battle that day and he won." At the time, Rosenberg was in his second year in law school, pursuing a degree in music law. He had given up rapping years before, but was intent on representing Detroit's untapped talent. "I talked to Em after the battle that night, told him who I was, and he was really stand-offish and shy, as he usually is when he first meets somebody. I just got his phone number and I bought his tape off him for six bucks. Best investment I ever made."

Rosenberg became a friend first, a manager-lawyer second, as he is today. Eminem's circle at the time were his classmates in rap school, the peer group with whom he honed his skills: Proof (born DeShaun Holton), Denaun Porter (a.k.a. Kon Artis), and Rufus Johnson (a.k.a. Peter S. Bizzare). Proof had made his own reputation as a battle MC, an omnipresent figure at Detroit open-mike nights. By the mid-nineties he'd begun hosting the Saturday-night proceedings at Maurice Malone's Hip-Hop Shop. Proof was Eminem's mentor and sponsor on the scene, encouraging him to rap at events where Eminem would otherwise be a spectator, banking his own name on Eminem's skills. Eminem began to write and rap with Proof and the others, throwing down at the Hip-Hop Shop and other local venues, such as St. Andrew's Hall, the Rhythm Kitchen, and anywhere else they had the chance. Proof and Kon Artis, whom Eminem approached for production assistance on *Infinite*, gathered the rap troop that now call themselves D12, short for Detroit Twelve and Dirty Dozen. Proof's goal in creating D12 was to form a band of MCs in a loose collective like the East Coast's Wu-Tang Clan. He approached the rappers he felt were skilled but were stylistically on the outskirts of the Detroit scene. The D12 concept evolved further on a car trip back from a rap convention in New York, when Proof floated the idea that each rapper in the group create a dark-half alter ego to allow each of them to experiment with hardcore styles unlike their own. "The whole thing in D12 was to have a personality where you would just say anything," Proof says. "You just didn't give a fuck. Your persona was almost like a mask to hide behind, know what I'm sayin'? We all took our different identities, and Em took Slim Shady and he ran with it. He took it way more serious than all of us, that motherfucker." With each member of the group in a new guise, they wrote the most abrasive raps they could think of, a cocktail of serial-killer-ology, black comedy, and ultraviolence.

Eminem was the last member of D12 to create his alter ego because the summer of 1997 was a rough one for Marshall Mathers. He worked a lot when he had a job, he drank a lot, he fought a lot, and one ordinary morning found himself on the path to his dream. Slim Shady became his D12 character, and Eminem immediately created a list of words to rhyme with it. Slim Shady became his avenging angel, a figure he pictured as a mummy with its wrists slit; a fiend without feeling and beyond life, death, or caring; a monster freak who only knew how to say and do what no one was supposed to.

"I was taking a shit, swear to God," Eminem says about the morning he thought up Slim Shady. "I was sitting on the toilet and *boom*, the name hit me. I started thinking of all of these words I could rhyme with it. So I wiped my ass and got off the pot and went and called everybody I knew. I was like, 'Bada-boom, bada-bing, wanna go with it, or no?' Once I came up with the Shady concept, I wrote the *Slim Shady EP* in two weeks." He had found himself and he was serious about it: Eminem showed up to record what became the *Slim Shady EP* with the Bass Brothers with a $50 "Slim Shady" tattoo on his left arm, complementing the "Eminem" on his right.

The *Slim Shady EP* laid the groundwork for *The Slim Shady LP*, executive-produced by Dr. Dre and released February 23, 1999. That included seven songs, three of which made it onto Eminem's full-length major-label debut: "I Just Don't Give a Fuck," "If I Had," and "Just the Two of Us," Eminem's first murder ballad to his baby's mother, Kim. The EP has all the Slim Shady essentials: flippant nihilism, self-loathing, destruction, acute battle raps, fucked-up family pathology, and comedy, both subtle and slapstick.

Although the EP is seven songs long, two are shortened, radio-edit versions of other songs on the album. So in just five main songs are the roots of the blueprint of Eminem's success. Slim Shady is his avenger, anointed for bad behavior, but the album also hints at the three-character harmony that would soon develop in Eminem's music: Slim Shady, Marshall Mathers, and Eminem.

In 1997, Eminem and Kim Scott made their way through a few houses in drug-infested neighborhoods further into the city limits than either had ever lived. After stray bullets hit their house and chronic burglaries cleaned them out, Kim and Hailie moved in with her mother in the white suburb of Warren, while Eminem couch-surfed, eventually renting a room with a few friends in a house on 7 Mile Road. "We were paying this guy rent because his name was on the lease," Eminem recalls, "but he was keeping all the money." Everyone got evicted. "The night before I went to the Rap Olympics in L.A., I had to break into that fucking house and sleep on the floor because I didn't have anywhere else to go. No heat, no electric, everything was shut off. I woke up the next day and went to L.A. I was so fucking pissed then. I had gotten fired from Gilbert's for the second time, we got evicted, and that guy ran off—we still haven't found that motherfucker."

Paul Rosenberg, recently signed on as his manager, had been raising awareness of Eminem in New York, and met up with Wendy Day, CEO of the Rap Coalition, an influential artists' advocacy group that co-sponsored a competition for up-and-coming MCs, dubbed the Rap Olympics. When Paul met Wendy, she already knew Eminem from one of the many rap conventions he attended in the midnineties. "Wendy had met him at some music seminar in Detroit," Rosenberg recalls with a sly grin. "He used to walk around with, like, a stack of vinyl after he ran out of his tapes. He'd pressed his whole *Infinite* album onto one piece of vinyl. You're not even supposed to press vinyl when you're putting out an independent album on your own, but he did. He had this whole album on vinyl, that's how he used to shop himself around. So he gave her one when he met her." The Rap Olympics featured team competition and categories for the rappers to compete as individuals. Day wanted Eminem for her Rap Coalition team for the same reason Eminem had become a fixture in the Detroit freestyle pecking order: no one had ever seen anything quite like him before. "When he came to New York, he freestyled at one of Wendy's workshops and she added him to the team," Rosenberg says. "Our thing was great. He was going to do the team battle, but our focus was the individual battle. That battle ended up taking so long that he didn't get to compete in the team battle. Actually, the individual battle took so long that they didn't really get to finish the Rap Olympics."

By the time he reached the Olympics, Eminem was at the end of his rope, financially and spiritually. He was hungry for a break. "Right before the battle in L.A., I took him to a bar," Rosenberg says. "I said, 'I know you want to win, but if you don't, it's okay. Do your best.' My God, he was unbelievable. I was sitting in there next to this big black guy and after the first round he shouted, 'Just give it to the white boy, it's over. Just give it to the white boy.'"

"I went in there just shitting on everyone, man," Eminem says of the competition. "I had nothing to lose. I took second place and I was very unused to that. Everyone said I looked like I was ready to cry. And I was so mad. Steaming, dog. I had nowhere to live back home. The winner of Rap Olympics got, like, five hundred dollars and a Rolex. I could have used that, man. Second place got nothing."

By most reports, Eminem was defeated twice at national MC competitions in 1997 by the same man, J.U.I.C.E., a talented freestyle MC from Chicago, who took first prize away from Eminem at the Rap Olympics as well as at Scribble Jam in Cincinnati, Ohio. Many who witnessed both called it a victory for Eminem or a tie that Eminem lost to his competitor's loyal fanbase or a color bias. Many others don't even remember who won, just who was good. For his part, Paul Rosenberg remembers otherwise.

"This guy named Other-Wize beat him [at the 1997 Rap Olympics]," Rosenberg says. "I'd have to see a tape of it to see how he actually won. I think Eminem won. But it doesn't matter. He really wanted to win; he could have used the money. But I knew that, even though he didn't, it was great for us—it was exposure we could turn into something." Rosenberg was right; Eminem didn't win that battle, but he did win the war. Two Interscope assistants, Dean TK and Evan Bogart, son of deceased disco king-pin and Casablanca Records founder Neil, approached Rosenberg and Eminem after the Rap Olympics. They felt strongly about Eminem but were careful about pushing his music across the boss's desk. "We stayed in touch with them," Rosenberg says. At the time he worked as personal-injury lawyer for a firm and stayed late at the office to call labels on the West Coast on Eminem's behalf. "At some point I called the guys we knew at Interscope and was like, 'OK, we're coming to town; I'm bringing Em out and I want to set up a meeting because he's starting to get really dis-couraged.' There were a whole slew of labels flirting with it, but nobody was biting because he was white. Aside from the moderate success of 3rd Bass, there really hadn't been a success-ful, credible white rapper. They thought he was talented, but they were scared of it." This time Rosenberg's push worked: the tape made it to Jimmy Iovine, the Interscope Records president, then to Dr. Dre.

There have been many versions told of how Dr. Dre came to hear Eminem. In one Dre heard him rap on the nationally syndicated Friday-night hip-hop showcase *The Wake Up Show*, with King Tech and DJ-rapper-turned-MTV News correspondent Sway Calloway, and phoned the studio. Other variations of the story of Eminem's discovery state that either Dr. Dre, Iovine, or both approached the rapper at the end of the '97 Olympics. A third says that Dr. Dre happened upon a tape of Eminem's *Slim Shady EP* on the floor of Iovine's gym. The truth is that the night after taking second place in the Rap Olympics, Eminem freestyled on *The Wake Up Show* along with a group of rappers who had also com-peted. Dr. Dre did, in fact, hear him, and remembered Eminem's voice when Iovine handed him a tape some time afterward.

"I was at Jimmy's house and he played the tape for me," Dre says about hearing the *Slim Shady EP* for the first time. "He asked me what I thought of it and I said, 'Find him. Now.' I thought the tape was incredible, know what I'm sayin'? In my entire career in the music industry, I've never found anything from a demo tape. Usually somebody knew somebody or someone was brought up to the studio. When I heard it, I didn't even know he was white. The content turned me on more than anything, and the way he was flipping it. Dark comedy is what I call it. It was incredible, I had to meet him right away."

The Bass Brothers and Paul Rosenberg pooled some money to fund their trip to L.A. to meet Dr. Dre; the accommodations were as luxurious as Eminem's back home. "We were in some shitty-ass motel with a hard-ass cement floor," the rapper says. "When Paul told me that Dre called I was like, 'Get the fuck out of here, man.' I thought he was lying. We had gotten jerked around by so many labels by that point."

Soon after, the contracts were signed. It wasn't long before Dr. Dre introduced Eminem to the world as he'd done with Snoop Dogg about half a decade earlier (Snoop's 1993 debut, *Doggystyle*, became the first debut album to enter the national charts at number one). Though FBT would work on Eminem's debut, furnishing their services to Interscope Records, Dr. Dre would be the influential face man and public mentor, bestowing upon Eminem a flawless hip-hop credibility to silence naysayers from the start. After they broke the ice, Dr. Dre was eager to begin recording with his new apprentice. "When I met Dre I was nervous, man," Eminem says. "I was just like, 'What's up,' and looked away. I didn't know what to say to him. I didn't want to be starstruck or kiss his ass too much. I told him later that I've been a fan of his since I was little, since N.W.A. He was like, 'I didn't even think you liked my shit.' I was like, 'Dog, you're motherfuckin' Dr. Dre!' I'm just a little white boy from Detroit. I had never seen stars, let alone Dr. Dre. That shit was bananas."

"Em just couldn't believe he was sitting here and that Dre liked his music," Rosenberg says. "What else can you say? The guy's sitting in a room with Dre, and Dre is like, 'I want to fuck with you.'"

The first day they worked together, Dr. Dre and Eminem

recorded four songs in six hours. Two of them, "My Name Is" and "Role Model," made the album and distinctly defined the Slim Shady persona. They are an invitation and a warning, an arrival with a disclaimer of all that will follow. Like Snoop Dogg's "Who Am I (What's My Name)?," "My Name Is" is a hummable anthem that trademarked Eminem in just one song. "My Name Is" is nursery-rhyme catchy, a showcase of Eminem's humor over a bouncy beat built around the funky piano hook of the eclectic, openly gay, African vocalist Labi Siffre's "I Got the . . ."—ironic, considering the accusations in Eminem's near future.

"My Name Is" did more than introduce Eminem to the world, it established a tradition: the caliber and tone of the singles that would announce each of his following albums ("The Real Slim Shady" for 2000's *The Marshall Mathers LP* and "Without Me" for 2002's *The Eminem Show*). "My Name Is" set the precedent of prediction that now flows through all of Eminem's lyrics: it is a debut single from the point of view of the already famous. It is a dictated message to a huge, preexisting fan base by an artist who had barely been heard outside of his hometown.

When *The Slim Shady LP* was released on February 23, 1999, the pop-culture landscape wasn't ready. Owing to the heavy rotation "My Name Is" had gotten on radio and on MTV for nearly a month, the LP debuted at number two in the nation on TK, selling more than 300,000 copies in a week.

"When 'My Name Is' was released on MTV, his underground buzz was as big as an underground buzz could get back then," says Paul Rosenberg. "The underground has changed, but at the time you had a scene that was really anti-MTV and all of the Puff

Daddy jiggy videos. The underground wanted some real rap. These kids bought vinyl and really searched for something different than mainstream hip-hop. Eminem did a show at Tramps in New York that was completely sold out and he didn't even have an album out. And that is a pretty big deal. It was a great show. That crowd was all fans, some who had seen him perform before, some who had bought tickets just to see him. From the beginning he was an MTV staple, so that puts him automatically with the kids. It depends on where he was playing or what tour he was on, but Eminem played to a lot of different crowds."

The album holding on to number one the week *The Slim Shady LP* was released was TLC's *Fanmail*, anchored there by its mooching-men caveat, "No Scrubs." The number three spot was held by *The Miseducation of Lauryn Hill*. The spotlight for the past year had belonged to women: Celine Dion, the chest-beating diva whose chart-topping ballad "My Heart Will Go On," from the film *Titanic*, went on and on; Lauryn Hill's string of hits, "Ex-Factor," "Doo Wop (That Thing)," and "Everything Is Everything," blazed across the charts; Shania Twain's "Man! I Feel Like a Woman!" rallied for girls' nights out; and Madonna returned with *Ray of Light*. The Backstreet Boys and the Spice Girls rode atop the first wave of teen pop, the Spice Girls enjoying a pair of albums on the charts simultaneously, and both groups logging well over one hundred weeks on the Top 200 Albums list, while newcomers such as Britney Spears and *NSYNC nipped at their heels. In rap, Will Smith's *Big Willie Style*, Mase's *Harlem World*, and Puff Daddy's *No Way Out* led a celebration of all things fly and material with, in the case of Puffy and Mase, a side salad of gangsta posturing. Jay-Z and DMX represented the hip-hop streets in quality while multimillion-dollar record cartels, selling mountains of CDs, such as Master P's No Limit Records and Cash Money Records, did in quantity, yet remain virtually unnoticed by the mainstream media. Will Smith, for his part, made a point of succeeding in rap without cursing or killing in his records—a fact Eminem would point out in "The Real Slim Shady" before asserting that he couldn't do the same with an emphatic "Fuck him and fuck you, too." The rock world of the day was drowning in Pearl Jam's legacy: the insipid, introspective warblings of anonymous bands such as Matchbox 20, Creed, and Third Eye Blind. They would soon be pummeled by the sound of testosterone: the amped frat-boy rock of Limp Bizkit, the aggressive weirdness of Korn, and all those who followed.

The forty-first annual Grammy Awards celebrated the music of 1998 and were held in February 1999, weeks before the release of "My Name Is." The ceremony might well have been a wake: the acts commanding the public eye suggested a mood about to change drastically, a takeover of sensitive diversity so complete that it could only give way to the extremes of teen pop, hardcore rap, and rap-rock. The year of the woman, with females dominating nearly every major award, would be the last for some time. The Grammy for Album of the Year (among others) went to Lauryn Hill for *The Miseducation of Lauryn Hill*; Record of the Year and Pop Female Vocal was "My Heart Will Go On," by Celine Dion; Madonna won her first Grammy after sixteen years in the business for *Ray of Light*, the year's Best Pop Album; while Sheryl Crow won Rock Album of the Year for *The Globe Sessions*, and

Alanis Morissette's "Uninvited" took home Best Rock Song and Rock Female Vocal. The Beastie Boys' *Hello Nasty* took home Best Alternative Music Performance, while in the rap categories Will Smith's "Gettin' Jiggy Wit It" and Jay-Z's *Volume 2—Hard Knock Life* took home Best Solo and Best Album respectively. The top-grossing films of 1998 were *Saving Private Ryan* and *Armageddon*, while the Best Picture Oscar went to *Shakespeare in Love*. In 1998, the only hint of the coming of Slim Shady consciousness on the big screen was the politically incorrect gross-out opus *There's Something About Mary*. Just a year later, tastes sure had changed. Along with the shoo-in box-office monster of the year, *Star Wars: Episode I, The Phantom Menace*, Americans flocked to all things Shady: slapstick, violence, horror, and the pathology of the American family. The top-grossing films of 1999 were the creepy ghost story *The Sixth Sense*, *Austin Powers: The Spy Who Shagged Me*, *The Matrix*, and the gritty scarefest *The Blair Witch Project*. The Oscar for Best Picture that year went to the brilliant, dark, dysfunctional family drama *American Beauty*. The world was not only ready for Slim Shady, we were looking for him.

In the previous few years, the music world had seen too many heroes die, and with them the idealism inspired by what seemed like transformative revolutions in rock and rap. Kurt Cobain's death stopped the progress far too early, while hip-hop's reigning rappers, Tupac Shakur and Christopher Wallace (a.k.a. the Notorious B.I.G. and a.k.a. Biggie Smalls), were gunned down in their prime, just as their music could no longer be ignored by the mainstream. Tupac and Biggie Smalls did get covered, of course, like so many rappers before them, for the violence that surrounded their lives, deaths and music. In the face of such real tragedy, record companies and consumers' taste turned to the positivity of the earthy, female variety as well as the low-calorie sweetener of teen pop. By 2000, the year Eminem released *The Marshall Mathers LP* and *NSYNC released *No Strings Attached*— the album that, at 2.5 million, still holds the record for the most albums sold in one week—these two were each other's foil, the equally popular camps polarizing teen music consciousness: on one side, the coy sexuality and synchronized dance of Britney Spears and company; on the other, the bird-flipping angst of Eminem.

In 2000, the American mood was also growing skeptical of the government and the good-times high began to dissipate as the economy turned downward. The country watched as Bill Clinton renamed the Oval Office and O. J. Simpson evaded a murder charge. Eminem was a joyous irreverent Bronx cheer, be it in the face of the marketed, pre-fab talent of teen pop or the authority of and blind belief in society's leaders. It was solace to fans who found nothing for them on MTV and nothing but lies on the evening news. From the beginning, Eminem's music was as hard to ignore as a turned-on television and every bit as saturated with images. How could a generation bombarded with sound-bites and jump-cut visuals since birth not be immediately drawn to him?

The playful, vicious stylings that caught the world's attention on *The Slim Shady LP* skewed darker on *The Marshall Mathers LP*, released May 23, 2000. One week later, Eminem was arrested outside of the Hot Rocks Café, a Warren, Michigan, nightclub, for allegedly assaulting a man he caught kissing his then wife, Kim Scott. Less than twenty-four hours before that event, Eminem brandished an unloaded gun at Douglas Dail, tour manager for Insane Clown Posse, a schlocky white Detroit rock-rap group whom Eminem had mocked on stage and off for quite some time. The famous was turning infamous, as the rapper's new album too closely predicted his life.

Despite his brushes with the law and the curse of the sophomore slump (in which an artist follows an amazing debut with a rushed, less-than-stellar follow-up), Marshall Mathers thrived. On his second album, Eminem evolved into a grade-A pop instigator—the Sex Pistols' Johnny Rotten and a top-notch lyricist like Rakim rolled into one—who delved deeper into his own pathology and commented on the taste of celebrity he'd had in the past year. The snapshot of Eminem's private life hinted at on *The Slim Shady LP* grew into a detailed collage on *The Marshall Mathers LP*. Gone is the predominant mood of *The Slim Shady LP*, the gleefully violent zaniness. *The Marshall Mathers LP* is rarely as perversely upbeat. It exudes a raw darkness, at once a challenge to and defense from the eyes of the world Eminem had begun to feel on him. The antics of his debut had won him the class-clown attention he craved; for better and worse, he now had more than he needed.

The Marshall Mathers LP, more than Eminem's debut album, anticipated and assumed—and rightfully so—the fame and infamy that followed. The theme of the album isn't a closer look at Marshall Mathers the man, as the title would suggest, but an explanation, criticism, and visualization of how and why he is the most misunderstood man in America. Eminem points out his deliberately inflammatory ways but he also portrays himself, Slim Shady, and Marshall Mathers as he would soon be seen by the mainstream—as one and the same, a moral criminal, a menace in the eyes of the nation, not as an artist but as a Pied Piper whom the kids love and the parents fear. In this sense, the album is aptly titled: after its release, Marshall Mathers was the man held accountable.

The Marshall Mathers LP sold nearly two million copies in the first week of its release, nearly breaking *NSYNC's 2.25 million record. It debuted at number one, blowing Britney Spears's *Oops! . . . I Did It Again* out of the top spot it had held on and off for nearly five months. At number twenty-nine the same week was *The Slim Shady LP*, enjoying its eighty-fourth week among the Top 200 records sold in the nation. In the following two months, eight million copies of *The Marshall Mathers LP* would be sold and the mainstream media would begin to comment, realizing this wasn't a novelty. Only a year after Dylan Klebold and Eric Harris killed twelve students and one teacher in a shooting spree at Columbine High School in Littleton, Colorado, mainstream culture was still searching for scapegoats in society. People were not ready for an artist so directly confrontational as to rap about his stolen machine guns and black trenchcoats ("Remember Me?") or the sonic murder cinema of a song like "Kim." Eminem would spend the year explaining himself by blaming everyone else: parents who would rather blame entertainment than own up to their shortcomings, the media who judged an artist by his words out of context, and everyone incapable of digesting a complex piece of entertainment no more violent than an R-rated film.

Many didn't agree with him. Throughout 2000 and 2001, Eminem's concerts were regularly picketed by women's rights and gay groups, culminating in a protest outside the forty-third annual Grammy Awards, at which, to illustrate the fiction-and-reality axis in his music, Eminem performed with openly gay singer Elton John and took home three statues to match the two he won for his work on *The Slim Shady LP*.

Though Eminem was reduced to the sum of his controversies in most of the newsprint around the country in 2001, the publicity brought record sales and exposure that eventually landed his name in Congress, delivered to a committee on the tongue of Lynne Cheney, the vice-president's wife, who led a hearing on unsuitable violence in music. Despite and to some degree because of an older generation's reaction to Eminem, he became a unanimous hero to the teenage music-buying public, even those who enjoyed the teen pop acts that Eminem routinely lampooned. His singles were played on classic-rock stations, alternative-rock stations, as well as Top 40 and hip-hop stations. His disaffected stance appealed to rebels of all stripes. To mainstream teens *The Marshall Mathers LP* was to boy bands what Nirvana's *Nevermind* was to Guns N' Roses in 1991, when hair-metal bands held the top of the charts even as the Seattle trio turned rock upside down.

Eminem spoke of situations many of his fans shared—broken homes, dead-end jobs, drug overindulgence—while exploring taboo emotions many couldn't face—parental hate, gender hate, self-loathing. Eminem was the antihero who had ambushed the pop show.

By the end of 2001, Eminem had five Grammys in his trophy case and millions of albums sold worldwide. His fans were so diverse that he could carry a festival with rap-rock bands like Papa Roach on the Anger Management Tour as easily as roll with the hip-hop elite if they had organized a festival that year. He had the attention of the country—between his weapons-possession arrests, his foul-mouthed agitation, and his runaway success, even the unimpressed were watching.

Between 2000 and 2002, Eminem had lived a reality-TV life, his every move broadcast, his rhymed confessionals recorded. He touched his audience with music that is the equivalent of a cinematic, panoramic *Survivor*, *Big Brother*, and *Making of the Band* all in one—you could call it "*The Rapper*." From the first line of his first single "My Name Is," Eminem had provided a running commentary on his world, expanding the breadth of the subject matter to suit the steady increase in "viewers." Unlike other reality shows, *The Rapper*'s star makes all the creative decisions, crafting the plot of his show in the editing room without an audience vote. As usual, Eminem's elocution of the times was impeccable: America's hunger for reality TV in 2002 and 2003 was insatiable. The Roman Colosseum of bad taste mediated by Jerry Springer in the late nineties evolved into a more stylized desire to be concerned and improperly involved in the lives of strangers for amusement. Shows like *Married by America*, *The Bachelor*, *The Bachelorette*, *Joe Millionaire*, *The Family*, *American Idol*, and the ironically titled (considering the B-level talent) *I'm a Celebrity—Get Me Out of Here!* filled a voyeuristic void in America and established a societal addiction (or affliction) fully entrenched in Britain and Europe.

Always evolving his sound, Eminem characterized *The Eminem Show* as being inspired by the seventies rock he'd grown up with, particularly among his relatives in Kansas City, Missouri, and in the white Detroit suburb of Warren. The beats on the album are generally not syncopated or complex; they are straight-ahead rock-and-roll rhythms that lay a simple foundation for Eminem's verbal gymnastics. The album also ties together Eminem's various styles—the lunacy of Slim Shady, the intensity of Marshall Mathers, and the savvy of Eminem—often in the same song, as in "Square Dance." In this song's second verse, Eminem interlocks polysyllabic rhyme patterns into consecutive lines, compacting the language until it is no longer possible to continue the structure, all while laying down as much of an antiwar state-ment as Slim Shady is bound to make: "Yeah you laugh 'til your motherfuckin' ass gets drafted / While you're at band camp thinkin' the crap can't happen."

Despite critiques to the contrary, Eminem did not soften up to win mainstream acceptance. *The Eminem Show* is every bit as demented as his other albums. There is less homophobia, but there is just as much misogyny on this album, if not more. "Drips" is a cautionary tale about easy women who are out to steal your money and leave you with venereal diseases, while "Superman" revels in a harsh groupie fantasy. Songs like "My Dad's Gone Crazy" and the before-mentioned "Square Dance" turn Eminem's eye to terrorism by comparing Slim Shady to Saddam

Hussein and claiming that Eminem has more pain in his heart than a little girl in a plane heading for the World Trade Center.

In a post-9/11 world, Eminem is less shocking, and understandably so. Zealots who don't like America have beaten up on our country. The violence and hate in Eminem's music that was once such a bone of contention for Lynne Cheney is the sound-track of the times: America is angry, poor, out of work, misunderstood, and gunning for revenge, a country which has had it up to here and is ready to flush reason and act rashly. America had to understand Eminem in 2002—America had *become* Slim Shady.

The Eminem Show debuted at number one in the United States the week of May 23, 2002, and sold 1.3 million copies in its first week, going on to sell 7.6 million copies by the end of the year. The narrator here hasn't created a monster, as he says on the album's first single, "Without Me"; he's written a play and he's playing every part, including the audience and the theater critic; it is the stance of a savvy media manipulator. The release of *8 Mile* in November 2002, however, brought a new demographic, or several, to Eminem's table.

The film took in $54 million in its first weekend, and it ranked twenty-one in the year's top grossers, landing $115 million in just two months. The film reflected the American dream just as Eminem reflected the American mood: like a Horatio Alger story from the turn of the last century, the film's protagonist, Jimmy "Rabbit" Smith, struggles against poverty and adversity and strikes out alone in pursuit of his dreams. The film is as full of hope as Eminem's lyrics are full of rage; it's as much a story of unity as

Eminem's lyrics are of alienation. It is the kind of story that renews a belief in the American way.

If Slim Shady had directed 8 Mile, it would be an X-rated horror porno. Left to Marshall Mathers, the hurt and angry misunderstood underdog, the film would be a controversial after-school special. But Eminem, the Hollywood player, was behind 8 Mile—the only one of the three personas who would think to wield the power of the big screen. The film was an outlet for Eminem to elevate his story to the universal plane, by translating it into more accessible terms. It was also an opportunity for him to recast preconceived notions, to explain himself better than a Barbara Walters sit-down, without the coaxed tears and soft lighting. The film showed exactly where Eminem was from, simultaneously reasserting his street cred and capturing a time and place where hip-hop was pure.

Eminem's acting leap is logical: it is phase two of rap-career expansion, which generally follow the launch of an artist's record label and clothing line and, if they're as talented as Eminem, their efforts as a producer. By the end of 2002, Eminem had bagged them all, signing a deal with Macy's to feature his Shady Ltd. clothing line, to be manufactured by Nesi Fashion Brands, the company that makes Jay-Z's Rocawear, which made about $200 million in 2002.

8 Mile was the jewel in the crown, a showcase for Eminem's considerable acting skills, before only seen in his videos. But, above and beyond the end product, the film was a stroke of public-relations genius, effectively distancing and differentiating Marshall Bruce Mathers III from his life on record better than any

disclaimer of his or any critic's analysis had. It allowed Eminem the space to express a range of emotions at once and in the eye of the public, so that he became, in playing a real, rounded person, a character, once again. The result is like watching a well-executed interview, conducted and edited by the subject. After so much self-defense, it was the rapper's only recourse to clearing up the misconceptions about him. As with film reinterpretations of classic literature or world history, *8 Mile* became, for those who weren't already fans, the story of Eminem. It accomplished what Eminem had been trying to do all along: show the world where he came from so that everyone would understand who he was and, maybe, why he felt the way he did. It focused the story for those who couldn't see it through the music.

To paraphrase *New York Times* contributor Neal Gabler in his 1998 book *Life the Movie*, Americans are so enslaved by cinematic and televised entertainment that we are no longer satisfied watching it on a screen, we want to live on that screen. So at the turn of the millennium we took a logical next step—we brought the screen to us and made entertainment out of our lives. From the billion-dollar beauty industry (including Botox and home chemical peels) at the ready to make anyone appear more like a celebrity to the continued popularity of *America's Funniest Home Videos*, *Real TV*, and the bushel of other reality programs that dominate prime time on the major networks, it is clear that, in one way or another, Americans want to be on the screen any way they can be.

Eminem is an example of the next level: a celebrity turning his life into entertainment before the public can. He does so, as it happens, while mocking the same trend. He's the reality-TV music star, one whose series was expanded into a film after its third season. He exists as a whip-smart wiseass sitting in his own living room, watching his life unfold on the tube and laughing at it with his friends. Eminem's view isn't the gritty documentary eye of hip-hop's best-known black lyricists such as Nas and Tupac. Eminem's stance is in the control room, reveling in the camera angles, re-creating, in his image, the hours of television watched and comic books read as an antisocial introspective child.

8 Mile puts a twist on Eminem's reality art that echoes fictionalized celebrity biographies past, all of which gained an advantage in the retelling. The film adaptation of Howard Stern's autobiography, *Private Parts*, brought out the New York shock-jock's sensitive side, portraying him as the odd, sex-obsessed nerd whom radio listeners knew him to be, but more empathetic than his years of berating strippers could allow. Perry Henzell's *The Harder They Come*, starring reggae artist Jimmy Cliff as Ivan O. Martin, is an example closer to *8 Mile*. Inspired by a legendary Jamaican 1950s gangster named Ivanhoe Martin, Cliff's character was a more loosely veiled version of Cliff than of his gangster namesake. Set in the early seventies in Jamaica, the story starts with Cliff's character leaving his family's farm for the big city of Kingston with dreams of becoming a reggae star. Like the character he plays, Cliff spent his early years struggling against the corruptions of payola and poverty before making a name for himself, though the heightened international fame Cliff reaped from the role can't compare to Eminem's big-screen rewards: a seven-time platinum album, a five-time platinum film soundtrack, and

an Oscar win for "Lose Yourself" in the best-song-from-a-sound-track category. Eminem's big-screen debut also bears a resemblance to Elvis Presley's role of Vince Everett in *Jailhouse Rock*, not so much in the plot similarities of the two films, but in regard to the effect *8 Mile* had on Eminem's public profile. In *Jailhouse Rock*, Everett, a convict serving his time, meets a country-western singer who inspires him to pursue a life in music upon his release. Everett is quickly disillusioned by the music business until, with the help of a friend, he paves his own way to overnight superstardom. Everett is given a new lease on life by the music business, just as the movie business transformed Eminem from a sinner to a saint in the eyes of mainstream America.

The timing was right for *8 Mile* and Eminem's redemption in the American pop-culture landscape. The country needed a *real* American story, that of a hero overcoming obstacles. In a year full of escapist fantasies such as *Spider-Man; The Lord of the Rings: The Two Towers; Harry Potter and the Chamber of Secrets; Star Wars: Episode II, Attack of the Clones;* and *Men in Black II, 8 Mile* reasserted a philosophy that America was built on (as Eminem says in the film's theme song, "Lose Yourself"): "You can do anything you put your mind to, man." *The Lord of the Rings* allowed Americans to root for the allies' fight against a shadowy evil in a far-off land while our nation moved closer to war with a nation similarly portrayed by the government. But *8 Mile* reminded people why they were fighting.

In 2002, Eminem was the cultural locus of America, the man who in just one year seemed to have garnered the entire world into his card-carrying fan club without having campaigned. In the weeks following the release of the film, "Eminem awareness" was even greater than it was when he was infamous. It was surreal watching who came on board as an Eminem fan. Even those he had cruelly lampooned had nothing but kind words. At the *8 Mile* premiere, Christina Aguilera gushed, "Everyone has that right to get out and be artistic in any way, shape, or form and express themselves. I'm a big supporter of someone who's trying to go out there and do their thing." Barbra Streisand's reaction was supremely strange: "Most of the language I couldn't understand," she said of *8 Mile*. "It was like watching a foreign film. But it's a real slice of life. This kid Eminem is really interesting, I can relate to the truth and I can relate to the emotion and I can relate to him in some strange way. I was raised in the projects, I was born in Brooklyn. We were poor. I relate to that stuff because it's my heritage. That's a big part of me, that kid playing in the street." Strangest to see, though, was Eminem as the topic of coffee talk on *The View* in December 2002. Cohost Meredith Vieira admitted to liking him, as did guest Whoopi Goldberg. A short discussion ensued when the raspy-voiced Joy Behar reviewed *8 Mile* as if it were a home movie from the Mathers' family archive, and predicted that Eminem would lose credibility with his fans for appearing vulnerable in the film. "Once a tough guy like that shows he's vulnerable, it's over," she said. "No one wants to see that."

Time will tell, but I'm not putting my money on Joy. One of Eminem's strengths is his instinct to critique himself first, the world second. He has been pointing out his faults and weaknesses nationally for four years and it has hardly hurt his profile.

After the release of *8 Mile*, Eminem avoided the spotlight as much as possible. In paparazzi photos he looked somber, and at the forty-fourth Grammys on February 23, 2003 he looked stoic but emotional. After the ceremony, Eminem passed on the parties much as he did at the L.A. premiere for *8 Mile*, where he left the business of Hollywood to his costars and ran the red carpet like a fifty-yard dash. Eminem stopped for just one interview that night, with the hosts of a local hip-hop radio station. At the premiere party for the film, he sat surrounded by his friends, separated from the two thousand or so guests by a phalanx of security. I didn't go to the *8 Mile* premiere, although I was invited. I preferred to see the film on opening night, premiering to a crowd without VIP parking. I was glad to hear, though, how Eminem navigated his big night. He went to Hollywood on his own terms; he showed up, but he didn't play any game but his own.

I only cuss to make your mom upset

2. A lot of truth is said in jest

"Buuuuhhhhhpp," the blond kid says from inside the bathroom stall. There is silence for a minute, then he emerges, his face red and his eyes watery. He wipes his mouth on his sleeve and leans on the sink. He looks at me, then washes his hands and his face. I don't know him yet, so I stand a little to the side, not knowing whether to say hello. I must look like I want something from him, maybe just a clear path to the stall, because he stands there tense, his body language betraying his awareness of my presence. When he's done washing, before I can even say "Hey," he swaggers by me woozily, eyeing me on the way out.

"I just threw up everything I had," he announces to the people in the conference room down the hall. "All I ate today was that slice of pizza and that fifth of Bacardi. Feel good now, though." He ducks into his manager's office, leaving the rest of us, his fellow rapper Royce Da 5990 and his boys, Dennis the security guard, and me to chat among ourselves. When he comes back in, it is to crack jokes on every topic in the air and every person in the room but me. Sure, he sees me, but he says nothing to me for the first twelve hours that I'm in his orbit. It's a blessing and a curse: I'm never the target of his pointed jokes, but that only means that to him I don't exist.

Two hours later, nine of us get into two limos, one of them white and immense, the other black and shorter. DJ Stretch Armstrong ducks his lanky frame through the car door and sits next to Eminem; he is singing, as he was in the elevator, an appropriate interpretation of a Cream song: "In the white room, with white people and white rappers." The long white limo is now full; Eminem is deepest in, sitting behind the passenger seat. His manager and bodyguard are on one side, and as I get in, I am last on the bench. The radio is tuned to New York hip-hop station Hot 97 and Jay-Z's "Can I Get a . . ." from the soundtrack to *Rush Hour* pumps from the speakers. "Can I get a fat fuck to all these chickens on these nuts," Eminem says, substituting lyrics. There is a rap at the window, and the security guard rolls it down. A guy in a hood looks in at me with his hand out, nodding for me to do the same. I do and a pile of pills falls into my hand. I feel a kick in my knee and turn to see Eminem, crouched forward with his arm outstretched, holding money at me. I exchange the pills for the cash through the window.

Eminem's manager, Paul, puts his head in his hands. "I don't believe this. Are you fucking stupid?" he says. "Do you know what you just did? The guy from *Rolling Stone* just bought your drugs. That's it, fuck it. You're on your own tonight." Paul gets out of the car. He will rejoin us when we leave thirty minutes later.

"Hey, Paul, you're already fired, you fat fuck," Eminem yells at the slammed door. "You're so fired and rehired, you're tired, you skinny fat fuck! Fuck you, you bald fat fuckin' fuck. Fuck you fuckin' fuck, your life, it's over." Eminem loves the word *fuck*. He uses it like a basketball player uses a dribble, to get from here to there.

"Ohh, yeahh," Stretch Armstrong says, imitating Eminem's lecherous gay character, Ken Kaniff, from his albums' skits. "Paul's sexy when he's mad. Oh, yeah." Ken Kaniff was the goof persona of underground rapper Aristotle, who recorded a skit of a prank phone call to Eminem on *The Slim Shady LP*. After the album's success, as with so many relationships ruptured by unequal fame, Aristotle and Eminem had a falling-out over who had the right to play Ken. On his next records, Eminem, an able mimic of any voice, performed the Ken Kaniff skits. For his part, Aristotle recorded anti-Eminem songs in the Ken Kaniff persona and set up a website to sell an album of Ken Kaniff raps.

"Yo, pass me a ginger ale," Eminem says. "I need some shit to settle my stomach." He swallows a hit of ecstasy with his first gulp.

"Ohh, Eminem, yeah, I bet you melt in the mouth, not in the hand," Stretch says, bugging out his eyes and baring his teeth.

"Ohh, yeah, you fuckin' fuck," Eminem says. "Fuck you, you fuckin' fuck. You're Stretched, you fuck. You're so thin you can't spin, you skinny fat fuck."

The car moves away from the curb and heads downtown, slowly, through traffic toward the Verrazano Narrows Bridge to Staten Island. We're already two hours late. As the E starts to hit him, Eminem becomes a word dervish, a rhyme tornado, a spaz, and a force that can't be reckoned with. In most people, ecstasy brings on a state of bliss. In Eminem, it brings out Slim Shady. Right now Slim Shady is cranked up to eleven and bristling with energy he can't contain. His drug-fueled rhymes are sharp, and he cannot sit still. When the radio catches his ear, he'll rap along perfectly with OutKast's "Rosa Parks" or DMX's "Ruff Ryders Anthem," until the next bit of stimulus redirects him. At a red light, behind the black-tinted windows that keep the New York noise out and the riders' noise in, he starts talking to the Sikh cabdriver next to us in Shady's version of Hindi.

"S'cuse me, talkin' a me, no?" he says, banging hard on the window. "S'cuse me fuckin' a talkin' a me? No? I'm a fuckin' a talkin' a you!"

The man sits resolute and unaware, less than a foot away through the glass. He doesn't hear and doesn't respond, so Slim Shady fills in his half of the dialogue, too, all the while banging on the window. He's soon conducting both sides of the "conversation" in a wacked-out language known only to him. The rest of us can't even hear it because we're laughing so hard.

"You're all fired!" he yells at us, as the cab pulls away. "You fat fuckin' fucks!"

At the next light, a couple sits next to us in a Lexus. "Oh, yeahh," Eminem says. "Mmm, yeah. Ohh, yeah. I'm Ken Kaniff from Connecticut. Can I ride with you? I wanna ride in that car of yours, mmm, yeah." The more oblivious the other motorists, the more incited the joker. When a nearby driver suspects something, it kills us even more; the poor guy might hear Eminem pounding on the window or might be trying to divine who is in the stretch, but when he stares at Slim Shady while the rapper screams, "Oh, talkin' a me!" it's like witnessing a police lineup, performance art, *The Tom Green Show*, and the greatest *Candid Camera* episode ever imagined, all combined.

"Somebody tell Paul he's fired," Eminem says. "Right now. Fire that fat fuck. Then rehire him. He's over. He's done. His life is garbage. Ay, yo, Paul, what's up?" At the opposite end of the limo, Paul cocks his head and looks at Eminem, then back out the window.

Eminem is starting to burn—his face is flushed and his eyes are wild and hungry. They twinkle with the unbalance of a madman and the steel focus of an athlete; his pupils are the size of pennies. Five blocks from Staten Island's Club Carbon we see it: a mass of kids in the street, blocking traffic. It's hard to tell how big the club is, but this mob looks big enough to fill it—and they're the kids who didn't make it inside. They are a teen amoeba on the black-top: every time a car comes through, they separate in blobs to let it pass, then rejoin. The limo creates a frenzied reaction. As we inch slowly into the crowd, the kids realize that the show has arrived and they move in to consume it. They surround the car entirely, forming a layer of insulation between us and the building. Guided by two harried beat cops trying to direct traffic, the limo turns around slowly, honking constantly, and pulls up to the curb. Kids are trying to look in, waving, banging on the windows, and pulling the door handles.

"Look at this place, man," Eminem says, dead serious for a moment. "Fuckin' *fuck*."

"Staten Island in the house," Stretch Armstrong says, grinning ear to ear. "We've got white rap in the house, Staten Island. We've got white people and white rappers in this white car for you."

We sit in the limo at the curb and wait while the police and venue security clear a path for us. Along with Eminem's body-guard, we form a phalanx at the car door as the crowd starts to freak out. The kids push forward, some getting stuck between the cops and our ride, some climb over the limo's wide hood. They yell at Eminem, or just about him, as if he were in front of them, not live, but still in two dimensions, on their MTV.

"You look *good!*" shouts one girl, who can't be more than fifteen.

"Oh my gawd, he looks so much better in person," another says, as much to us as to her friends.

We are in a tight circle, being pushed and pulled along, the kids packing in against the guards who can't quite surround us. It is slow going, like swimming upstream, and we won't fit through the doors of the venue without breaking rank. I'm holding on to one of the crew members as we push through the doors, flatten-ing a few teenagers on the way. I start slipping behind as bodies push in against me and try to break our human chain. Eminem's security guard pulls me forward by the neck of my shirt just before I'm squeezed out of the pocket and into the mob. Kids are screaming all of his names now—Shady! Em! Slim!—and trying to high-five him over the human wall.

Inside, this former movie theater is pitch-black except for the tiny toothpick-size glow-sticks that dot the dark. The fans have them stuck in loops of their clothing, in their hair, in their nostrils, and in their mouths. A boy trying to push through me into the circle has them jammed in his braces. It is the grand opening of this all-ages spot, and either the club handed out several gross of these glowing party favors or Staten Island teens are oddly obsessed with disposable light sources.

The club is basically still a movie theater. There's no backstage and little security, and the dressing room/storage closet is a well-lit attic located at an end of the top row of seats at the top of a ladder. We make our way up the aisles, and while I hold on to the jacket of one member of the entourage in front of me, I look to the side and watch as the seated kids in the rows realize who leads this human train. Their faces change to those of tots on Christmas morning: they shake themselves out of a groggy recline and rush at us as if to tear the paper off Eminem like he's their new video game. After we are all up the ladder, a trapdoor shuts the fans out.

Waiting in the room, between boxes of plastic cups is a man sporting *Sopranos* chic. "Hey, nice ta meet ya," says the club owner in a thick Staten Island accent. "This is our big night. My daughter told me to get Eminem, so I got Eminem. It's her fourteenth birthday today. Come on over here, say hi to her and her friends."

Eminem is ruddy, bewildered, high, and suddenly shy. He looks pissed off. But he switches gears, takes off his coat, and poses for pictures while answering statements pronounced as questions, such as "You've got a cool video?" The girls say little beyond how much they totally love "My Name Is." These fourteen-year-olds, little women, are like many of their peers downstairs, dressed older than their years, carrying themselves with a disturbing self-aware sexuality.

When his guests leave, Eminem retreats to a back corner by

61

the chips and salsa with his stage gear: a towel and four bottles of water. He sits backward on a chair, resting his arms on its top. He is brewing, silently fuming. He's quiet for the first time in hours, giving Paul Rosenberg a break in the hire-fire cycle and not talking to or about anyone else in the room. The rest of us chat, Stretch Armstrong cracks jokes as we all steal looks at Eminem. I'm trying to read him, wondering how much of his static stare is raw intensity, how much meditation, how much preparation or chemical side effects. I'm wondering if he's freaked by the crowd, their numbers, ferocity, or demographic. He must see, as I do, that these aren't all underground hip-hop heads; these are MTV kids waiting to see him, their Total-ly Request-ed favorite, Live.

We climb down the ladder and once again fall into a tight pack, gripping each other's clothes and pulling and pushing our way to where the screen used to be. These predominantly white kids are in such a frenzy, shouting, waving, and shoving so much that our entire entourage is corralled onto the tiny stage. We take positions along the back wall, forming a semicircle that touches the front edge of the stage at both ends. We're told by venue security, military style, that after the last song we must immediately exit stage right, where police officers will escort us through the side door into the alley to our vehicles. Venue management and the present law-enforcement officials are concerned about the possibility of a riot. I stand third from the edge of stage right, an arm's reach from kids piled on top of each other. It doesn't matter to the trio of girls at my feet why I am there; I am some avenue to Slim Shady, and they wave to get my attention. They ask if they can dance with me onstage and ask where we're going afterward.

They want backstage passes, but I point out that there isn't a backstage to have passes to, so they ask me if they can come wherever we're going or just meet us at Eminem's hotel later.

The entire front row is young, shouting, and female, most with long nails and skimpy tops, and don't notice the crowd piling up against them. I wonder how well they know Eminem's lyrics and if they'd heard the last verse in the song "As the World Turns," where Slim Shady kills a "trailer park bitch" with his go-go-gadget dick: "I shouted, 'Now, bitch, let's see who gets the best!' Stuffed that shit in crooked and fucked that fat slut to death!"; or his devilish advice in "Guilty Conscience" to Stan, a twenty-one-year-old minding a drunken fifteen-year-old at a party: "Fuck this bitch right here on the spot bare / Till she passes out and forgot how she got there." If *The Slim Shady LP* came with lyrics, and these teenagers read them, I wonder if the girls would even care about these lines.

Eminem grabs a mike and flips the Shady switch on. "Ay, yo, how you doin'?" he says to the screaming mass, tossing water over their heads. "Hi! Fuck you!"

The loudest teens can still be heard over the roar.

"He's so fuckin' hot!"

"Oh my god!"

"I wanna *fuck* you!"

"You're hot!"

"Shady!"

"Over here! Hi! Hey!"

"*Yeah*, dog!"

Stretch Armstrong drops the needle on "Scary Movies," a track

63

by Bad Meets Evil, a.k.a. Eminem and Royce Da 5'9" that was released as a twelve-inch single in 1998. It's two long battle verses of breath control and verbal dexterity. Eminem paces the stage, crouching lower, holding his crotch and slowly losing his pants. He spits his words furiously, breaks a sweat, and strains the veins in his neck. His verse builds, skipping topically from migraines to Monica Lewinsky, from being hit by a Mack truck to *Celebrity Deathmatch* to Tupac Shakur and Biggie Smalls.

The crowd flips for "My Fault," a tale as adolescent as they are, about a mushroom trip gone wrong. They shout along to the shuffling funk chorus with their hands in the air: "I never meant to give you mushrooms girl / I never meant to bring you to my world." Eminem heads over to the front of the stage, in front of me, and leans out over the audience. One of his more aggressive female fans reaches up and grabs his crotch, then looks at her friend with the wide-eyed pride of a victorious daredevil. Her friend gives her an "I don't know" look, spying Eminem's crotch where it hovers a foot in front of her face before she foists a demure grab of it. If Eminem feels the action through his baggy pants and boxer shorts, it doesn't show; he's so engaged in rapping the third verse of the song that it sounds like he may inhale the mike. He's rattling off words, and heaving, and he looks like he might fall down, but instead he wanders back to the front of the stage as the beat stops and for a second there is silence.

"I touched his dick!" one of the two girls says loudly to the other.

"I love you!" screams a different girl, directly in front of him, with her arms outstretched.

"I love you, too," he says, and in a moment of ecstasy-fueled affection and poor judgment bends over to give her a hug. She lays a kiss on his lips, and instantly the girl next to her clasps his head with talon-tipped hands and pries his face away. She kisses him, completely, with opened mouth and tongue. A forest of arms reaches out and nearly pulls Eminem forward into the crowd.

"Ohhh, *shit*!" he says, pulling free and falling back on his ass. "I'm going to jail tonight!"

As promised, after the last song, "My Name Is," we're immediately escorted into an alley where the limousines await. Some of the fans break through the security and chase us out the door where those who didn't get into the oversold show are already waiting. We pile into the car, flushed with the adrenaline rush of our exit. As we wait for the police to clear a drivable path, a sexy young girl who looks no more than fifteen taps on the window, inches from Eminem.

"I want to fuck you," we see her say. She pulls down the front of her halter top, exposing all of her cleavage. She flicks her pierced tongue at the window.

"I want to fuck you, too," Eminem says. "But I won't." He looks at her a moment longer and then sits back, his head deep in the corner of the seat, his eyes darting about, taking us in.

"Hey, you fuckin' fucks! Why is everybody so quiet, you fuckin' fat skinny fucks! Fuck you, you fuckin' fucks! You're so quiet, you're tired, you're so boring you're snoring, you're so garbage, your life is over!"

*

WHETHER WE ADMIT IT OR NOT, SLIM SHADY IS THIS MILLENNIUM'S JESTER, THE pop-culture punk come to piss us all off, the underachieving class clown bent on disturbing the peace. He'd be a bright student if he applied himself, but Slim Shady spends his mind on jokes. Slim Shady is a cracked-out crack-up who boasts in "Role Model" that he gets so high because he hits the trees (i.e., pot buds) harder than Sonny Bono. Slim Shady claimed victory in defeat. He is Eminem with exhausted options, a victorious last stand, gleeful and amoralistic, a demidemon with nothing to lose but his bad mood.

Slim Shady transformed Eminem's life and troubles into pop-culture iconography. The character's nihilism defied all that was fake and polite in popular entertainment with a smile as fake and unsettling as the testimonials on late-night infomercials. Slim Shady embodies the angry young white misanthrope who feels marginalized by society and feminized by feminism and who rejoices in the freedom of his uselessness. The sheer bitterness at the heart of Slim Shady's extremity is presented in a cartoonish excess that waltzed into the mainstream like a Trojan horse, subverting societal norms rather than defying them as Eminem's labelmate, the Goth shock-rocker Marilyn Manson, had done. Manson manipulated perceptions of gender and organized government and religion to upset convention in the midnineties, but his image as an androgynous space alien is too easy to relegate to the freakish outskirts of popular culture, rendering his message, as it were, easy to ignore. Manson became a two-dimensional effigy for disaffection and was burned as such in the wake of Columbine: Marilyn Manson was the perfect scapegoat god for teens so disenfranchised that they would shoot up their school.

Eminem's lyrical instigation left less room for misinter-pretation than Marilyn Manson's artier façade. The rapper's neatly cropped blond hair, blue eyes, cute earrings, and boy-band good looks were too normal to ignore. On the strength of his out-sider alter ego with nothing to lose, Eminem's wit and dark humor entertained or repulsed casual observers, sometimes achieving both at once. He used Slim Shady to voice the deepest evil in his mind and make an example of bad behavior, then hid behind Slim when critics asked him to explain. Slim Shady did the deeds and thought the thoughts, not Eminem. This stance both criticized the importance of entertainment and acted as a con-venient, infallible alibi, but the nuances of Eminem's creation were, of course, lost on the mainstream. Among teenagers, Eminem was the Ferris Bueller of popular music, the shadowy legend who got away with everything, while Slim Shady, his rebel soldier, brought home Eminem's dreams. Slim Shady landed him a record deal and won him hip-hop respect, MC battles, and starhood on a par with legend—in four short years.

In a hip-hop edition of Shakespeare's *A Midsummer Night's Dream* in which rappers or their personas were the players, Puck, the comedy's fairy instigator, could be no one but Slim Shady. The comparison's valid when you closely examine Eminem's use of Slim Shady as a humorous device. Slim Shady is like Shakespeare's Fool: the character who darts across the plot to tip the audience to truths unseen by the other characters. The Fool is sly, smarter than he lets on, and concealed by his comedy. He may annoy or illuminate, but he won't be ignored. Like any mischief-makers worth their weight, be they political, like Abbie Hoffman, or mythological, like the Greek god Pan, Slim Shady is a savior in a nuisance suit—a needed, uninvited messenger. Slim Shady is also compulsive, neurotic, and in possession of both the knack for getting into trouble and the cunning to extricate himself from it.

"I'm bringing cutting-edge humor to hip-hop," Eminem said a few months before *The Slim Shady LP* debuted. "It's been missing that for a while." In 1999, mainstream hip-hop was serious and seriously materialistic, fuelled as much by industry standards as consumer taste: Jay-Z's *Volume 2—Hard Knock Life* and *Volume 3—The Life and Times of S. Carter*, Puff Daddy's *Forever*, Missy Elliot's *Da Real World*, as well as the Notorious B.I.G.'s first and 2Pac's third posthumous albums were the dominant barometers of the time. Humor, sarcasm, and the exploration of anything other than the spoils of the hip-hop life were in short supply. *Volume 2—Hard Knock Life* is one of Jay-Z's most somber offerings, fueled by the single "Hard Knock Life," which featured a sample from the *Annie* soundtrack. It was the most crossover-minded collection of his career. His follow-up, *Volume 3—The Life and Times of S. Carter*, was a favorite buoyed by the boasting single "Big Pimpin'." Puff Daddy's *Forever* depicted the high life as a full-time job, complete with Cristal memories and forty-carat dreams. Missy Elliot's sober second album relied more heavily on hip-hop cliché than she had ever before and would ever again. In 1999, Cash Money Records and Master P's No Limit Records, two Southern labels whose image epitomized ghetto excess, made their mark. Both labels had been raking in tens of millions of dollars since 1995 with minimal mainstream exposure and no major-label distribution; but deals with Universal Records and Priority Records respectively brought their sound to the masses. Rapper B.G. of the Cash Money family put a term to the material age with the anthem "Bling Bling," from the 1999 album *Chopper City in the Ghetto*. The phrase was slang for all things shiny and pricey, from having enough ice (diamonds) to skate on, to Lorinser rims and Yokohama tires on every (note the "every") ride in the garage, a combination that can average $2,000 per wheel. The bling-bling philosophy was really more eighties than nineties: it was conspicuous consumption, the belief that you were only living when you were blinging.

Flaunting possessions and referring to brand names in rap lyrics are as old as hip-hop itself, but in the late nineties the trend grew elitist. Where goods were once a piece of the picture, they took center stage and were upgraded exponentially, making hungry bystanders of much of the hip-hop nation. Where Run-D.M.C. once rapped about their Adidas, Puffy now rapped about Prada; where rap gear once meant a Troop tracksuit and boombox, it had become diamonds, designer clothes, and cars. Hip-hop's material lust complemented the pseudo-Mafioso imagery that dominated the East Coast groups of the day, and suggested a new pecking order, in which skills were honored but a stylish package was an equal priority. Hip-hop's mainstream image in the bling era, to paraphrase the theme song to *The Jeffersons*, moved on up to a deluxe apartment in the sky. Sports jerseys were replaced by suits, and thuggish aliases gave way to pinkie-ring personas. Puff Daddy's Bad Boy Records disseminated the style widely, transforming its artists from gangst-a to gangst-er. Puffy protégé Mase, formerly Mase Murder, became a white-suited Harlem mobster. Biggie Smalls' cohorts, the Junior M.A.F.I.A., which launched Lil' Kim and Lil' Cease, toed the same line. Even Nas was caught up in the moment, mixing his literate street honesty with tales of gangster high life, and his street garb with fancier attire on two albums, *I Am … The Autobiography and Nastradamus*, both released in 1999. Many fans believed Nas's classic first album, *Illmatic* (1994), to be a fluke until the rapper returned to his roots with *Stillmatic* in 2001.

At the same time, socially conscious hip-hop was left for dead. Acts such as Arrested Development and Digable Planets had charted hits in the early nineties, but aside from superstars like the Fugees, worthwhile "alternative" rappers like Black Sheep and Pharcyde received little record company promotion for their sophomore albums in the age of gangsta rap. Even the legacy of KRS-One—socially aware songs by rappers with a thug image— fell out of style, not to achieve any kind of mainstream chart success until Nas's "I Can" in 2002.

Premillennial mainstream hip-hop was thug life lite: an allegiance to the fruits of rap success and violent imagery without a celebration of the violence and death-obsession that surrounded the Tupac–Biggie Smalls years. At the same time, hip-hop artists and fans were obsessed with "keeping it real": not putting on airs, telling lies, or forgetting your roots, even as the scene moved inextricably further from those roots. From late 1997 through 1999, following the deaths of Tupac Shakur and Biggie Smalls, it was as if hip-hop went on spring break and sent MTV footage of the good times: pool parties, speedboats, and more squadrons of

Hummer SUVs than the marines had in Operation Desert Storm. The climate was even sunny and friendly enough for the G-rated rap of Will Smith, who scored with "Gettin' Jiggy Wit It" and "Miami" from 1997's *Big Willie Style*, although by 1999's *Willennium* he had become a punch line for that nice-guy image. The rare artist such as Jay-Z, could be street and bling, while eccentrics like Busta Rhymes stood out from the pack with hits such as "Put Your Hands Where My Eyes Could See."

The dominant face of hip-hop in the late nineties reflected mainstream culture, whereas in the previous decades it had reflected a culture apart. Hip-hop's material extravagance paralleled the technology-boom economy that turned lucky stockholders into lottery winners, while the benefits of a fatter economy were celebrated by all. Both the limitless Internet gold-mine and the bling-bling universe broadcast on MTV portrayed a state of indelible rich bliss, but the high wore off and depression followed: the economy dipped, the dot.coms closed down or sold out, and hip-hop fans hungered for change.

Well-heeled rap imagery was soon mocked by fans and dropped by artists. Mase, Puffy and Bad Boy Records' shining star, saw diminishing sales, as the label affiliation that once worked to his advantage became a hindrance. He was so disillusioned by his days in rap that after a multiplatinum debut, he retired and became a minister, just as his second album, *Double Up*, was released. The LOX, the Bad Boy Records act who wrote, among other hits, Puffy's bling-bling anthem "It's All About the Benjamins," deserted Bad Boy publicly for a rap coalition closer to their thug-image roots, DMX's Ruff Ryders. The LOX blamed

Puff Daddy for their momentarily cleaned-up, well-suited image, and songs like "If You Think I'm Jiggy" (a reinterpretation of Rod Stewart's "If You Think I'm Sexy") and "Get This $" on their debut, *Money, Power & Respect*.

It was fitting that the LOX, arguably some of the game's most underrated rappers, fell in with DMX, the New York lyricist who took the throne of hardcore rap after the fall of 2Pac and Biggie Smalls. DMX and his Ruff Ryders were the most popular and contrary rap acts to thrive in the face of bling-bling hip-hop. His ascent was ten years in the making, by which time DMX had mastered his craft, combining street credibility and commercially appealing song-writing so well that he remains the first artist to have his first four albums debut at number one, beginning with *It's Dark and Hell Is Hot* in 1998. DMX tapped into what Eminem would a year later: rap and music fans didn't want to hear artists keeping it real, they wanted to *feel* artists keeping it real. DMX brought an intense, confessional, no-frills individualism to rap, unearthing his life's uneasy contradictions and conveying them in gritty detail. DMX was the new style, a composite rap persona, a thug without excess; tough enough to kill but brave enough to cry. He and Eminem, in stylistically different forms, embodied a new rap paradigm that connected deeply with fans: real skills, real stories, complex emotional terrain, and no undue ceremony. DMX and Eminem made honest revelation respectable, paving the way for even Jay-Z to dive deeper on his 2001 stunner, *The Blueprint*, with tracks like the heartfelt "Song Cry." DMX and Eminem proved that the pop-music-consuming public would not subsist on fantastical tales alone. They wanted to hear tales like theirs—lives they might have lived, not those they'd never know.

In the ramp-up years to the millennium, while popular hip-hop checked its reflection in its diamonds, the synchronized dance of teen pop dominated popular music with a manufactured sunny-day reality. Members of *NSYNC and the Backstreet Boys, competing acts managed by talent agent Lou Pearlman, had cut their teeth on the Orlando, Florida, theme-park circuit and turned Disney cheer and adolescent longing into multimillion-selling albums mostly produced in Sweden, the pop mecca that birthed Abba. Videos of rain-swept Backstreet Boys, some then close to thirty, dominated MTV. Britney Spears and Christina Aguilera, former costars on *The All-New Mickey Mouse Club*, similarly competed for fans as they once competed for solos. In the late nineties, marketing to teens became big money. Business studies identified teens and their disposable allowances as an untapped resource and refocused their products and marketing accordingly. Corporate America churned out teen-oriented films; launched magazines such as *Teen People*, *Cosmo Girl*, and *Elle Girl* in a sliding publishing market; and conducted frequent teen focus groups to track trends.

On MTV, sandwiched between the boy bands, Britney Spears's sassy schoolgirl act, and microdiva Christina Aguilera's active acrobatics, Eminem played a humorous hip-hop stereotype: the crazy white boy. In the "My Name Is" video, which begins with a television broadcasting "*The Slim Shady Show*," starring Marshall Mathers, the rapper imitates Bill Clinton, a flasher, a puppet, a science-show host, and Marilyn Manson, and he plays himself as a

73

patient on Dr. Dre's analysis couch. The video's irony is Eminem at his best. Playing a wacked-out nerd, he satisfies and mocks the expectations of a white rapper: that he must be insane for even trying, because white rappers, in a genre founded on street wisdom and style, are as smooth as a geek in plaid pants. As his life story became public, Eminem became less parody than reality. Compared to the pop songs of the day, "My Name Is" was dynamic, harnessing brattiness and self-destructive frivolity to a chipper point of view detached from the implications of it all. The emotional scope of Eminem's music was as irregular as life itself, while in teen pop the pieces fit just right.

Eminem stuck out, as he says in "Role Model," from *The Slim Shady LP*, like a green hat with an orange bill. In his first interviews with MTV, one of which caught the eye of Brian Grazer, the producer who developed *8 Mile* around him, Eminem shape-shifted from sarcastic to serious and goofy to gangsta in the space of an answer. He lit up his MTV performance debut on the Music Video Awards in 1999 with a medley of "My Name Is," "Guilty Conscience," and "Nuthin' but a 'G' Thang," performed with Dr. Dre and Snoop Dogg, which highlighted his hip-hop pedigree and a theatrical, high-energy stage presence. At the MTV Awards and the Grammys that year, Eminem looked like he might actually laugh during his acceptance speeches, as if he couldn't believe he was being rewarded by those he mocked. A year later, in 2000, as his negative media image loomed and his personal life began to unravel, Eminem played to his reputation. Accepting one of a handful of MTV Awards for *The Marshall Mathers LP*, Eminem pulled a speech from his pocket, allowing a pile of "pills" to fall on the stage, and he summed up the event as "The one night where you can fit all these people I don't like into one room."

In his first appearance on MTV's *TRL*, the same week *The Slim Shady LP* was released, the rapper was subtly hilarious. The show's co-guest of the day was pop-rapper-turned-underwear-model-turned-actor Mark Wahlberg, there to promote his current film, *Three Kings*, to the channel's teen audience. The contrast between Eminem and Wahlberg's Jazzercised take on hip-hop less than a decade earlier couldn't be missed by the viewers old enough to remember when he called himself Marky. Wahlberg represented two pillars in Eminem's hate files: crappy white rappers *and* teen pop. The screaming youths in the studio audience probably were not aware of Wahlberg's rap career, coincidentally as an Interscope Records artist too, fronting the pop rap outfit Marky Mark and the Funky Bunch. The Bunch sold a million records in 1991, thanks to the high-energy hit "Good Vibrations," but failed to connect on their second and final album, *You Gotta Believe*. Their brief notoriety did, however, pave the way for 1993's *Form . . . Focus . . . Fitness, the Marky Mark Workout*, clearly a stepping-stone to Wahlberg's film career.

"Marky Mark, fucking asshole. Bastard prick," Eminem told me about that day on *TRL*. "I don't know what the fuck his problem was. He walked up in there like fuckin' 'What, is there supposed to be some fucking tension in here?' He's a fucking little faggot. I'm standing with Carson Daly and we're off air. And some dude who works for MTV tells us Mark Wahlberg is coming in, says he'd appreciate it if we don't call him Marky Mark. I thought that was kinda funny. I wasn't planning on doing that shit anyways.

75

Little fucking homo. Then he comes up and he's standing on the side when we was off air and he's like, 'What, is there supposed to be some fucking tension in here or something?' I pretended like I don't hear him and shit. Then we're on air and Carson calls him on set and I'm like, 'What's up, Mark?' He shakes my hand but he don't even look at me. He goes, 'Where do you want me to stand?' Carson's like, you can just stand there. I'm like, 'We'll just stand around here like one big fun bunch!' So I threw a stab at him. He didn't want me to say Mark-y. Probably didn't want me to say funk-y neither." Eminem punctuated the "fun" moment with a bug-eyed look at the camera. Wahlberg looked as if he had forgotten his next line in a scene.

"Marky looked away and shit when I said that," Eminem said, "with a look that was like 'fuckin' dick.' So Carson congratulates me on my sales for the week and Marky Mark is like, 'Oh, you got an album out?' Fucking dick! Nah, you fucking bitch. You already heard it everywhere, you fat fuck. You probably got six copies, you fucking little queer. After I leave, Carson and Mark are talking about Korn on the air and Marky Mark says, 'I like Korn. Ice Cube turned me on to them. I usually don't like white people who do music, though.' Trying to throw another stab at me, I guess. What the fuck is he? Because he don't do music now, he don't like white people who do music? How'd he do albums? I've never even mentioned his fucking name anywhere!"

As with every other pop star who comments about or otherwise irks Eminem, Wahlberg showed up in a lyric soon afterward (in "Drug Ballad" on *The Marshall Mathers LP*). The reference to Wahlberg was minor because his slight wasn't too serious.

Christina Aguilera, on the other hand, revealed Eminem's marriage to Kim Scott on MTV before the couple made it public knowledge. The comment landed her in "The Real Slim Shady" from *The Marshall Mathers LP*, complete with characteristically inventive accusations that she gave Eminem a venereal disease and oral sex to both Limp Bizkit's Fred Durst and MTV's Carson Daly. Moby's later intellectual dissection of Eminem at the 2000 Grammys and MTV Video Music Awards landed him a mention on "Without Me" from *The Eminem Show*, and a simulated beating in the video and live show. Former House of Pain rapper-turned-would-be-bluesman Everlast's attack on Eminem in the song "Ear Drums Pop" by Dilated Peoples warranted "Quitter," an entire unreleased song complete with a death threat. Eminem's response to Wahlberg was minor, merely reminding the public that the now-serious actor was once a cheesy rapper. But it started what is now a tradition in Eminem's music of skewering, for the benefit of his audience, anyone who insults him—a fitting outlet for a sarcastic and entertaining battle rapper.

At a time in American history when the president was on televised trial for intern-management worthy of Larry Flint, Eminem voiced the lunacy of the day and the pent-up male psychology beneath it. "Eminem's style is incredible," Dr. Dre said a few months after finishing up *The Slim Shady LP*. "He has his own thing and he sounds like nothing else out there. He's saying some shit your average MC isn't even going to think about. He has this one line on 'Role Model' that sticks out for me, it's kind of grotesque: 'Me and Marcus Allen were buttfucking Nicole, when we heard a knock at the door, must have been Ron Gold [*sic*].' You know what I mean? It's dope, it's entertaining, it's just bad taste."

While Puffy and company sipped champagne and documented hip-hop's *Great Gatsby* era, Slim Shady got high on model-airplane glue, his mom's pills, and other people's hallucinogens. His lyrics were often an exercise in uselessness, carelessness, failed suicide, and self-immolation that the crew of MTV's show *Jackass* wouldn't even try, like hanging from a tree by your penis. Slim Shady got off ripping Pamela Lee's tits off. He soothed Hillary Clinton with sherbet after ripping her tonsils out, and killed a fat girl who taunted him in gym class by having sex with her, using his mortally expandable go-go-gadget dick. The character inverted Eminem's handicaps as a man and a rapper, from his color, to his mother, his temper, and his taste for drugs, into his greatest advantage; his frustration turned to fuel. Slim Shady is inappropriately funny, like a Ritalin kid off his meds or a scatological joke at a funeral, inspiring irrepressible laughter. Eminem fused the crazy white boy and angry young man stereotypes, playing both to their fullest with ironic, unmerciful insight into white, dysfunctional family values, all the more real for the self-loathing present throughout. "Nobody is excluded from my poking at," Eminem says. "Nobody. I don't discriminate, I don't exclude nobody. If you do something fucked up, you're bound to be made fun of. If I do something fucked up, I'll make fun of myself—I'm not excluded from this."

Eminem was hesitant to flaunt his natural sense of humor earlier in his career for fear of seeming more ham than hardcore— a crazy white boy without a clue. On his independently released album *Infinite*, his wit was buried in wordplay, expressed in the rapper's ability to wield complex mouthfuls: *lamination*, *intimidator*, *telekinesis*, *unconditionally*, *cumbersome*, and *Christianity*. But the jokes were there, and every bit as deft: "Cause you can be quick, jump the candlestick, burn your back / And fuck Jill on a hill but you still ain't Jack," from "313," a standout on *Infinite*. Even on the album's title track, among serious musings about a superstar career and being able to feed his daughter, Eminem revealed the reason for his lack of success: he's currently serving a sentence in hell for murdering musical instruments but still compulsively tries to rap his way to repentance every time he hears a new beat. Witty, sure, but nowhere near the lunatic limits to come. "I was always a comedian, since I was a kid," Eminem says. "That's why *Infinite* wasn't a good album, it was way different."

Eminem laughs both with and at himself, as well as at popular media and anyone else who doesn't get the joke. His humor is part of an arsenal that allows him to subvert popular culture while being a card-carrying member of the mainstream, a stance that stands out in rap and pop music as much as his consistently singsong melodies and unique, pent-up delivery do on the radio. Eminem thrives amid opposition, uniting hummable hooks and blunt lyrics, enticing his now very diverse fan base into off-color sing-alongs. Take the misogynistic bridge of *The Eminem Show*'s "Superman" ("I do know one thing though / Bitches they come, they go") or his update of Sex Pistols creator Malcolm McLaren's hit, "Buffalo Girls," echoed in the introduction to *The Eminem Show*'s "Without Me" ("Two trailer park girls go round the outside, round the outside, round the outside"); such phrases are used to refrains as G-rated as a Barney song and as tough to purge once heard. Eminem's knowing smirk shines through his harshest moments, which include their own disavowals. The anti-women assertions of "Kill You" (*The Marshall Mathers LP*) and the anti-American society rant of "White America" (*The Eminem Show*) contain spoken "just kidding" conclusions. "Kim" and "'97 Bonnie and Clyde," Eminem's murder ballads to his wife, Kim, contain no clear indication of parody, but for their contrast to reality: despite years of fighting, a marriage, a divorce, a suicide attempt, a custody battle, and the birth of another man's daughter, Eminem and Kim are still connected beyond the bond of their own daughter, Hailie.

If there is one song that makes Eminem's point once and for all, it is the final song on *The Marshall Mathers LP*, "Criminal." Over a grooving chorus, Eminem says that every time he says what's on his mind, each rhyme of his is seen as a criminal act. The verses of that song lay out Eminem's key to success in hilarious lines, telling his mother, preachers, and teachers that they can't reach him because he learns everything he needs to know from cable television. Imitating a televangelist (in the voice of Mr. Mackey, the *South Park* elementary-school teacher) who asks the Lord for a prostitute, new car, and the healing of Eminem's soul, Eminem raps that he won't be ignored because his blond hair, blue eyes, and pointy nose can't be missed. To reinforce the point, the song begins with a spoken introduction in which Eminem warns listeners who believe he is as dangerous as his lyrics that they should be very, very afraid, because that means they believe that Eminem is really going to kill them. He inverts the expectations that rappers and musicians must live by the word of their art, turning the critique back on the audience that expects this to happen, while feeding their interest by his pointed mixture of fact and fiction, seriousness and sensation.

Without the ironic twists, Eminem's music would have no message. It would be the rap equivalent of the one-dimensionally macho comedy of late-eighties goombah Andrew Dice Clay, whose misogynistic brags grew nothing but tiresome. Unlike Eminem, Andrew Dice Clay was banned for life from MTV for foul language during a presentation at 1992's Video Music Awards. Maybe Clay is the true rebel, playing his image against the world without compromise, even to his disadvantage. Maybe Eminem is just a huckster, changing costumes to suit the occasion, donning his joke side to hit big on pop radio and his hardcore stance to maintain his credibility, playing the two sides off against each other to keep from copping to the extreme themes of his art. The world is still listening to Eminem because his art can be what you make of it; there is evidence to suit every point of view.

Rock and rap stars have long stirred controversy, and the best of them have done so with an inherent sense of the improperly funny. But most do not or cannot integrate it as well as Eminem does. From Marilyn Manson to N.W.A to Ozzy Osbourne to fellow Detroit native Alice Cooper (whose slapstick gore was as hilarious onstage as his booze-soaked behavior was problematic offstage), musicians dubbed "controversial" never turn sinner to saint, as Eminem has, in the space of just one album. Marilyn Manson, America's most hated musician before the release of *The Marshall Mathers LP*, was targeted by morality watchdog groups such as the PMRC and blamed by a number of mainstream media outlets for coloring the lives of Columbine killers Dylan Klebold and Eric Harris. Unlike Eminem, Manson's art did not contain any kind of explanation or image disclaimer to tip off the literally-minded that he is not a cult leader, despite his stage surname. As happened to Eminem in Daytona, Florida, in 2001, Manson has been banned from performing in several U.S. cities and boycotted by activists for the point of view expressed in his music. In spite of an eloquent defense of free speech in interviews as well as in his 1999 autobiography, *The Long, Hard Road Out of Hell*, Manson has never been entirely accepted in the mainstream, with or without his stage makeup and prosthetic breasts. It has taken Ozzy Osbourne and Alice Cooper twenty-odd years and their middle-aged bloat to become cuddly elder statesmen of rock in the eyes of America. Both have grown up and, as a key point in the metamorphosis, generally sobered up into respectable, average citizens, the kind who loves his dogs (like Osbourne) or loves golf (like Cooper). In comparison, Eminem circumvented one-dimensional shock-rapper status with cunning, by issuing his defense with his offense and serving them up with a wise-assed grin. This was the only way that Eminem's views of society, himself, and everything in between could have made it into so many homes, both as an intruder and a welcomed guest.

A good deal of Eminem's zaniness relies on his gift for mimicry, lending him comedic possibilities that other rappers do not have. He can halt his most self-important swagger, as he does on "Criminal" from *The Marshall Mathers LP*, with a wacky voice introduced flawlessly into a verse. He has pulled off manic imitations of his mother ("My Dad's Gone Crazy" on *The Eminem Show*); rappers Snoop Dogg ("Bitch Please II" on *The Marshall Mathers LP*), Method Man ("Get You Mad," from King Tech and Sway's *This or That*), and Slick Rick ("Quitter," unreleased on album) as well as *South Park* characters, including Eric Cartman, the obese, careless, short-tempered kid ("Marshall Mathers" and "The Kids" on *The Marshall Mathers LP*, clean version). All of the voices and backup vocals on his albums, unless otherwise noted, are by Eminem, including the high-harmony parts sung in "Hailie's Song," from *The Eminem Show*. But, even when imitating others, Eminem is one of the easiest rappers to understand, with enunciation that remains crystal clear regardless of the slang, mispronunciations, or truncations he employs to force dissimilar syllables to his rhyme patterns. "The way he raps is one of the main things that sets him apart," says *Village Voice* critic Sasha Frere-Jones. "People shouldn't discount for a second how important that is to him being popular. The first time I heard 'My Name Is,' I was walking into the Virgin megastore, and it was so loud and crowded, but I heard his voice and knew it was him, over everything. He has the kind of voice you can recognize from one thousand feet away."

In his early freestyle days, Eminem also had a visual rap style that was as impossible to miss as the color of his skin. "I remember the first time I saw Eminem rap," says Sway Calloway, MTV News correspondent and host of the influential L.A. radio show, *The Wake Up Show*. "I noticed how he really assumed this identity when he started to rap. He looked kind of weird in the face, kind of crazy, and that was his thing. He was this little white guy, who when he rapped, looked kind of like a jerking mannequin. Every punch line he would jerk and bob his head really hard and he was saying the craziest shit, just the most extreme, outlandish, and really humorous metaphors. Before he showed up at our show the first time and I saw him do his thing, I remember we had a copy of his tape, I think it was just *The Slim Shady LP* on cassette. We were the first people in L.A., on commercial radio at least, to play 'Just Don't Give a Fuck.' At the time, that was very extreme; nobody would dare to touch that lyrical content. But we banged it right off the cassette because this guy was just so extreme and crazy as shit, sayin' 'Fuck the world, like Tupac,' and telling you 'Put my tape back on the rack.' That's funny shit."

When Eminem debuted many hip-hop heads had spent the past two years cheering on the all too real Slim Shady: Ol' Dirty Bastard of New York's Wu-Tang Clang. This rapper spent 1999 celebrating the success of his second album, *Nigga Please*, with a string of bizarre arrests ranging from failing to pay a year's worth of child support (about $35,000) for three of his thirteen children, to making "terrorist threats" (i.e., threatening to shoot up the House of Blues nightclub in L.A. after he was kicked out for drunken behavior during a concert by R&B singer Des'ree). He was also arrested—and this list is by no means complete—for lounging in the nude on the balcony of a Berlin hotel, driving repeatedly without a license, and shoplifting a pair of $50 sneakers that he wore out of a store in Virginia Beach. Ol' Dirty Bastard's antics made as much sense as his often incoherent, hilarious lyrics and frequently unrhymed, off-the-beat ramblings that put the scat in scatological. While other rappers flashed their cash, Ol' Dirty Bastard demanded—via a dance groove—his girl's money after accusing her of lying about being pregnant with his child. Though his free-associative leaps and cracked warbling are disturbingly entertaining, hip-hop heads didn't come to Ol' Dirty Bastard for lyrics, they came for the show, to hear the only lunatic in the mainstream. But with a character who was this erratic, the fun couldn't last. Whether it was the crack and alcohol abuse that landed Ol' Dirty Bastard in a court-ordered rehab program (which he violated) for six months, or genuine mental instability, the same behavior that made Ol' Dirty Bastard hip-hop's beloved loco also earned him a two-to-four-year jail sentence that began in April 2001. ODB was a mere mortal version of the God of Mischief: He could get himself into trouble, but he couldn't get out. Slim Shady, the crazy out-of-place white boy fed the same desire for a freakish hip-hop joker. In "Cum on Everybody," a deliberate "dance song" caricature of the jiggy hip-hop singles of the late nineties, Eminem gets down getting down on himself. He claims that his best chance with the ladies in East Detroit is pretending to be a Beastie Boy, admits that he's one tablet short of a full medicine cabinet, and says he wants to murder every rich rapper who makes him jealous.

The attention that heavy MTV rotation brought Eminem soon changed him. "When you don't watch MTV much and the few times you do turn it on, you see yourself there somewhere, it's weird," Eminem told me in the middle of 1999. "Whenever I see it now, I'm talking or it's a video, or MTV News or something. If I'm up there and I mention something, anything that I might do, it might be an MTV News thing later on." Eminem was plucked from the hypothetical visions of success in his underground freestyles and, after years of rejections from record labels, given the opportunity to live up to it. In a four-year span, he's created three albums, one film, one soundtrack; he has toured worldwide; and he's produced albums and tracks for other artists. But in the words of Biggie Smalls in 1997, Eminem's success brought mo' money, mo' problems. When his royalty checks started rolling in, Eminem, Kim Scott, and Hailie Jade moved from Kim's mother's house, where they had been living since they moved out of their trailer, and into a large home in Sterling Heights, a middle-class suburb, complete with a pool, a few bedrooms, and a beautiful piece of land that, in an irony worthy of Eminem, was situated across the road from a trailer park. "Literally the entrance to the whole development was across the street from his driveway," says Jonathan Mannion, the celebrated hip-hop photographer who shot the artwork for *The Marshall Mathers LP* and *The Eminem Show*. "It was about twenty feet away—you step out of his front door and you're looking directly into the main entrance of this trailer park. His house was beautiful, too. It was a phat crib, it had a lot of land in the back, a pool, whatever. It had everything, and then you look out the front and, what is this?"

The township did not allow Eminem to build a fence around his property, which left his home and its inhabitants exposed to passing fans, some of these helping themselves to a dip in his pool or his entire mailbox as a souvenir. Despite his performance persona, Eminem is shy around strangers yet quick to anger if he feels violated, so it's no surprise that he handled fan invasiveness with more than an alarm system. The rapper bought a few guns, kept one on him, and boasted to *Spin* magazine just days before his arrest in 2000 for alleged assault and weapons possession that anyone who came to his house unwanted would be met by a barrel in the mouth.

Eminem's critics believed his music's celebration of violence would spawn copycat activities, just as WWF wrestling inspired young men in makeshift rings to pummel each other in their backyards. Children have always imitated art, from staging light-saber fights with flashlights after watching *Star Wars* to acting out their own kung-fu choreography based on that of Jackie Chan. The MTV series *Jackass*, despite the onscreen warnings, inspired a flood of moronic, injurious pranks to be caught on tape and sent to the station's offices—so many, in fact, that the show's disclaimer was changed to inform viewers that these tapes land in the trash, unseen. Faced with the platinum-selling popularity of Slim Shady, parent watchdog groups foresaw a teen apocalypse of drugs, lewd behavior, and violence, and spoke out against Eminem in 2000.

If public enemies weren't enough, Eminem found worse drama at home, as his family members reached out in bold new ways. The rapper's father, who lives in San Diego, California, contacted him for the first time since his son was a child. Eminem did not return the favor but answered instead in songs like "Cleanin' Out My Closet," from *The Eminem Show*, calling his father a "faggot" and wishing him dead for his deadbeat ways. Eminem's mother, Debbie, took her son's success personally. During the time we spent together for the *Rolling Stone* cover story in March 1999, Eminem told me confidentially that his mother had threatened to sue him for his claim on *The Slim Shady LP*'s "My

Name Is" that she does drugs. After my *Rolling Stone* cover was published, she did, filing suit against her son on September 17, 1999, for slander to the tune of $10 million, claiming that his comments in his lyrics and in a handful of magazine articles caused her emotional distress and sleepless nights. She later filed another million-dollar lawsuit against her son for emotional damages suffered during the proceedings of the first lawsuit. The trials would drag on for two years, after which Eminem's mother took home, after legal fees, approximately $1,600 of the $25,000 awarded her by the court. As he says in "Marshall Mathers" off the album of the same name, Eminem discovered that he had more relatives than he realized, all of whom wanted a part of his new, televised life. The only upside to success in the private sphere of Eminem's life was the stability that money brought and the fact that, for the first time in years, he was welcomed by Kim Scott's family. In the summer of 1999, in a private ceremony among his mother's relatives in St. Joseph, Missouri, Marshall Mathers and Kim Scott were married.

It took less than a year for them to go from marital bliss to the parking-lot brawl that could have cost Eminem jail time. The incident set off a downward spiral in their relationship that ended with Kim Scott's suicide attempt about a month later. While her husband played a show at Joe Louis Arena and her mother watched a video with Hailie downstairs, Scott slashed her wrists in an upstairs bathroom. She was discovered in time by her mother. After Kim recovered, Eminem filed for divorce, and the legal wranglings over the custody of their daughter began.

Considering the possibilities, Eminem got off easy. In 2002, he settled the lawsuits with his mother and won joint custody of his daughter. A variety of litigation over Eminem's music was settled favorably or dismissed. The most entertaining suit was filed by Jacques Loussier, a French classical jazz pianist who demanded that all copies of *The Marshall Mathers LP* be recalled from stores and who requested $10 million as compensation for alleged unauthorized sampling of his piece "Pulsian" in "Kill You." More important, for his criminal offenses, Eminem was given two years' probation. He moved into a home within a gated community that, with his new indoor pool, home studio, and movie theater, eliminated any need he might have to leave.

Eminem escaped the legal pressures through his work. During this time, he produced D12's debut, *Devil's Night*; toured with Dre and Snoop on the Up in Smoke Tour; toured with Limp Bizkit on the Family Values Tour; filmed *8 Mile*; recorded *The Eminem Show*; and produced beats for Jay-Z, Nas, and most of his own album. It was a relentless schedule that kept him focused and out of trouble. "I'm on probation now," Eminem said in the spring of 2002, "so I'm a lot more calm because I don't have a choice. But I probably would have done it anyways. I'm growing up, and I figure there is a certain level of maturity that comes with that." He then picked his nose to illustrate his point. "Really, though, perhaps all of that was a blessing in disguise. I'm more focused on my job than I've ever been."

Eminem met fame as a trickster would, by trumping expectations. Slim Shady, the vehicle that announced his arrival in 1999, was sidelined at the height of his fame in 2002, as humor took a backseat to technique. "I do most of my stuff at my home studio,"

Eminem says. "I make the beat and, depending on how late it is, I'll either write the rap there or wait until the next day. I'm taking whole days to write songs now—before I might do them in twenty minutes. Once I lay down the vocals, then I see what the beat can do, where it can drop out, what else can come in—most of that shit I learned from watching Dre. Sometimes, though, I get a couple of lines in my head and find a rhythm for them, then I'll go downstairs and make the beat to that rhythm. That's why a lot of my drum patterns are kinda crazy and offbeat because they were made to follow my rhyme. Now more than ever I try to make my rap go right with the beat. I listen to my older shit, even from just two years ago, from the second record, and I can't stand it. I think I fell behind the beat too much." If one song can be a turning point in a musician's style, for Eminem it was "The Way I Am" on *The Marshall Mathers LP*. One of the last songs recorded for the album, it was produced by Eminem, a role he has grown into as his career has progressed. But the song marked an evolution toward his surging, anthemic musical style. Eminem's pugilistic defense of himself in this track is emphasized by a skittering snare drum, ominous bass, and church-bell toll to dramatic effect. Where his voice once ranged high and low in an enticing lilt, on "The Way I Am" it is spit through clenched teeth and vocal cords. "I was out in Detroit to shoot pictures of his house where he grew up and bits and pieces all around town for the inside of *The Marshall Mathers* album," Jonathan Mannion says. "Afterward we were hanging out and I had heard just a couple of the songs they had finished for the album and a couple of others that were just vocal tracks and I was already, like, blown away. So he says he's going to play one more and he puts on 'The Way I Am.' And he spit that, word for word, the whole thing, man. I took my friend's camera right out of his hand and started shooting, like, 'Sorry, man, give me that.' Just to hear that song for the first time with him spittin' it like that. Oh my God, I was floored, the kid was just fucking amazing. He's out of here, no question."

Eminem has left the joking aside in search of serious, heartfelt, and technically superior explanations of himself. His zany wit has been replaced by sarcasm and his earlier rhyme styles with dexterous manipulations of language. He has become a stylistic feat in motion like the footwork of welterweight champion boxer Roy Jones Jr. or a dunk shot by Alan Iverson. Whereas Slim Shady lagged behind the beat, then rushed up to it and around it, lending an added level of humor and mania to Eminem's delivery, the rapper has become an expert at laying his rap on the beat, sinking into it, making for a more powerful presentation. *The Eminem Show* is full of brilliant moments that sound like the breaking of linguistic laws for the sake of free association. A few gems are: "cocks per second" / "gospel record" ("My Dad's Gone Crazy"); "verse starts. . .MC's heart" ("Till I Collapse"); "closest pal" / "poster-child" ("White America"); "prescription . . . kitchen" ("Cleanin' Out My Closet"); "crayons . . . chaos" ("Square Dance"). This isn't Slim Shady's ecstasy trip; a more serious, more skillful ride.

"I fucking hate 'My Name Is,'" Eminem said in 2002. "I didn't hate it when I first made it. When I do a record now, there's an instinct thing that kicks in when a song could be big. When I listen to a song a few times and it starts to become cheesy to me, that's when I know it could be a big record. Like 'The Real Slim

Shady,' that started to get cheesy to me and I said, 'I think people may like this.' You know, the shit I really, really put my heart and soul into I don't get recognized for. My serious shit like 'The Way I Am' is where I really dump out my true feelings. There's a difference between being funny and being real, and I feel like I don't get recognized for the real shit, my best shit."

Fame and this sense of not being noticed when he's serious steered Eminem away from humor, toward earnest looks at his life, leaving the public fewer chances to miss his point. Songs like "Sing for the Moment" and "Cleanin' Out My Closet," from *The Eminem Show*, as well as "Lose Yourself" from *8 Mile* are concise, cinematic stories, in contrast to Slim Shady's slapstick.

"I sampled 'Dream On' for 'Sing for the Moment,' and Aerosmith cleared it," Eminem says. "That's really great of them because it's one of my favorite songs in the world. I was talking to Steven Tyler about it the other day and he said some true shit. He said if I have to make songs that appeal to everybody—like to get people to listen to my realer songs—that's what I'll do. Basically, my theory is the same: if I have to make cheesy songs to get people to listen to my harder songs, then that's what I'll do. That's the theory that everyone in the business sticks with, but it's cool to see, especially those guys, they've been in the business so long, it's great to hear that you have the same theories. You gotta play the fucking game, man, you gotta play the game I guess."

Eminem is a perfectionist, a rapper who prefers the studio to the club and who has evolved into a producer quickly. "He's a studio jockey, man," Dr. Dre says. "He wants to get in there and make records. I admire that kind of energy, it keeps me on my toes." Eminem's growing production prowess is in the rolling, bombastic vein of his mentor, but with a rock-and-roll sense of drama.

"It really bugs me out that Eminem has this conception of himself that he thinks his older music was silly and his real music is this incredibly grimacing method acting shit he does," says *Village Voice* critic Frere-Jones. "I thought that early music was a little bit happy and maybe him being a little bit silly, but none of it is exactly happy; it's a strange hybrid of happy and twisted."

Hip-hop in 2003 has become a similarly strange hybrid of itself. Popular rap is at once more thuggish, hardcore, and hedonistic, with an even greater premium placed on a basis in reality—when that reality is thuggish, all the better, it seems. At the same time, the juxtaposition and celebration of the sacred and profane so central to DMX's oeuvre is the hip-hop rule. What would be considered "conscious," positive rap must come swathed in thug imagery, and a greater degree of confessional expression is to be found in rap of all stripes. Talib Kweli, Mos Def's collaborator in Black Star, is the epitome of the thinking tough man on his second solo album, *Quality*. Nas, in "Made You Look" on *God's Son*, advises ladies to look for men who are intelligent thugs, "like a real thoroughbred is."

The king of hip-hop in 2003 is a real thug, 50 Cent, a former drug dealer who has been shot nine times and suits up each day in a bullet-proof vest. The Queens rapper has a long enough list of enemies, professional and criminal, that after Columbia Records released him from his record deal, following his shooting, no record label would sign him. Eminem sought him out, and his interest sparked a bidding war, which ended when 50 Cent accepted $1 million—less money than others offered—to sign with Eminem's Shady Records and Dr. Dre's Aftermath Records. Upon the release of *Get Rich or Die Tryin'*, 50 Cent broke the sales record for a debut album, selling almost 900,000 copies in just five days. Eminem's zeal for 50 Cent as well as his verses on the album taunt his newfound audience with threats more real than the parody of "Criminal" from *The Marshall Mathers LP*. In a verse that begins with Eminem's saying that he's got to be what fans see on TV, he says he's bullied his way into the rap game and he'll take on any challenger. 50 Cent is a far cry from Eminem's benevolent on-screen pals in *8 Mile*. So, too, is Shady / Aftermath Records' continuing beef with Ja Rule's Murder Inc. family more potentially dangerous than a street fight with the Free World, Eminem's *8 Mile* enemies. This is yet another reinvention for Eminem, from potty-mouth comedian to strung-out delinquent to sobered thinking man; his next incarnation looks to be gangsta mogul.

"His persona, to me, has changed almost entirely for the worst," says Sasha Frere-Jones. "But to be sympathetic to him, instead of just looking at the text of all the shit that happened to him in the last two years, with him hitting people you could see him completely mythologizing himself. He got famous really quickly, seized up, thinking everyone's looking at him and thinking he has to act tough, doing all this stupid shit because he's in this tornado of people looking at him all the time and asking him for things. That's also just what happens to people. We should all be glad he's not dead, because it wouldn't have been very surprising."

"I don't know if you're going to see Slim Shady more on the next album," says Eminem's publicist Dennis Dennehy. "With the stuff going on around him, and I don't mean this in a bad way, but he's had a lot less fun. It has nothing to do with his probation, he's just working his ass off. He'll hang out with his friends and have a good time, but he doesn't take a break. He is always working and thinking about music. Everything that happened to him in the past year and a half was a lot more serious than what came before that. The music that's going to come out of a time like that is definitely going to be more serious. If you look at it as Eminem, Slim Shady, and Marshall Mathers, he hasn't had a lot of room for Slim Shady in his life lately."

Damn! how much damage can you do with a pen?

3. Marshall and the media, from pans to fans

The Townsend Hotel in Birmingham, Michigan, is Midwestern plush, four-star Ethan Allen chic—a layman's White House. Outside, it is a redbrick modular block with beige stone trim; it's short enough that the windows open on every floor. Inside is an orgy of gold, indirect lighting, black-and-white marble floors, fireplaces, and deep couches. A wedding party has unfurled on three of the couches, soaking in whiskey, wine, cigar smoke, and the post-rehearsal-dinner glow. At the bar, a salt-and-pepper-haired man in a merlot-colored turtleneck sweater is talking to me.

"So you're here on business?" he says.

"Yeah," I say.

"Well, you know the one thing to always forget on a business trip, don't ya?"

"No, what is it?"

"Your wife!" he says through a gusty laugh. "But you probably don't have that problem yet, son!"

They think that I'm a
motherfuckin' Beastie
Boy: Eminem in New
York City, 1999.

Photo by Michael Schreiber

The boy who would be
Shady: Eminem at age
eighteen in 1990.

Photo courtesy of WENN

You do want a piece of me: Eminem performs at the Palladium in Worcester, Massachusetts, April 14, 1999. Photo by Steven Tackeff

A Mr Shady to see you: Eminem in 2001.

Photo by Salifu Idrisa

Where he'd live if he could: Eminem in the studio with rap legend Rakim in Los Angeles.

Photo by Estevan Oriol

A snapshot of things to come: Staten Island shorties show Shady mad love at Club Carbon, March 5, 1999.

ABOVE

The reeling rhyme animal in action at the Universal Amphitheater in Los Angeles, September 10, 1999.

Photo by Robert Gauthier

LEFT

Moon over Barcelona: Eminem accepting one of his three MTV Europe Awards in Barcelona, Spain, on November 14, 2002.

Photo by Dave Hogan

BELOW

Fans in Times Square await their hero on MTV's *Total Request Live*, November 8, 2002.

Photo by Scott Gries

"No, not yet."

"Well, just remember one thing," he says, looking at me intently, his eyes a little red. "There's only one difference between your wife and your job after five years. You know what that is?"

"No," I say, "but I think someone's uncle told me once."

"Your job still sucks!"

Upstairs in the Presidential Suite, kicked back in the living room of the three-room spread (dining room with wet bar, bedroom with deluxe bath), Eminem bites into a tuna melt.

"Damn, they didn't get me fries with that," he says. "What the fuck? I'm off that no-carb diet now." He keeps eating.

There is a twelve-pack of Mountain Dew on the floor, hip-hop magazines on the coffee table, a big FedEx box on a chair, and an enormous security guard outside in the hallway.

"So I was thinking," Eminem says. "About the angle for this here article. And I think it should be all about what school I went to and how I dropped out."

"I'm with you," I say, smirking. "That's a good place to start. And then I'd like to cover your family life, and I'm kind of wondering if you've ever felt, as a rapper, judged for your race?"

"Well, you know, not really, no," he says, picking at his food. "And I've got a good relationship with my family. I spend most of the day with all of them. We just sing songs and pick flowers. And that's me, that's just all the me there is to me. We done?"

"Yeah, I think that covers it. Well, just one more question. I was wondering, do you get any kind of presidential treatment in this room? Does it come with, like, hotel Secret Service or some Oval Office special massage or something?"

"Yeah, you get dirty whores," Eminem says with the half-cocked smile of a kid about to pop a wheelie. "You want to get some? We can get some dirty whores up here. We could get my mom up here."

Eminem has done other interviews today, some for television, some for Britain, and at least one for another magazine, but I don't think those started like this. Then again, you never know. He's one-third slaphappy and two-thirds tired, as if he's coming down from a Mountain Dew rush, even though the box is unopened. This is his first meal today, but he's not complaining. I flash back to how he could barely contain his energy back in 1999. He see-sawed between manic and shy in proportion to the size of the crowd. He was living moment to moment then, expecting the roller-coaster ride to end.

"So I'm thinking," I say, "that we should forget the music—no one who reads *Rolling Stone* cares about it anyway—and make up new rumors about you, because everybody knows all the old ones. We could call the article 'Eminem, the Born Again.' Or 'Eminem, Saved by Scientology.' What do you think? Would the public bite?"

"The public?" Eminem says. "Oh, I've got something for them to bite on. Yes, I do. And I feel like I have a story to tell, man. I've got things to say. But I've got a better idea. We'll sit here, crack jokes for two days, and then you can just read the *Source* interview I just did and then rewrite my bio. Fuck it, we're done! Let's go."

Eminem looks healthier than he has in the last four years—his skin is clear and he is toned from the workout regime he started for his film debut in *8 Mile*. There is a clarity to him I've not seen before, a kind of bright-eyed aura coupled with restraint. At first his new mood seems odd to me. In a few days, I'll realize that this is Eminem calmer than he's been for the better part of his life. The past year for him was sobering, dotted with lawsuits, his divorce, Kim's suicide attempt, and his two-year probation sentence. Professionally, his responsibilities were daunting: a film, producing and writing for three albums, touring. The pressure in his personal life has lifted, but his professional trials haven't even begun. I know why he's calm. He can handle the entertainment. It's life that's scary.

I watch Eminem pick through the rest of his food, and I listen to him talk about the calm he enjoys in Detroit. His speech has changed, too. The stretched vowels of his hip-hop patois are now a clean Midwestern dialect for the most part. He is still quick to respond when he's passionate about a topic, but now he takes his time to structure the answer. When my tape recorder is rolling, Eminem is forthcoming, but the situation is more of an interview than it has ever been.

This makes my job easier, but it makes me want to finish quickly, too. We break up the questions with the kind of banter that editors cut and only musicians and fans care about, discussing in nontechnical terms (e.g., "I like old keyboards because you can get those, like, music-box kind of sounds") the science of mixing and mastering, the uncelebrated genius of the Pharcyde's first album, *Bizarre Ride II the Pharcyde*, and the side effects of over-analysis (paralysis, paranoia) brought on by too many interviews or too much psychotherapy, which are more or less one and the same. We skip tangentially over the past two years of his life and the album and film that capture and encapsulate it, and I feel like he's practicing, testing out subjects and answers for future meetings with writers he doesn't know. In the months to follow, I see some of those same answers in print in other magazines, said better than today, with the afterthoughts born of repetition.

Eminem sits hip-hop style in a lounger: leaned way back, legs akimbo, one arm hanging over the armrest, a pose at once stately and disheveled. We're talking about the pains he's taken to be clear in his lyrics on *The Eminem Show*, about how he's tired of being misinterpreted, about how the controversy in the past few years took attention away from the music. We're talking about the mainstream press, the mainstream listener, the casual MTV viewer tuning in to Eminem for the first or second time and whether they'll see "Without Me," the first single from *The Eminem Show*, for its high-speed irony. I ask him if he thinks fans and critics who have followed him from the beginning will appreciate a thematically heavier Eminem. His eyes widen and he stares straight ahead at the horizon, along the top of his right Nike Air Max where it rests on the coffee table. He's seized by a thought. I've seen him this way before. We were on a plane and Eminem was talking about his mother, he was telling me a story about food poisoning and hot dogs and about being arrested on his birthday. He froze like he did now in the retelling, picked up a pad covered with his small, crooked scrawl, and proceeded to scribble rhymes with his left hand, keeping time with his right. He doesn't do that now; this Eminem has probably already made a lyric of this feeling.

"I have to tell it like it is," Eminem says, not looking up from his shoe. "What I sit around and talk about, you know, I have to go say to the world, otherwise what would I be? If I've got any balls at all, I'll come out and say it, which is what I do. That latest *Source* article— I'm just not happy about it. I felt like there could have been more said and it could have been said in a different way. Whatever."

When Eminem is angry, he'll say he's not and then dissect the object of his irritation until it lies in pieces. The May 2002 issue of the *The Source* featured an Eminem cover story for *The Eminem Show*. The self-proclaimed "Bible of Hip-Hop" had covered the rapper before, starting with a piece in their "Unsigned Hype" column in March 1998, but their latest installment reflected a disintegrating relationship between two mutual admirers. *The Source* cofounder Jonathan Schecter, who sold his interest in the magazine in 2000, had released Eminem and Royce's twelve-inch "Scary Movies," and the rapper's coverage in the magazine's pages had been regular. *The Source* had the chance to be the first national magazine to feature an Eminem cover story and had taken steps toward it, but balked like so many of the record-label executives who had heard Eminem before Dr. Dre. A year later, in July 2000, Eminem was the first white face to appear on the magazine's cover since its inception in 1988. The *Rolling Stone* cover story I wrote was the first in-depth feature in a national magazine about Eminem and proved to be far more thorough and revealing than *The Source*'s article. Since then, the magazine's coverage of Eminem had been a game of catch-up. The May 2002 issue focused on the rapper's family history by talking to peripheral players, at a time when Eminem's past had been regurgitated ad infinitum. In addition, the rapper's albums never ranked among the magazine's "Five Mic" Hall of Fame, where even a cursory glance at the roster highlights the omission: the Beastie Boys' *Licensed to Ill* is the only album by white artists, and two albums (one from 2002) by Scarface, a skilled but not sublime rapper, are honored. Eminem had lived by *The Source*'s word in his youth and now, justifiably, felt disrespected. In the magazine's "Quotables" column, copy devoted to the best rhyme of the month, Eminem felt his best rhymes never made it to their pages.

"It's funny, it's like that, though," Eminem says. "Every rapper, especially me, always dreams of getting a Quotable in *The Source*. When that magazine first started, it was the bible of hip-hop to me. The first thing me and my friends would do is open it to see whose verse got the Quotable—whoever it was was God for that month. I've gotten them now, but the shit I've gotten Quotables for is, to me, not my best shit. I can't believe I got a Quotable for my verse in 'Forgot About Dre.' To me, that's nothing compared to my third verse in 'Criminal.' In all my songs, I try to start the song off real slow, then in the second verse I amp it up a little bit, and the climax is the third. I think that last verse in 'Criminal' is one of my best. Or my verse in 'Fight Music' on the D12 record. The things of mine that I like most get slept on, and the shit that's routine for me ends up becoming Quotables. It's weird."

This was only the beginning. *The Source* and Eminem would become outright enemies a few months later. That day in the Townsend Hotel, Eminem kept coming back to the topic, angry that the magazine he'd been loyal to gave him superficial tabloid treatment. All evening and the next day, he said it didn't matter, and yet he made statements about *The Source* ripe for bold print. I knew he wanted to slap the magazine in my article, to air his gripes in the same pages that had scooped *The Source* in 1999. I also knew that no matter how much of his venom I included, it would be cut by my editor. The bits I did include were cut—they were regarded both as free publicity and taboo; media featuring media-bashing was deemed akin to cannibalism.

The Source, to Eminem, was a betrayal after years of history, a mentor turning its back, then attacking. As the year 2002 drew to a close, *Source* cofounder and rapper Ray "Benzino" Scott called Eminem "Vanilla Ice 2003," and he recorded a handful of tracks that lambasted Eminem as "the rap Hitler," "the rap David Duke," and the leader of a white coopting of hip-hop. Eminem responded with two blistering tracks—"The Sauce" and "Nail in the Coffin"—that buried Benzino lyrically and closed the door of *The Source* to Eminem and, unfortunately, other artists on his Shady Records, such as D12 and newcomer Obie Trice. Case in point: in the magazine's "Top Thirty in Hip-Hop," a list of the most powerful players and biggest sellers in 2002, Eminem, Shady Records, and his manager, Paul Rosenberg, were *not* cited, despite selling 7.5 million copies of *The Eminem Show*, the year's top-selling album in any genre. They had also sold 3.5 million copies of the *8 Mile* soundtrack, a film that took in more than $100 million at the box office. Eminem's yearly gross in 2002 was about $300 million, while Shady Records won a bidding war for rapper 50 Cent, whose *Get Rich or Die Tryin'* broke the sales record for a debut album, selling more than 800,000 copies in less than a week and three million in about a month. In the same issue, 50

Cent was listed as one of the acts to watch in the coming year. Yet in the "Power 30," Eminem and Shady Records were passed over in preference to Réné McLean, CEO of McLean Entertainment Group, a marketing consultant firm who worked on *8 Mile*, and Flavor Unit, Queen Latifah's management firm and record label whose cofounder, Shakim, admitted that first-week record sales of five thousand copies was good enough for Flavor Unit's artists.

The hate between Eminem and *The Source* grew, blurring the border between journalism, cultural community, favoritism, and racial prejudice for the worse. MP3s of co-owner Benzino's anti-Eminem tracks were posted on the magazine's website as he churned them out, and they were sent to journalists from a *Source* editor's e-mail address. At the same time, Kim Osorio, the magazine's executive editor, issued an official statement in defense of Benzino against Eminem online, on TV, and on the radio, proclaiming that the magazine's involvement with Benzino was separate from their objective role as critics of hip-hop.

This drama was months away from our Townsend Hotel interview, but *The Source* was already under Eminem's skin when we met. He had idolized the magazine and felt that if any media outlet would represent him properly, *The Source* would. It was, in fact, an old gripe all over again. On the song "If I Had," from *The Slim Shady LP*, Eminem derided Detroit hip-hop station WJLB, an operation with the motto "where hip-hop lives" that only played 2Pac and the Notorious B.I.G. and never local artists, especially Eminem.

"I know that plenty of artists, not just rappers, who sell a lot of records are looked up to, and sometimes it's deserving and sometimes not," Eminem says. "A lot of people could be saying that I don't deserve it. You know, failure has always been the scariest and biggest motivation for me, just the fear of losing and somebody getting the last laugh on me. In the back of my mind my worst fear is that I wake up tomorrow and I won't be able to write nothing. That's why this is good. If people stop writing about me tomorrow I might not have shit to write about. If there's not drama and negativity in my life, and all that shit, my songs would be really wack. They'd just be boring."

IN 1996, WHEN EMINEM'S FIRST ALBUM, *INFINITE*, WAS RELEASED, IT WAS ONE OF many independent rap releases. Zero newspapers, even in Detroit, reviewed it. In 2002, Eminem and *The Eminem Show* were discussed in one column or another of *The New York Times* alone 153 times, up from 20 in 1999, 78 in 2000 and 96 in 2001. In 2002, Eminem was the *New York Times*'s mirror, angled to reflect aging critics who donned ill-fitting zeal (Maureen Dowd, Frank Rich), a critic who saw commercialistic shtick defeat innovation in Eminem's new music (Jon Pareles), another critic's love-hate-love relationship with him (Neil Strauss), and an infamously unmerciful editor's summary of post-9/11 art (Michiko Kakutani).

In November 2002, as the *8 Mile* buzz inebriated the nation, newspapers that had printed uninformed, anti-Eminem articles at the height of anti-Eminemism circa February 2001 featured columns by nearsighted fuddy-duddies who, somewhere between then and now, had come to terms with Eminem's misogyny, gotten over his corrosive influence on the youth of America, and decided that *fag* was an acceptable term (probably because he wasn't saying it as much). Either they'd been seduced by the magic of the big screen, where they were won over by the familiar Hollywood outsider-makes-good template, or maybe seeing Eminem act convincingly on the screen convinced them that he acted on his records, too, that all of his statement—antistatement somersaults really were the fun of it. Andrew Sarris, in an article in the *New York Observer* titled "Guess Who Thinks Eminem Is a Genius? Middle-aged Me," stated that Marshall Mathers is today's James Dean. Paul Slansky, a Los Angeles writer, theorized in the same paper that middle-aged suburbanites identified with Eminem's anger and frustration, brought on not by hard times but by the pressures of childrearing. *The New York Times*'s celebrated theater-critic-turned-cultural-analyst Frank Rich covered Eminem in a Sunday-magazine cover story, comparing him to Elvis (a tag Eminem predicted in "Without Me" from *The Eminem Show*) and equating the violence in his lyrics to nothing more threatening than that of Hollywood fare.

"Chiming in on Eminem gives older critics a sense of vitality," says *Village Voice* executive editor Richard Goldstein, a political and cultural critic since the sixties. "Discussing Eminem makes them feel connected with their young. It's kind of a testosterone producer, which is a big issue for middle-aged people."

The pick of that litter was New York Times political reporter Maureen Dowd's piece "The Boomer's Crooner," a Sunday editorial in late November of 2002, brimming with tales of her middle-aged friends dropping the kids off at school, then rolling down their SUVs' windows, childproof locks be damned, and rapping along with Eminem as he lyrically rapes his mother. Dowd reported that a friend's eleven-year-old daughter called her mother "psychotic and weird" because parents should not like people who talk about "drugs and sex and hard lives." Dowd collected the juiciest bits of her fellow fogies' Eminem praise and expressed disdain for her peers, who, "frantic to be hip, eager to be young," she asserted, were doing no more than "trying to rob their children of their toys." The thesis that seemed to emerge from her stream-of-consciousness piece was that her crowd's "suffocating yuppie love" rendered Eminem as cuddly as Beaver Cleaver. Like long-standing anti-Eminem critics such as Jim DeRogatis of the *Chicago Sun-Times*, Dowd claimed that acceptance among the demographic he loved to annoy signaled the end of Eminem. Like her friends who only "got" Eminem when the parody was removed, Dowd still missed the point. Her piece's punch line claimed that Eminem's jacket and tie on the cover of his latest album, a trade-off for his "do-rag and baggy Nikes" (baggy Nikes?), were a surefire sign of a sellout and that if Eminem weren't very smart and wicked, he'd soon hear his music in elevators. If Dowd had taken the time to buy that CD and leaf through the booklet, she might have followed the story told in the photos. Laid out as simply as an AOL news report, the inner sleeve of *The Eminem Show* is a photo story of Eminem being stalked by paparazzi bent on making his life a show, while, in reality, the rapper is seated in a control room, reading a newspaper in a suit and tie, watching the action on monitors, collecting footage for a show of his own. If

Dowd thinks the positive praise being currently heaped on Eminem won't annoy him more, she obviously hasn't been listening.

Of course, if Eminem's new "older" fans were wondering why they had missed the joke before, they should have asked their children. The Kids, the group Eminem shouts out most often in his records, seem to have known the difference from the beginning. It also seems that only after older eyes realized that Eminem wasn't going away was he examined, a process made easier with the printed lyrics provided as they were for the first time with *The Eminem Show*. The music is equally large-type: though thematically as disturbed as the other two, Eminem relied less on bizarre imagery than precise explanation to make his point, allowing for literal-minded access. Maybe the older newcomers found that in a post-9/11 world, Eminem's immoral anger wasn't threatening in the face of pending war, or that the sing-along rage forum he provided exorcized their fear, anxiety, and Osama hate. Maybe they were impressed that Eminem worried about the same things as they did, juxtaposing the claim that he was a destructive force to American youth with the very real threat of war and the draft in the first song on *The Eminem Show*, "White America."

In 2002, there were other op-ed columns about Eminem in regional and national papers such as *USA Today*—that great barometer of the middle—by middle-aged writers. Most of these scribes, the type who usually devote their columns to musings on the raking of leaves or that crazy Christmas shopping season, suddenly waxed on about family bonding after seeing *8 Mile*: how they related to America's bad boy and then happily head-bobbed to Eminem with their kids. It was a reaction that record-company marketing and sales execs dream of but couldn't plan for; a re-action more overtly subversive than Eminem would ever have predicted. At the time, I wondered if these new fans weren't offended by the words *bitch* and *ho*, or Eminem's critique of the Bush administration in "White America," or his comparison of his pain to that of a little girl inside one of the planes heading for the World Trade Center on "My Dad's Gone Crazy," the same song that features the voice of his then seven-year-old daughter, Hailie, and simulated sound of Eminem doing cocaine. It was just weird; it felt like a PMRC conspiracy to declaw Eminem by manipulat-ing his acceptance; sterilizing him with an injection of parental approval.

The widespread embrace by the Boomer generation was a pre-diction Eminem didn't make, and one that freaked him out. Looking back on 2002 in December, he told the *Detroit Free Press* that he may be getting too big for his own good and that he never really asked for that, just a chance to make a living in rap. Shortly after, Eminem retreated from the public eye. He dove into production work for artists on his label, and passed on award shows, while his publicist turned away never-ending interview requests and his booker started planning a limited summer tour that included just two American appearances: consecutive nights in Detroit. With *The Eminem Show*, the rapper had released his most self-absorbed, least funny, most detailed vision of himself. The album is Eminem for Dummies, for those who can't take a joke or differentiate fiction from reality. The content isn't much softer, as some reviews of it suggested. The homophobia—and its converse, graphic descriptions of gay sex—are lessened but intact, and though there aren't as many uses of the word *fag*, they are there, referenced as censor bait, and labeled as such, for example in this line from "My Dad's Gone Crazy": "If y'all leave me alone, this wouldn't be my M.O. / I wouldn't have to go 'eenee meenee meini mo, catch a homo by his toe." There are no murder ballads about his wife, but the album still gives Kim and all women plenty of jabs. Yet, strangely, no one has criticized *The Eminem Show* on moral grounds, not even the factions who attacked him just one album ago. As his list of fans grows, his list of obvious "muses" for his next albums grows smaller.

Eminem's nonmusic press profile has evolved in three stages: from nonexistent to begrudgingly acknowledged, from a problematic titillation to a blight on society, from surprised enlightenment to rabid, irrational, illogical, unprecedented love.

It is strange, but it hasn't always been that way. "No one will admit to it," Interscope Records president of publicity Dennis Dennehy said in early 2003, "but when I started doing the press on *The Slim Shady LP*, Eminem had done a few big interviews, and at the tail end of it we tried to get him higher profile press and some TV spots. He'd sold two million records, and people didn't want him on their shows. At that point, people at the big shows and the others were like, 'Eh, I don't know.' I don't want to name names, but it was a bit of a hard time. It was actually difficult, because he got a lot of press, but there was an attitude like 'this is a fad,' and people questioned whether he would even be around for the next album. Of course, all of those people were delightfully proven wrong."

Major-label publicity folk receive a pile of clippings every morning; faxes of the press their artists have garnered overnight. Dennehy has watched Eminem's pile grow rapidly in the last year alone; at the height of the hype, it reached two inches daily, then leveled out at around an inch.

"If you look at the press he's done, in terms of the quantity," he says, "it's been fairly static, album to album to album. He always does about the same number of real interviews—it's the stuff around him that's grown. It's gone from press interest to press fervor on *The Marshall Mathers LP*, when he was public enemy number one, to a long and heated debate that's still going on, about whether it's okay to like him or not. When this started, I had friends giving me crap for working with him at all."

The debate in music and traditional media outlets about whether or not to like Eminem can be tracked to the start of his national career. In the (white) rock music press, even reviews that praised Eminem were tempered with conscience and pause for his more violent rhymes. Many critics also exposed their ignorance of the terrain. More traditional outlets such as *USA Today* redundantly labeled him a "foul-mouthed shock-rapper," a category which could potentially include everyone from Sir Mix-a-Lot to Public Enemy. *Entertainment Weekly*'s review of *The Slim Shady LP*—a negative one, by David Browne—portrayed Eminem as a backlash against the hip-hop soul positivity championed by Lauryn Hill, Erykah Badu, and the Roots. Browne must not have noticed that 1998, the year of Lauryn, was also the year of ascension for DMX and Master P, two artists who celebrate thug life to the fullest. Browne's conclusion was a ludicrous assertion that Eminem was a product of "the post-gangsta era of hip-hop," which hadn't truly died, and a reaction to the "anti-macho, almost asexual world of alt-rock," as well as a victory for the "millennial-caveman mentality bum-rushing the culture," via the WWF and men's magazines such as *Maxim*. On the last point, Browne was on to something (and mentioning the rising popularity of the frat-rock band Limp Bizkit would have strengthened his argument)—the culture at large was then and has continued to grow even more comfortable with casual sexism and misogyny. Eminem didn't do that to our culture's values, nor can it be said that his albums alone increased it, but he certainly wasn't hurt by the trend. Yet timing alone did not define *The Slim Shady LP*'s success; America's love of controversy did. Eminem had it all: he rapped better than most MCs on MTV at the time, he upset the color hierarchy in rap, he lambasted every norm and accepted celebrity in sight, and did it to a melody you couldn't forget.

What is lacking in Browne's review and plenty of others is the assumption that Eminem should be judged first and foremost in a hip-hop context, which implies a supposition that he isn't a real rapper, that he must be a white artist coopting the style, or that since he is white, this must not be real rap. It isn't natural to see a white MC, and memory of white rappers past only serves to make the image stranger. In fact, a number of *Slim Shady LP* reviews read like a review of a punk-rock band. Perhaps these writers saw Eminem as an alternative act, a novelty act, or a hybrid of rap and rock, black and white. It was a strange discrimination by those paid to analyze pop culture. The "My Name Is" video made Eminem an MTV darling, while the song's lyrics lampooned his peers on that medium the way Beck's "Loser" trumped macho rock with slack beats and surreal sarcasm. But anyone who missed that Eminem is a card-carrying member of the hip-hop nation, from his walk to his product, wasn't spending enough time on him. This wasn't a charade by a clown who learned rap from MTV, it was a deft underground MC who had paid his dues.

"There were a few other underground rappers coming up when Eminem did who stood out as innovative lyricists," says Sway Calloway. "Eminem found a way to do things better. And Eminem stayed on the grind. He just continued to come by our show and drop freestyles. I got so much stuff that he did. He was doing his footwork. And the thing about him I noticed each time I saw him back then—and it's still going on—is that he keeps getting better and better. He came to our studio to record 'Get You Mad' [on Sway and King Tech's 1999 album, *This or That*], and that's when I first started noticing, damn, this dude keeps getting better. His metaphors are ridiculous. I could just tell he wasn't going to run out of things to say or how to say them after one album. So many rappers do when they lose touch with the reality that got them there in the first place."

Regardless, the critics were coming. Eminem's first high-profile detractor was Timothy White, the now deceased *Billboard* editor in chief. White devoted his page-long column the week *The Slim Shady LP* came out to a benefit album for Respond, an organization for battered women, as part of his denouncement of the misogyny in Eminem's music, which he felt perpetuated cycles of violence against women and made "money off the world's misery." Eminem made White insult fodder in "Bitch Please II," from *The Marshall Mathers LP*, and speculated on the validity of White's assertions in "Criminal" and other songs.

"He's a fucking asshole," Eminem said about White the week the *Billboard* issue hit newsstands. "Fucker. He took everything I said so fucking literally it disgusts me. He should be able to tell when I'm serious and when I'm not—it's not fucking rocket science. He didn't even realize that 'Guilty Conscience' was a concept song. It's about the way people are in the fucking world and how evil always seems to outweigh good, whether it's in your conscience or in the world and in America especially. In the song, we're talking about the devil half of you and the angel half of you. Nine times out of ten, the devil's gonna win."

In the hip-hop press, Eminem was received cynically until he had proved his abilities. *The Source* put Eminem in their "Unsigned Hype" column before he was pursued by Dr. Dre, a pedigree Eminem shares with DMX and the Notorious B.I.G.

That column anointed Eminem in 1998 as "an MC in need of some nurturing from a record company . . . this rapper of the Caucasian persuasion's got skills . . . Point blank, this ain't your average cat. This Motor City kid is a one-of-a-kind talent and he's about to blow past the competition, leaving many melted microphones in the dust."

The hip-hop press dissected the power of Eminem's rhyme skills as much as they heralded the twisted terrain of his content: *The Source* called "Just the Two of Us," the precursor to "'97

Bonnie and Clyde," a "guaranteed rewinder." The hip-hop press already knew what even many of the (white) men and women who made their living critiquing music overlooked: black rappers have spit rhymes as gory as Eminem's for years, full of misogyny, homophobia, and street violence, traditions entrenched in the machismo of the gangsta pose, however close it may or may not be to the rapper's reality. On the microphone in every hip-hop style, exaggeration rules supreme, an extension of the tradition of hyperbole that began on wax in 1979, in the second verse of the Sugarhill Gang's "Rapper's Delight," but with roots far older. At the same time, Eminem's upbringing, among poor blacks and whites, was closer to the black and minority experience reflected in rap, lending Eminem the added credibility of similarity. Eminem, without a doubt, is the first white rapper with true street cred to cross over. The Beastie Boys, though they did all right musically, boasting the backing of Russell Simmons and Def Jam, were the well-educated New York City kids of wealthy upper-middle-class families whose debut album was nothing but bad behavior draped in hip-hop's gold chains. The rapper Everlast of House of Pain, whose "Jump Around" hit large in 1992, was born on Long Island but grew up in the San Fernando Valley of L.A.—not exactly cushy, but not exactly Compton. He was signed to Warner Brothers on the basis of his association with Ice-T's Rhyme Syndicate, a loose group of L.A. rappers. Everlast's debut, *Forever Everlasting*, was a flop. It took the funk of Cypress Hill's DJ Muggs's produced single "Jump Around" to get House of Pain to the top of the charts once—and never again. One-hit wonder Vanilla Ice grew up comfortably in Miami Lakes, Florida, attending the racially mixed Miami Palmetto Senior High School for two years, a history he recast when his debut album *To the Extreme* sold seven million copies and stayed at number one in the nation for sixteen weeks. Eventually, the gangster past he fabricated was exposed for the fraud it was, and by the time Vanilla Ice's film, *Cool as Ice*, was released just a year later, he had become such a joke that the film's soundtrack remained among *Billboard*'s Top 200 best-selling albums chart for fewer weeks than *To the Extreme* remained at number one.

The moment his debut single commanded the airwaves and his bottle-blond visage dominated the small screen, Eminem walked into this novelty legacy. But he was none of what the others had been—he was white trash who had lived poor. He had lived and breathed hip-hop since hearing his first rap song at age nine and started break-dancing at eleven. If he hadn't had street cred from the start, he'd have never even made it out of Detroit. As it was, getting out was a feat in itself. "We talked to everybody, every label," Eminem's manager, Paul Rosenberg, says about landing Eminem a record deal. "I mean, at the point that he did get signed by Dre, we just wanted a deal. Everybody passed on him. To them, it was a risk. Most people don't officially pass on an act; they sort of string you along because if something happens they don't want to be sitting there looking like a dickhead. So that's how they handled it. They didn't know what they had, but, honestly, neither did we."

At the start of Eminem's career, the music press across the board spent most of their words on what set him apart: how he boldly went where no rappers had gone before, turning his anger and spiked tongue on himself. The album includes at least fifteen references to self-mutilation of one kind or another on *The Slim Shady LP*. Eminem was seen as credible and joyously improper, an heir to the antics of the Beastie Boys circa *Licensed to Ill*, with a twisted and shocking background story that explained the misbehavior and rendered it harder to swallow.

There was one negative exception in the hip-hop world: *XXL* magazine called Eminem a "culture stealer" years before *The Source* waved that banner in 2002, by which time *XXL* had rescinded their comments from four years before and made an ally of Shady Records. Initially, though, *XXL* mirrored the doubt that had met Eminem for years at rap conferences from Miami to L.A., and at more MC competitions than he can count: How can a white MC truly be a part of hip-hop culture? Years later, when *The Source* copped the same line, running a caricature of Eminem as Elvis and launching a months-long dialogue about the white theft of hip-hop culture, the predicament was more complex. Citing Eminem's landmark year as a performer, one unparalleled by a rap act in terms of projects, profits, and press, the magazine saw Eminem as a greater evil, a threat to the black identity that is hip-hop. Befitting a complicated topic, *The Source*'s stance vacillated between insulting Eminem for the advantages his race afforded him in connecting to a wider white audience (insinuating that his dysfunctional family shtick was a greater asset than his rhyme skills) and worrying beyond Eminem, predicting that his success would close opportunities in radio play that would otherwise be afforded to black rappers.

Regardless, *The Eminem Show* still ranked in the magazine's ten best albums of the year.

There were, of course, the critics who just got Eminem from day one. Robert Christgau, the music critic laureate of the *Village Voice* who sits alongside legends such as Greil Marcus, Lester Bangs, and Dave Marsh (who all popularized music criticism as we know it today), hit it on the head as usual: "Anybody who believes kids are naive enough to take this record literally is right to fear them, because that's the kind of adult teenagers hate," he wrote in March 1999. Christgau's only critique was that toward the end of *The Slim Shady LP* Eminem "turns provocation into the dull sensationalism fools think is his whole story."

Yet there were plenty of those "fools." Chicago writer and devout contrarian Jim DeRogatis has attacked Eminem on all fronts and has never swayed. "He's a charlatan and a fraud," DeRogatis says, "who is as bad musically as he is content-wise. There is talent there, but he could be doing so much more with it. I cannot forgive him the rampant misogyny or the homophobia. There is *Psycho*, which is one of the best films ever made about a serial killer, and then there's *Friday the 13th, Part 8.*" Kevin M. Williams, one of DeRogatis's peers at the *Chicago Sun-Times*, referred to Eminem in a review of a 1999 concert as a "rap-impaired mediocrity" and proclaimed that his "meager skills . . . gain greater impetus simply because of his skin color," naming him a rapper "propelled to dizzying heights by an irresistible song and major label backing."

"The most dishonest observer of the hip-hop scene I know could not listen to Eminem and say 'He's really not shit, musically,'" says rock critic Dave Marsh. "A common assumption among critics is that the people making this music are not quite as bright as they are or at least not as intellectual, analytical, or well informed about what it is that they do. People think the manipulation of an image is an accident. My assumption is that there are no accidents. Anyone who reaches the level of fame of Floetry, let alone Eminem, wants it, they want it bad. Their job is creating a complete package that starts with the performance of the music. You have to be a performer and you have to have desire. People are taught in media theory that the creation of the image is the foundation of the art. I think the creation of the image is the byproduct of others seeing somebody who has set up a foundation for their art."

The release of *The Marshall Mathers LP* is certainly the defining moment in the history of Marshall Mathers and his media perception. Eminem's character-juggling defense of his most graphic lyrics to date stirred listeners into a froth over what he did and didn't do—and what that did and did not mean. Eminem may have played characters on *The Slim Shady LP*, but like those of the best comedians— Richard Pryor, Lenny Bruce, Chris Rock— his imitations (nerdy devil, violent burnout, pathologically alienated baby-daddy) were permeable masks demarcated by a lighthearted delivery, interspersed with enough comedic flourishes to reveal the joke. On *The Marshall Mathers LP*, Eminem loosed a slew of obvious yet confusing contradictions, typically within the same song, that America, for the most part, got lost in. The word *fag* was tossed around generously. There was homophobia, but there was also the line "if we can hump dead animals and antelopes / then there's no reason a man and another man can't elope" ("The Real Slim Shady"), as well as graphic descriptions of gay sex, complete with sound effects, to rival the lyrics of gay punk rockers Pansy Division. For every "Bleed! Bitch bleed!" ("Kim"), there were sweet nothings to Eminem's daughter, Hailie Jade: "Baby, you're so precious / Daddy's so proud of you" (also "Kim"). For "Bitch, you just a girl to me" ("Kill You"), there was "I'm just playin', ladies" (also "Kill You"). For all the moral fire alarms Eminem pulled, there was the last verse in the hit single "Stan," which captures the thoughtful side of Eminem, the man, as he truly is in person more than any other song he has recorded. In "Stan," the rapper apologizes to his obsessed, unbalanced fan Stan for not having written back sooner, sends him a cap for his little brother, reminds him that Eminem doesn't mean everything he says, and advises Stan to get counseling. "And what's this shit you said about you like to cut your wrists, too? / I say that shit just clownin' dawg, c'mon, how fucked up is you?" The album was a masterful manipulation. And the media jumped all over it.

Eminem's brushes with the law in 2000 gave credence to his haters' theory that bad words promote bad behavior, but it almost didn't matter. The press was divided, among themselves and within themselves, over Eminem. He had created an "indefensible and critic-proof" (*Entertainment Weekly*) "call-your-local-congressperson offensive" (*Time*) album in *The Marshall Mathers LP*, "with all the production values and skill money can buy" (*Billboard*) that "isn't just a twisted joke; the rapper's sociopathic façade masks the lingering hurts of his

Dickensian childhood" (*Newsweek*). It was the "first hip-hop album to assume universal attention" (www.salon.com) that "contains the most blatantly offensive, homophobic lyrics the Gay and Lesbian Alliance Against Defamation has seen in many years" (GLAAD alert). It was also "dangerously close to being a classic" (*Vibe*), a "grueling assault course of lyrical genius" that "somehow feels completely conversational, the musical backdrop (calypso/Caribbean, Gothic etherea, jiggy disco evolving into P.M. Dawn) is frequently, of all things, beautiful"; it was a "car-crash record: loud, wild, dangerous, out of control, grotesque, unsettling" (*Rolling Stone*) and an album in which "nothing rises above the level of locker-room insults—nearly every song seems to feature Eminem giving someone the finger" (*New York Magazine*). It contained "some of the most explicit descriptions of violence ever to make their way into people's homes" (National Organization for Women, public statement) but it was "funny how much controversy can spring up over an album that is, musically, not all that noteworthy . . . what could have been a brilliant statement instead elevates Eminem to the rarified air of true platinum rappers, i.e., those that drop outstanding rhymes over frustratingly mediocre beats" (*Spin*), a condition that just "isn't that much fun this time around, no matter how fresh Dre's beats are" (*L.A. Weekly*). In the end, "there's even less point moralizing about this one than there was the last" (*The Village Voice*, Robert Christgau), and "*Marshall Mathers* is music about what one man doesn't know, doesn't even know if he wants to know, and on that road anything can happen" (*Interview*, Greil Marcus).

After *The Marshall Mathers LP* became the fastest-selling rap album of all time, racking up 1.3 million copies sold in one week, his dissenters, just like Chief Brody (Roy Scheider) in *Jaws*, were in need of a bigger boat.

"The controversy didn't surprise me," Eminem says. "I knew there was something coming. I didn't know exactly what it was yet, but Dre told me I'd better get ready for some shit. He was like, 'You're gonna go through it. Believe me, I went through it with N.W.A.' But I had no idea all of that was gonna happen. You know, selling all the records I sold off *The Marshall Mathers LP* out the gate was strange to me. Not that I feel undeserving or anything like that, but I was just like, 'Holy fuck, this is me doin' this.' That's the biggest weirdest thing to live with. I had no choice but to get used to it. But it's still strange."

By September 2000, the "Eminem question" reached the floor of the Senate, where the vice-president's wife spoke out against Eminem.

"So here's a name," said Lynne Cheney, former chairwoman of the National Endowment for the Humanities, "Marshall Mathers. It is truly astonishing to me that a man whose work is so filled with hate would be so honored by his peers." The week before, Eminem had won three MTV Music Video Awards, in addition to the two Grammys and one MTV Music Video Award he'd won the year before. "This isn't the first time," Cheney said, "but Eminem is certainly, I think, the most extreme example of rock lyrics used to demean women, advocate violence against women and violence against gay people." All the while, an unlikely rainbow coalition of gay, Christian, and women's groups were doing their best to boycott Eminem and his album through letter, e-mail, and phone campaigns to his management office, record label, and the Grammy Association, who nominated *The Marshall Mathers LP* for four Grammys. They also protested outside his concerts on both coasts and in Europe.

"Somebody called me during that time, around *The Marshall Mathers LP*, who is a homosexual," recalls publicist Dennis Dennehy. "He's with a website and he supports art that's labeled obscene— Robert Mapplethorpe and other artists that Middle America find obscene. He called me to say that of all the controversial art he does support, he could not support Eminem. Yeah, you know, because it pissed him off. It's fine to promote art that doesn't piss you off, that pisses someone else off. But once it strikes a nerve, it's a different story. You'll defend something until it actually affects your world."

To hip-hop fans, Eminem was different, but the harsh themes and violence in his music weren't too terribly new. But the attention afforded him indicated a subtle racial prejudice. Eminem's opponents, by singling him out, suggested that the same themes, as chronicled by black rappers, were somehow more acceptable. "I think it was about the messenger," Sia Michel, *Spin* magazine's editor-in-chief, says of the controversy surrounding *The Marshall Mathers LP*. "It was sort of this kind of weird racism, where it was like, 'Oh, well, you know how those gangsta rappers are, they say lots of crazy shit.' As if we don't expect anything more from them. And then a couple of years later, the white guy comes out saying similar things and it's like, totally shocking. This white, blond man is saying these things, we're going to take umbrage at this. It is kind of racist, just assuming that Eminem

123

should be any less violent or use any less offensive language than anybody else, simply because of his race. It was harder for people to stomach."

"With Eminem's Grammy nominations viewed as a seal of approval, many more people have stepped forward to voice their outrage," read a call to arms released by the National Organization for Women (NOW) in early February 2001. "Young women, parents, people of all political persuasions are writing to NOW, asking what they can do. While Eminem continues to make lots of money for lots of people, he will most likely be everywhere. But we can certainly shame those who profit from and promote him and his music." They did their best, outside of the Staples Center in Los Angeles on February 21, the day Eminem won three more Grammys and performed his most ambitious single, "Stan," with Elton John singing the hook sampled from Dido's ballad "Thank You."

"While Eminem certainly has the freedom of speech to rap whatever he wants," read a GLAAD public statement, "it is irresponsible for Universal/Interscope Records as a company to produce and promote such defamatory material that encourages violence and hatred. This is especially negligent when considering the market for this music has been seen to be adolescent males, the very group that statistically commits the most hate crimes."

NOW must have been dismayed by Madonna's open letter to the *Los Angeles Times* in defense of Eminem: "Since when is offensive language a reason for being unpopular? I find the language of George W [Bush] much more offensive. I like the fact that Eminem is brash and angry and politically incorrect. At least he has an opinion. He's stirring things up, he's making people's blood boil, he's reflecting on what's going on in society right now. This is what art's supposed to do. And after all, he's just a boy."

Elton John's jump from outspoken gay activist to Eminem supporter disparaged Mrs. Cheney and GLAAD. "Elton John has been good in the past about speaking out on issues of equality for gay people," Cheney said in a press release just after the Grammys, "on issues of being against violent language against gay people. I am quite amazed and dismayed that he would choose to perform with Eminem." Elton John, in my opinion, understood what the moral gatekeepers didn't: if Eminem was smart enough to push the buttons he had, he was smart enough not to hate homo-sexuals and to know that anyone who took his songs as a mission statement were the extremists one really needed to be worried about. In post-Columbine America, having been honored by the Grammys and hounded by the PC watchdogs, Eminem found himself the world's new pop monster.

"Eminem wasn't even as extreme as some stuff that had existed in hardcore rap before him," says Sia Michel. "But he said it and wrote about it in such a crazily, amazingly cinematic way that it made it seem even more graphic. He said it over these friendly kind of singsong riffs, too, so you really heard the lyrics in a different way. But part of the controversy was the fact that for a while there, hip-hop was the mainstream but it wasn't treated as the mainstream in the media. R. Kelly was one of the biggest stars around but you weren't reading about him in the *Star* or the white mainstream press at all. When Dr. Dre came out with *The ironic*, it was huge, but it wasn't on the mainstream radar. It passed by the kind of people who would pick it up and make complaints. Then Eminem came out and here is this really photogenic white guy plastered all over MTV. He's just massive, as soon as his first single came out, and I think those same people took notice. And they saw him singing these singsong, fun songs and he's saying these things that are really going to get to the young kids, now. But they didn't know that those young kids were already listening to Dr. Dre and Snoop before Eminem."

When the mainstream tuned in to extreme rock music, they came up with a scapegoat. Now it was time to change the beat. "The Greeks and Romans used to put their monsters on stage for everyone to see and fear—they are what the society needs to see of itself but can't face," David Bowie said about Marilyn Manson in 1997. "Marilyn is exactly that. He's our most compelling monster right at the moment." He certainly was. Manson had been shoveling sludge Goth since the early nineties and finally hit his career apex in the same year as the Oklahoma City bombing, the Heaven's Gate mass suicide, the death of Princess Di, and the murder of JonBenet Ramsey. Manson held the indecency throne in PC America.

After the tragedy at Columbine High School, Manson became a household effigy. The two teen murderers who allegedly liked his music reopened the discussion on the detrimental effects of "devil's music" on youth deemed too unsophisticated to distinguish performance from reality, a discourse that began with rock and roll in the fifties and was blown open by Elvis's gyrating hips. Manson's guff was closer to the flak Judas Priest and Ozzy Osbourne received thirty-something years earlier when two teenagers, in separate incidents, took their own lives. Those parents blamed Osbourne's "Suicide Solution" and the allegedly embedded backward messages ("do it, do it") in Judas Priest's "Stained Class."

Manson, and Eminem after him, raised issues of the limits of free speech and the effects of music over other forms of entertainment on youth. Both performers challenge the ideals of the traditional American family held dear by so many; Manson by parodying gender and notions of beauty and organized religion, Eminem by parodying mass media and celebrity culture and white family dysfunction. Both harp on drugs. These artists and record label-mates sparked controversies different from other free-speech debates, however. The reaction to Manson and Eminem was a moral uproar; much different than the warning letter sent by the FBI to Priority Records after N.W.A's gun-blazing *Straight Outta Compton* went gold without radio support, or the campaign led by the NRA and police-support groups against the Ice-T-led Body Count's "Cop Killer" in 1992. Those artists were treated as rebel leaders encouraging inner-city chaos and racial revolution. Manson and Eminem were viewed as deviants who would lead God-fearing children into mass moral decline. Manson had shocked and titillated with self-immolation, gory imagery, and substance worship. Slim Shady farted his way onto the pop charts in 1999 and stole the show with jokes and whip-smart, wiseassed rhymes that taught the kids all the wrong (very wrong) nursery rhymes. Manson, for all the evildoing his denigrators believed he enacted upon the minds of Eric Harris and Dylan Klebold, was still easy to marginalize. With his praying mantis frame, Roswellian complexion, and buttless PVC wardrobe, Manson was the freakiest guy ever to be named Brian, an alien on the outskirts. Eminem was more subversive and ultimately more influential. With his bottle-blond hair and twin hoop earrings, he looks like a member of the pop system—the devil's Backstreet Boy. He's not from some Gothic underworld, he's from your neighborhood. A pill-popping metal monster like Marilyn Manson who lives in a drug-addled rock hell is just a guy with a bad case of Halloween. Eminem, the former dishwasher from the local grill who pops his mom's pills, dreams of killing his wife, and encourages robbery, date rape, and double homicide, is scarier. He looks like an average American young man and counts millions of them among his biggest fans.

The truth of the matter is that no crimes have come to light that were allegedly incited by Eminem's music. Perhaps because he's easier to hear and has more than a few controversial songs, Eminem was also not afforded the same artistic license as the great pop icons Nirvana, whose "Polly" from *Nevermind* recounted an actual kidnapping and rape from the rapist's detached perspective. On their next album, *In Utero*, "Rape Me" was written from the perspective of the angry victim in "Polly," whose recourse is to urge her attacker on. Though women's groups voiced opposition to "Rape Me," there were no picket lines outside of Nirvana concerts. "I've gone back and forth between regretting it and trying to defend myself," Kurt Cobain told *Rolling Stone* about the song in 1994. "Basically I was trying to write a song that supported women and dealt with the issue of rape. Over the last few years, people have had such a hard time understanding what our message is, what we're trying to convey that I just decided to be as bold as possible . . . I'm a big believer in karma and that that motherfucker [who rapes] is going to get what he deserves, eventually."

The first time I met Eminem, I asked him about the effect of his music on kids who may be too young to tell when he's joking and when he's not. He answered me then as he has everyone who has asked since. "My music is not for younger kids to hear," he said. "That's why there's an advisory sticker on it. You must be eighteen to get it. That doesn't mean that kids won't. I got 2 Live Crew tapes when I was twelve. I'm not responsible for every child out there. I'm not a role model and I don't claim to be. It's what the song 'Role Model' says. I say that I do everything in the song, but it's all fucking sarcasm. How can people not get it? . . . That's fucking ridiculous. It's obviously saying, 'You wanna grow up to be just like me? Fuck no, you don't!' The message is: Whatever I say, do the opposite. You do that, you'll be good, because my whole life is the opposite of good."

As soon as the National Academy of Recording Arts and Sciences (NARAS) announced that *The Marshall Mathers LP* was nominated for the Record of the Year Grammy for 2000 (as well as four Eminem nominations in the hip-hop categories), a letter-writing campaign was organized by the Family Violence Prevention Fund, while NOW, GLAAD, and a handful of other organizations organized the Rally Against Hate outside the ceremony. As the controversy heated up, NARAS president Michael Greene was forced to issue a defense of the album, claiming it was "the voice of rebellion."

In his defense of free speech in music, Greene didn't mention anything about the album that would win the Grammy for Best Album of the Year, Steely Dan's *Two Against Nature*. "Cousin Dupree," the Steely Dan song that would take Best Pop Performance of the year, is about an aimless lech coming on to his younger cousin. Another song on the same album, "Janie Runaway," is about an older man finding a muse in his teenage run-away lover and enticing her into a ménage à trois with one of her friends in return for a birthday trip to Spain. Though Steely Dan's Donald Fagen and Walter Becker are both in their fifties, no one treated their album as a mission statement or suggested their homes be searched for child pornography. It was considered a work of venerable song-craft by veteran musicians. Steely Dan wasn't protested by children's rights groups, nor was any suggestion made that the Grammy accolades for such songs would incite Steely Dan's demographic—middle-aged Baby Boomers, or their children—into sexual indentured servitude. Not to make light of hate crimes or domestic violence, but to think that a record alone will tip the scales in the mind of the monsters who commit such acts is to dangerously simplify both reality and the pathology of these criminals. Whatever music they might choose as a backdrop to their alienation doesn't create their sickness. If anything, visual arts are a stronger catalyst, film a more powerful influence over our culture. *8 Mile* proved this when it redefined Eminem, snuggle-sizing him to fit into the nation's outstretched arms. The film won over the Baby Boomers in particular, who took Eminem as their entrée into hip-hop, the first youth movement with as large a cultural impact as the hippies. At the 2000 Grammys, however, the academy, whose core voters are predominantly Boomers, voted for subtlety over hyperbole, Steely Dan's stylized taboo over Eminem's screamed "fuck you."

Eminem did take home three Grammys that year, one for Best Rap Solo Performance ("The Real Slim Shady"), one for Best Rap Duo ("Forgot About Dre"), and one for Best Rap Album (*The Marshall Mathers LP*), to place in his living-room trophy case alongside the two he won in 1999 for Best Rap Solo Performance ("My Name Is") and, again, Best Rap Album (*The Slim Shady LP*). Eminem's duet with Elton John at the ceremony was calculated to soften his tag as a homophobe. But Eminem couldn't resist stirring the waters again shortly after the event, claiming in an interview that he wasn't aware that Elton John was gay. The truth of the matter was seen backstage at the Brit Awards, the U.K. equivalent of the Grammy Awards, later in the year, when a writer from London's *Daily Express* observed Eminem, standing in the backstage bar, having a drink with his crew and being watched but left alone by the cream of the Brit pop-music scene, when he was greeted by John with a huge bear hug and a "Come here, darlin'!" If anyone still wondered about his views at that point, Eminem the homophobe didn't flinch or shy away from John, he just grinned.

"It amazes me that people can't see that what he is doing is a performance," John told the reporter that night. "He plays a part onstage and he pushes buttons. I think he's incredible as a performer and a person. The music industry needs people who can be subversive. As a nonsubversive songwriter, I particularly appreciate and admire his lyrics. I spent three days with him in

America and I can tell you, he's very calm, very modest, very sweet, and very shy."

When Eminem returned with *The Eminem Show*, an album released early to discourage rampant Internet piracy, it was a whole new world and a whole new Eminem. The cover art that intrigued Maureen Dowd featured Eminem seen through a stage curtain, taking a moment before stepping up to a microphone bathed in a spotlight. Unlike his other album covers—the shot of him in the gutter in a trenchcoat with an empty bottle of booze and pills, coupled with a shot of his childhood home on the back (*The Marshall Mathers LP*); the surreal night scene of him and Hailie on a dock, with a pair of legs sticking out of the trunk of their car (*The Slim Shady LP*)—this album art left no questions. The album was also the first to include his lyrics: another sign that nothing was to be misinterpreted.

The Eminem Show received accolades across the board for Eminem's production work, his more confessional lyrical content, and his improved rhyme skills this time around. The great Eminem question here was mapping his personalities—the bait dangled in the title. "On earlier albums," wrote Kelefa Sanneh in *The New Yorker*, "he turned his life into a cartoon, starring 'regular guy' Marshall Mathers and his 'crazy' alter ego, Slim Shady . . . Now he seems to be trying to turn the cartoon into a life."

"For all the raw hip-hop confessionals that line his body of work, this is perhaps the most emotionally naked he's allowed himself to appear in public," wrote Brian McCollum in the *Detroit Free Press*, referring to "Hailie's Song," the ode to his daughter that appears on this record. "One of the many aspects differentiating Eminem from other best-selling, vulgar pop stars is that there is so much pathos and honesty in his lyrics, especially on 'Cleanin' Out My Closet,'" wrote Neil Strauss in the *New York Times*. It's "a third album that avoids all the pitfalls of third albums: introspective without being self-pitying, expansive in scope without being pompous, exploring new directions without disappearing up its own arse," according to England's *New Musical Express. Q*, another British magazine, lamented Shady's early sabbatical: "As Eminem outgrows his old alter-id, so the obligatory pantomime villainy, skits, and crass cameos by Shady Records signings become a hindrance." "On *The Eminem Show*," wrote *Entertainment Weekly*, "he's still raging against the machine, while admitting that he's a deeply flawed part of that machine himself."

"His profile now is that he's obviously here to stay, he's obviously an artist with something to say," Interscope Records head of publicity Dennis Dennehy says. "There's no longer a debate about whether he is viable, or appropriate. The cultural argument, in this new world, is whether there's any point in getting wound up about this stuff anymore—obviously America's got more serious problems. Then it was the movie and more people talking about him. I wouldn't say he's a media darling, though. People, of course, want to talk to him, because who wouldn't tune in to see it? Even the people who hate him all want him on the show. The people who spend hours deriding him in the media? They all want him on the show."

Despite across-the-board praise, there are still two critics of stature in America who have not altered their stance against Eminem. Music critic Jim DeRogatis doesn't see the voice of a generation in Eminem; he sees a packaged product—a rebel yell manipulated by Jimmy Iovine, Dr. Dre, and Interscope Records, as he said in an interview for this book.

"We're talking about Generation Y, the second-largest generation of teenagers in American history. There are seventy-two million kids in Generation Y, after seventy-six million of their parents, who are the Baby Boom generation. There's a mere seventeen million of us Generation X-ers sandwiched in between them. This is a consumerist generation so far, and the vast majority of Generation Y has yet to wake out of its consumerist slumber. I think of the pod people in *The Matrix*, everybody plugged into the machine. It's a video game, television society, and everything can be solved with a quick trip down to Abercrombie and Fitch—and Eminem plays into that. He is product on exactly the same level that Britney Spears and Christina Aguilera and everybody else that he's made fun of in his lyrics is. There is no difference, except that his tactic is cheap sensationalism and shock, as opposed to showing your fake boobs like Britney. Pop music is inherently disposable trash, and I'm not saying there can't be great pop along those lines. But rarely has there been great pop that gives you that quick sugar fix, that had so much hatred intertwined, whether it's hatred for specific people or hatred for groups of people. If you have a serious problem with a woman, to fantasize about killing her and slicing her and dicing her—there's better ways to address your problem. Especially when you have vocal skills like he does."

DeRogatis cites a "critical overcompensation" toward Eminem to explain his widespread praise by an older generation of music writers. "There is a problem with forty-year-old white-guy critics, and now most of them are fifty," says the thirty-eight-year-old DeRogatis. "They desperately want not to seem out of step with young tastes, so they go overboard in praising something popular with young people. I don't have that problem. I know what my emotional reaction to Eminem is. I know what my critical reaction to Eminem is. I have no problem standing up and saying it's shit." DeRogatis sees wasted talent in Eminem—and no one is calling him on it. "He gets covered in two ways: by people who don't know hip-hop, who see him strictly as a sensationalistic scourge—and I don't think he's a plague on society, fuck that crap—or he gets covered with glowing hyperbole. There's very little in between. If Bob Dylan had released an album in the sixties praising Richard Nixon as a great force in American society, his wrongheadedness would have been attacked and assaulted by his generation. I think that's what the critical response should have been to Eminem. There's this thing of thirteen million record-buyers can't be wrong, to which I say, where is Hootie and the Blowfish today? America voted for Ronald Reagan—twice. Tell me again that the American masses can't be wrong. The tragedy is to have Eminem's talent and to do so little with it."

Richard Goldstein, editor-in-chief of the *Village Voice*, also came out against Eminem just as the national opinion rose to unprecedented pro-Em levels. Goldstein sees the rapper as part of a tradition of celebrity bigotry and aligns him more with conservative Republicans, such as George Bush, than free-speech liberals. "Eminem is a paranoid personality," Goldstein said in an interview for this book. "A paranoid male personality with an intense sense of aggrievement that is out of proportion to reality. That is projected through his music so that millions of people sign on to the paranoia. This is a dangerous phenomenon. What's happening now with 9/11 is that this came together with politics and is now a true orthodoxy, sublimated into militarism."

Still other critics were just bummed that Eminem had gone serious on us. "He's moved into something that seems like a Michael Mann movie," says critic Sasha Frere-Jones. "When he deals with the serious things in his life, he plugs in some very cheesy templates in his head. Now, I don't think he doesn't feel them, or it's not real to him or meaningful, I think it totally is. It just means it's harder for me with my Communist, pinko background and overeducated brain— I don't find it as effective as when he's doing acid and killing himself."

The release of 8 Mile opened the Eminem door to one and all. The film, like The Eminem Show, put him in a straightforward context that everyone could embrace—and they did. He became a common meeting ground for conversation, like a member of the celebrity machine that he lampooned on his first album. The tone of the mainstream press was reverential—the kind reserved for music figures such as Madonna. Rumors of Oscar nominations began to fly, and as the cast and crew of 8 Mile talked about Eminem's dedication to the film, his public image turned from bad boy to hardworking single father. To look at the coverage, Eminem's music career became secondary in the eyes of a public that was eager to fill out his celebrity profile with gossip of who he was dating and the life story they would have already known had they listened to any of his albums. Baby Boomer critics began to herald him as the icon of a generation, just a year after they'd declared him a blight on American values. "Unravel Eminem's pop DNA and you'll detect strands of Elvis Presley, John Lennon, and Bob Dylan. Heresy? Maybe, but so were initial appraisals of Madonna, another forebear to consider as Eminem's stock and stature rise" (Edna Gunderson, *USA Today*).

The Boomer comparisons to the rock idols of yore is a game played whenever an artist captures the ear of the country. Eminem is not the new Bob Dylan, the new Beatles, or the new Elvis Presley—these are unrealistic comparisons. The effect those artists had on pop music and culture is incalculable because of the times in which they lived. Elvis threw open the doors on American values and ushered into the national consciousness the age of the teenager as a cultural force in America—an age now fully institutionalized. Bob Dylan rewrote folk and rock into literature. And the Beatles in seven years took the history of pop music and turned it upside down and inside out. It is hard to measure anyone against artists who lived and innovated at such a fertile time of what we know as contemporary culture. If Eminem is like any Boomer pop icons, it is David Bowie, or John Lennon. Bowie was an adept thespian who changed with his times, but in every incarnation used a well-integrated façade, mystery, and shock to communicate the depths of his message. John Lennon as a solo artist was raw, honest, macho, and vulnerable, and made beautiful confessional art of his personal life.

When Frank Rich weighed in on Eminem in a cover story for

the *New York Times Magazine*, the end of the media conversation had been reached. The feature, like many others about Eminem in 2002, was uninformative outside of a writer's discovery of something he'd missed in the broader culture. Though the underlying feeling was that of a critic jumping aboard the Eminem train, it duly reflected the national Eminem meter. Later in that same month, November, Eminem was rumored to be in the running for Barbara Walters's "Person of the Year" accolade. It was an unprecedented degree of attention for someone with such a dirty mouth. All the Detroit newspapers ran stories featuring interviews of Eminem's neighbors in the plush gated community that he now calls home. They told reporters about Eminem's contribution to the neighborhood— sleigh rides for the children at Christmas. They chronicled his trick-or-treating with Hailie, dressed in a hooded sweatshirt and hockey mask as Jason from the *Friday the 13th* films, the same mask Eminem wore each night at the start of his show on the Anger Management Tour. "Marshall is a very good father and a very nice person—very down-to-earth," his forty-five-year-old neighbor Cathy Roberts told the *Detroit News*. The same paper interviewed another neighbor, fifty-seven-year-old Dave Crorey, who met Mariah Carey when Eminem brought her over to meet the Croreys during the pair's brief romance. "He seems a little timid," Crorey said of Eminem. "He's nothing like he's portrayed—a wild kid and all that. Seems a little on the shy side." There were Eminem cover stories gleaned from what seemed like twenty-minute interviews and endless articles about the concentric circles of his life, necessary since at the time the man himself was not doing press.

At the height of it all, three different houses in Detroit that were reported to have once housed Eminem went up for sale on eBay. The bidding price of the home pictured on the back cover of *The Marshall Mathers LP*, which had been appraised at $120,000, headed north of $10 million. It wasn't exactly a slow year for celebrity culture, but the excitement, curiosity, and embrace of Eminem outshone everything. America, for better or worse, must have seen itself reflected in Marshall Mathers, and rushed to join the fan club.

"Everyone seems to love Eminem," says Frere-Jones. "I think short of killing his own daughter, it doesn't seem like he could do anything that would repel people. You open the paper and Jimmy Carter is saying, 'Oh, I like Eminem'—they're clambering on top of one another to be offended less and less. I'm not trying to sell my cure or anything, but Eminem, what is this idea that people hate you? As far as I can tell, nobody hates you, other than Richard Goldstein—God bless him for being out there on his own."

"The challenge now is," says publicist Dennis Dennehy, "to keep from willfully overexposing him. I don't think he's overexposed, but he's everywhere. When you really get down to it, in the last year, he's done maybe seven interviews in this country. It's going to be a challenge with the next record, or the next whatever he does—but we've got to maintain the press he gets without giving him away. We could go out tomorrow and do an interview with almost any outlet in America—no one would say no to an interview with Eminem. But there's nothing to be gained by it. He's got a lot to say, he explains himself really well. But it's better to maintain some mystery. I think for anyone who really cares about artists, your favorite bands are always the most mysterious. You didn't read about them everywhere—so when you did, it was a big deal."

The truth is that Eminem doesn't like to do interviews; he prefers to save his soundbites for song. That's not to say he'll make the experience unpleasant. He is civil, charming in a subdued way, passionate, and if he's not too swamped or tired, a lot of fun to be around. He's learned to do interviews well over the years—probably to make them go faster, since he thinks they're pointless at their worst and redundant at their best. As for the storied past and personal life he chronicles in verse, he prefers to keep the intimate details private. "If you listen to the songs and don't take the words out of context," he says, "it'll tell you why I'm saying this or why I'm saying that. I might say it in the song later on, but you'll hear it. If you don't listen to the whole song, it's like watching the middle of a movie and turning it off and then talking about it. Just listen to the fucking songs. If you listen to them, they will tell you. The album's like a fucking instruction manual—and sometimes interviews are like somebody trying to put something together but they don't know how. Read the instructions! Why are you making me sit here and tell you?"

But Eminem being Eminem/Shady/Marshall/him/them, it can't be that simple. There are subtexts, metaphors beneath the metaphors—right? "Somebody asked me today in another interview," he said in 2002, "'When you said you feel like your father, you just hate to be bothered—what did you mean by that?' And I sat there for a minute and I was like, fuck! What did I mean by that? They almost had me thinking that there was a deeper meaning to it. No, dummy, it's a metaphor! My father didn't wanna be bothered with me. And I hate to be bothered by everything. Man, when people start to overanalyze, I tend to start overexplaining myself and in my head, I'm questioning it instead of taking it the way I meant it. It's like, 'I like to wear my raincoat in the rain'—what did I mean by that? I couldn't have meant, like, that I like to wear a raincoat in the rain! Could I? Do I? Do I like when it rains, so I can wear my raincoat?"

The four years of media angles on Eminem can be summed up with four questions: (1999) Is he a novelty?; (2000) Does he matter?; (2001) Should he be stopped?; (2002) How great is he? The year 2003 and beyond is interesting: What comes next? Since Eminem has been deposed from moral monsterhood by everyone but the most extreme right and left wings, he will be an MC with one less battle. And since he may have done some healing with his own "issues" over his past three albums, maybe he'll look around a little bit. America is a dark, complex, contradictory country—it shaped Eminem—and maybe Marshall will start a new dialogue about what he sees. He has the credibility, brains, and skill to catch everyone's ear on any topic, and by all accounts he's already got our attention.

"The truth is, at the end of the day," Eminem says, "I really don't care what people say about me because it's people like me who give half of these people their jobs. They keep their jobs if they have something to write about, and if they write about something good all the time they're not gonna sell papers, they're not gonna sell magazines, and they won't make a name for themselves. All of them dream of being a famous writer, and whatever it takes and whatever they gotta do to slap a fucking headline in the fucking papers that says 'Teen Murders Himself Because of Eminem's Lyrics,' they'll do. That's what's gonna sell papers and magazines, so that's why they do it. At end of the day, it doesn't really matter to me. Ya know, it's just kinda funny. I didn't blow me up half as much as the press did. I couldn't have sold myself half to these kids the way the press did. If they write that the Eminem album is gonna cause kids to go and murder and shit, they're gonna go fucking buy the album and see what it's about. And, you know, it ain't nothing but music."

This rap game

4. From kool herc to kool keith: a brief history of hip-hop

The headlights eat the dark between the traffic lights along four lanes sprawled each side of a wide divide. Electrical transmission towers form a spine up the median, carrying 200,000 volts through the city. Strip malls advertise sex and cars, mattresses and meals, glowing in the gray landscape. To one side of the road, the city's residents are 82 percent black. To the other, the suburban county's residents are 83 percent white. The white van slows to turn into a grid of streets. Each house we pass has a square patch of grass and a driveway wide enough for one car; some have fences, some have shingles, some are brick-faced. All are modest.

"Stop here," Eminem says, sitting behind the driver of the van, on the bench in front of me. "That was our house." The steep brown roof is broken by a deep-set window. The short porch is covered in snow, as is the car in the driveway. A light is on in the front room. The street is still. The house is sixty-two years old; as of this year, 1999, it's been in Eminem's family for nearly fifty years. Two years from now, Eminem will re-create the house's façade for a concert tour spanning America and Europe. He will begin each show standing before it in overalls and a hockey mask, wielding a chainsaw. Three years from now, his uncle, Todd Nelson, will sell this house for $45,000. Four years from now, the new owners, a lawyer and a real-estate developer, will watch eBay bidding on the house reach $12 million, then yield nothing.

"My room was upstairs," Eminem says, his breath fogging the window. "I was at my grandmother's a lot, but this is the house I grew up in. This neighborhood is all low-income black families. Across 8 Mile back over there is Warren, which is the low-income white families. We lived over there in a park; people think they're all trailers, but some of 'em are just low-income housing parks." He points past me at another house. "Some redneck lived over there," he says. "They were the only other white people."

No cars, animals, or people of any color stir the dusk. Eminem's eyes run over the house, scanning details. He has shared troubled memories of this place with me, but his eyes aren't melancholy, they're proud. "I want you to see the walk I did every day to junior high," he says.

Along the way, the van rolls past Osbourne High School, Eminem's rap alma mater. He attended Lincoln High School in Warren but snuck into this predominantly black school with Proof to battle-rap in the cafeteria, in the bathroom—anywhere a crowd might gather. We pass the junior high where D'Angelo Bailey, the bully he meets in "Brain Damage", beat up Eminem regularly. A week from now, I will call every "D. Bailey" in the Detroit Yellow Pages and find D'Angelo. When I do, I'll listen to him recount the beatings warmly, his memory blurred by either time or quasifame, denial or ignorance. Bailey once slammed Mathers onto frozen asphalt at recess, sending him to the hospital with a concussion, but Bailey will remember it as good fun. Before he will say good-bye, Bailey will ask me for Eminem's phone number so that they can catch up on old times. When I don't offer it, he will ask me for tickets to an Eminem show that is a few months off. Three years from now, Bailey will file a million-dollar lawsuit against Eminem for invading his privacy, defaming his character, and hindering the sanitation worker's efforts to launch a rap career.

We trace Eminem's old walk to junior high school. It is more than a mile from Eminem's house, farther from his grandmother's house in Warren, across 8 Mile Road. The van heads in that direction, on 8 Mile, and slows down at the entrance to the Bel-Air Shopping Center. There is a long stretch of grass, wider than a few cars, running along the parking lot. At one end is a wall, beyond it a few hundred feet of empty land.

"I got jumped by a whole crew right here," Eminem says, looking over his shoulder at me. "I was sixteen, I was skinny as fuck, and I couldn't fight as a teenager. I was walking home from my boy Howard's house through the Bel-Air and I stopped at Toys 'R' Us on the way to warm up 'cause it was winter. I came out of there and all these black dudes rode by in a car, flippin' me off. I was like, 'What the fuck?' and I flipped 'em off back. They kept driving and I didn't think anything of it. I'm walking down this long patch of grass right here to the wall at the end right there. Two dudes come from around one end of the wall and it's them. One dude walks past me. The second dude stops and asks me what time it is. I'm like, 'I ain't got a watch.' Dude who walked past came back and said, 'What you say to my boy?' And hit me in the face. I fell into all this mud."

Once on the ground, Eminem realized that he was surrounded. "I got up and was afraid to swing," he says. "I was like, 'What did you do that for?' And the dude's like, 'For the same reason I'm gonna do this.' And he pulls out a gun. I turn around and ran, right out of my shoes. That's what I thought they wanted. I had them new LL Cool J Troops and shit. I ran right out of them and didn't even mean to." Eminem had run past the wall in front of us, into the empty field on the other side, toward his grandmother's house.

"The other dudes from the car started chasing me, and one caught up to me and threw me down in the mud," he says. "I jump up and this dude is tall as fuck and I swing and hit him in the face and he just laughs. He hits me in the ribs and I fall down again. I'm in my socks, in the mud. I get up, start running again, and they don't chase me, and I'm thinking they're getting the car again. Then one of them shoots at me. Just one shot. As soon as I heard it, I thought I was shot but I couldn't feel it yet. I just start screaming and don't stop."

A car had pulled up next to Eminem, on the shoulder of 8 Mile Road. "This guy throws open his door and I don't even stop or look back—I thought it was one of the dudes chasing me. But this guy had seen what had happened and pulled a gun on them and scattered them. He drove to catch up with me, and I'm running on these train tracks over there past the field, cutting my feet up on 'em. This guy, he was a white guy, finally starts yelling at me, 'It's all good, it's all good, get in.' He drove me the rest of the way home, which by then, I had run so fast, I was almost there. I asked the guy to wait and tell my mom what had happened, but he took off. I was fucked up—face all swollen, feet bleeding and muddy. I slammed the door and screamed at my mom, 'Why the fuck do we live here! I'm getting fucked with every day!' It was totally racial. I know it because the next day I went back and my shoes and hat were right where they came off. At least they could have jumped me for my shoes. The only reason they could have done it is because I'm white."

Four years after our drive in his old neighborhood, I walk behind Eminem, up a flight of stairs in a Detroit club to a floor reserved for his party. Mirrors line one wall. Red velvet booths, with curtains, line another. The DJ mixes into "The Real Slim Shady" when he sees Eminem. Women in high-slit dresses proffer free shots of red and green liquor in test tubes. Eminem scans the room and takes a seat deep in a booth, behind the curtains. The half-circle of couch is visible from only one side.

Select guests arrive, more women than men. They line the walls of the room, and park on the dance floor. A few stare at the curtain that hides Eminem, but none approach. In the booth, he praises rappers past and present and describes new beats he's made. He tells me he thinks each new OutKast album is a breath of fresh air to hip-hop. His friends leave their seats to meet some women. Some return, some don't. Eminem remains, talking to me and whoever else sits down.

Two robust ladies appear at one side of the curtain.

"Hi, are you Marshall?"

"Yeah, how you doin'?" Eminem says.

"Why are you sitting in there hiding from us? Isn't this your party?" one of the ladies asks.

"Yeah, it's my party," he says. "I'm just chillin', you know."

"Oh, yeah? Well, come out here! Talk to us."

"Yeah, okay, in a minute," he says. One of his crew is happy to occupy these two in the meantime.

"This shit is funny, man," Eminem says. "Probation and all that sobered me up. It's a blessing in disguise." He watches the room, greeting the eyes that meet his when he shows himself. "Yeah, I'll be back," he says.

The dance floor is full now, but no one is dancing. These VIPs pose, striking a stiff posture of nonchalance while shifting to glimpse the party's honoree walk across the room. Eminem has seen enough of these events to expect that he's still onstage at private parties, that everyone here is either desperate or too proud to talk to him. Others are nightlife fixtures, the people who frequent VIP rooms, often sporting attitudes haughtier than the poutiest star. Eminem walks through the room, and I think of the awkward social machinations of an elementary-school dance. He moves slowly, looking at people, talking to no one. Guests approach him cautiously. A few women flirt with him. His friends circle around and joke with him.

He returns to the booth soon.

"See anything interesting?" I ask him.

"Nah, man," he says. "These things are all the same, you know. It's weird to meet people like this. It's funny, I mean, most of them want something from you. They might just want you to tell them stories and shit and entertain them. Some people are cool, but some don't realize when I go out like this with my friends, I just want to have a good time. I don't really take too many days off, so why do I want to entertain like that when I'm out with my friends? That's what I do on stage."

"You can't really let loose when everyone here is here to meet you, I guess."

"I can't really let loose at all right now, I'm on probation," he says, and laughs. "But yeah, I wouldn't want to anyway; you never know what people want from you or what they'd do. I've had so many fucking lawsuits, man, it just isn't worth it to me. I just hang out when I'm in Detroit. Just hang out with my friends, that's it." Eminem looks past me at a girl waving to him from across the room.

"I thought I knew her for a second," he says. "You know, all this shit really isn't important to me. All I care about is making music, man. If I could live my life in the studio, except to be with my daughter, that's what I would do."

The next day I drive a tan rental car in the middle lane of a three-lane road, following a silver-blue Mercedes. Behind the tinted windows, Eminem is in the passenger seat, and Paul Rosenberg drives. At the photo shoot we've just left, I heard Eminem quip about fixing the photos "in post," short for postproduction. "I can't believe I even know what that means," Eminem told me, chuckling at himself. "In the studio, I'm turning knobs that I never even knew existed. It's good, man, I feel more clearheaded, more focused now. I used to just come in the studio and drop my verse;

now I'm there all day. There's so much more to the process to me now."

It is sunny and brisk, and the road is busy. The snowbanks lining the road gleam under the blue winter sky. A rusted-out red Toyota sputters next to me; I hear the tattered muffler above the noise of the road and the stereo. Two black men in the car talk intently and nod. They lag behind, then cross from the left lane to the right. They drive beside me, then ahead. A red light stops the traffic, and the Toyota stops next to the Mercedes. The driver leans out of his window and talks to the one-way glass. Eminem rolls his window down and nods slowly as he talks. He is handed a tape. The traffic light changes and the cars drive off.

"Those guys shopping for a record deal?" I ask him later.

"Yeah. They had a tape they wanted to give me," Eminem says. "That's cool. I did that shit, too. Everywhere that I might meet someone, I'd show up with a tape. I never gave them to rappers, but everybody else that I could. That's what you gotta do, man. You gotta stay hungry, you gotta get your shit out there, you gotta show up places. You gotta just live for rappin', man. After my uncle Ronnie got me into it, that was it for me. As fucked up as shit got for me, I just lived for rap. It's the only thing that got me through the day."

FROM DAY ZERO, HIP-HOP WAS BUILT ON ALIENATION AND FREEDOM.
The freedom of expression in the face of oppression, the freedom to chronicle an unseen history. It was and remains the voice of the minority majority living in cities, born in a mecca wasteland called

the South Bronx. Today it speaks to citizens from Kalamazoo to Cambodia. In its earliest incarnation, hip-hop reflected the mores and traditions of a fragment of society within a greater one, and like other grassroots influences that altered the majority culture, from the blues to outsider art, it was created in isolation. Today hip-hop is an attitude, a lifestyle, a stance against the mainstream, and a voice of anger, frustration, alienation, sex, and rebellion for youth of all ages and backgrounds.

"To me, hip-hop is modern, mainstream, young, urban American culture," Russell Simmons, hip-hop godfather and Def Jam CEO, wrote in his autobiography, *Life and Def.* "I know there's a lot of ideas there, but hip-hop's impact is as broad as that description suggests . . . The beauty of hip-hop, and a key to its longevity, is that within the culture there is a lot of flexibility. So Run-D.M.C. and A Tribe Called Quest and N.W.A and Mary J. Blige and Luther Campbell and the Beastie Boys can all wear different clothes, use different slang, and have a different kind of cultural significance. Yet all are recognizable as being part of hip-hop."

Hip-hop, in comparison to other African-American musical traditions—blues, jazz, and rock and roll—has remained closest to its roots for the thirty years it has existed. It is possibly the most potent, least altered African-American cultural expression in history. Hip-hop has evolved technically, but its basic theme has remained: self-improvement with style. The earliest rap records, like those released a week ago, were about getting money, living better, having a party, having sex, defying mainstream society, and looking really good while you do it. In the beginning, hip-hop culture and rap music unified young black and Hispanic men and women, the original b-boys and -girls, at DIY parties in parks throughout New York City's five boroughs. It was celebratory, an alternative form of dance music to the synthetic disco and formulaic R&B of the time. It grew into sonic reportage with a scope that embraced the world the same way it did the end of the block. Rap broadcast inner-city realities and established-rebel stance—that no hardship would keep the minorities who pioneered hip-hop from living, to the fullest, on their own terms.

In the past thirty years, rock and roll has slowly faded away as the sound of teenage rebellion in America. Integrated into the system of mainstream culture by the aging Baby Boomers that drove its innovative 1960s phase, rock and roll has lost its outlaw edge; only rare talents such as Kurt Cobain or Radiohead stand out today. Cobain was someone as brilliant and broken as his music, while Radiohead channels anxieties into otherworldly rock opera. The majority of rock bands and rappers today, from Good Charlotte and P.O.D. to Ludacris and 50 Cent, act like rebels of society. From their dress to their lyrics, they stand apart from the norm. The only difference is that in hip-hop the stakes are typically higher, increasing the appeal to a voyeuristic audience. Where the average "misfit" rock band defies the jocks and cheerleaders, a rapper defies the police, the government, and anyone else who stands in the way. Rap rebellion, even when a pose, is closer to reality, as many rappers are or once were outlaws. Many more rack up arrests once in the public eye, simultaneously fulfilling a stereotype and bolstering their bad reputation. Their rebellion is more believable, more celebrated, and, to fans, more worthy of iconography. Many have prison records, gang affiliations, a history of drug dealing, or connections to all of the above. Most rappers redefined the reality of their upbringing and succeeded when statistics show that they shouldn't have. Rappers are the new icons of teenage disenfranchisement, and whether those teens are alienated by the suburbs or by selling drugs in the inner city, they all hear and feel the reality in the music.

Hip-hop is and always will be a culture of the African-American minority. But it has become an international language, a style that connects and defines the self-image of countless teenagers and that has been used to profit immense corporations. Chuck D once called rap "the black CNN." Today, it's more like a premium cable package, complete with QVC, five kinds of HBO, the Biography Network, NBA Season Pass, the Boxing Channel, and "Back-in-the Day" Television. It is closer to a cable corporation (plenty would say one owned by "the [white] Man") with internships and jobs and platinum perks for its employees, but no guaranteed retirement plan. In the rap game, street graduates with the highest rhyme-point average and style extracurriculars can land a corner office or prime cubicle. If they've got golden letters of recommendation and perform in the field, there's a chance they might make partner. Like the legal profession, though, there are more rappers in (and out of) school than there are job openings available in the charts—those chart spots require a specific profile.

In thirty years, hip-hop has proven itself the most expansive, mutable music of the twentieth century. The style and rhythms of hip-hop have altered everything from rock to techno as easily as they have integrated styles as diverse as calypso and East Indian music. It's as unsurprising that hip-hop's elastic subversion has taken its place in the fabric of American culture as it is that the innovative self-improvement capitalism at its root has been converted into a moneymaker for American corporate capitalism.

The lower classes in America have spent the last ten years (1990 to 2000) in the worst economic straits since the Great Depression and are characterized by high divorce rates and/or nonexistent nuclear families. Hip-hop speaks to and for these classes, particularly kids, like the church, reflecting and explaining reality, offering a code by which to live and a sense of community within a community. At the same time, in the middle-class suburbs, teenagers of all races meet on hip-hop common ground to relieve the stress of growing up in a downsized American dream, rife with divorce, academic and peer pressure, and the teenage angst that blooms as surely as zits. People of all types suffer ills that are voiced in hip-hop, a music that articulates community and alienation in the same breath.

The history of hip-hop can be set in contexts as flexible as the culture's boundaries. Books such as Nelson George's *Hip-Hop America*; Ishmael Reed's poetry anthology, *From Totems to Hip-Hop; The Hip Hop Generation* by Bakari Kitwana; *When Chickenheads Come Home to Roost* by Joan Morgan; and *Vibe History of Hip-Hop* all dissect the culture from within and without with clearheaded intellect. Others, such as the *Ego Trip's Book of Rap Lists* and *Ego Trip's Big Book of Racism*, make their point with fierce, bitter humor as freewheeling and embracive as hip-hop itself. Nineties academics such as Professors Herb Boyd, Cornel West, Tricia Rose, and Michael Eric Dyson bring the after-party to the ivory tower to dissect the breadth of hip-hop's implications, particularly now, when the culture has attained a global scope.

The following cursory overview skips over the three decades of hip-hop and the socioeconomic factors that shaped the hip-hop revolution. The purpose here is to trace hip-hop's path to national exposure via mainstream avenues such as MTV, to understand how the culture has spread and been perceived by generations so far. In doing so, I hope to shed light on the effect that Eminem has had on hip-hop at the turn of the century and how, when, and why hip-hop shaped him. Hip-hop is such an elastic-rich culture that tracing its artistic roots is a question of how deep to dig.

A musicologist bent on true beginnings would begin in Africa, tracing the slave ships and slave songs to the Caribbean and, ultimately, to America. In Africa, tribes used a variety of rhythm instruments to communicate over distance, including, as their instrument-building skills advanced, talking drums. Among the Ashanti of West Africa, the drums were the town criers and first newspapers. Flexing lengths of animal hide stretched along the sides of the drum, the drummer could achieve a variety of tones, bending them to mimic the octave changes that were employed in African languages to change the meaning of words. The intricate rhythms traditionally retold the tribe's past glories in celebratory ceremonies but were also used in war and in mourning, as well as for sending messages to neighboring villages more quickly than a swift runner could.

The talking drummers recorded history in soundscapes, conveying the past to the present and the present to an extended community like a deft DJ. They were later joined by the griots, who, like the bards of Europe, crafted the trials and tribulations of their nation into long oral poems, memorized and set to song and passed along to each generation. Griots were the first historians, the original MCs. Africans uprooted by the slave trade and brought to the New World turned the griot tradition into what we now know as the blues, arguably the root of all modern popular music.

A social-sciences professor investigating hip-hop might begin with the culture's sense of community and point out that hip-hop's closest ancestor is jazz, the musical form of the black working class from the forties to the sixties. From the bebop innovations of Charlie Parker through the mind-blowing redefinitions of Miles Davis and the intergalactic freedom of John Coltrane's late work, jazz has been a canvas of innovative African-American musical expression (that has since wilted, for the most part, into the vapid castrato of Kenny G). Jazz shares the scat vocal tradition with hip-hop as well; the storytelling being suffused with so much rhythm and feeling at times that only sound will do. Jazz swaggered with a cool confidence that defied segregation and racism with soul and style, and reflected the tribulations of black Americans. Like hip-hop, jazz connected with white audiences and was absorbed into mainstream white culture.

A historian studying hip-hop would couch the evolution of the form in the context of postwar, pre-eighties economic conditions in inner cities. The nutrients and waste products that fertilized the soil of hip-hop were America's edgy, depressed post-Vietnam mood, widespread speed and heroin abuse, the Orwellian control mentality of local and national governments, and decaying inner cities in the late seventies. In the years after the Vietnam War, the incentives of America's major industries—auto, chemical, and real estate—funded the development of suburban life, and urban-based families that could afford to move did. Those left behind had no choice; they were predominantly matriarchal households left to fend for themselves in eroding neighborhoods while city governments spent their budgets on police containment instead of on assistance. In New York, families moved to New Jersey and Long Island or better sections of Brooklyn and Queens. The Bronx, at the heart of America's biggest metropolis, was hit hardest. Gangs and drugs ruled in an area with no economic foundation to build on; it was depicted in the media as a wasteland, for example in movies such as *Fort Apache, the Bronx* (1981) and *Escape from New York* (1981), which predicted that in 1997 the federal government, in response to uncontrollable gangs and crime, would wall in Manhattan Island and declare it a maximum-security prison. On the music front, the righteous soul of Motown and funk of Sly and the Family Stone was superseded by disco's smooth elitist soundtrack and R&B singers in the disco vein.

In the seventies, at the northernmost tip of Manhattan, the southernmost section of the Bronx Borough of New York City, restless youth who either didn't like or couldn't afford to see hip-hop pioneer DJ Hollywood spin in Manhattan nightclubs found a dance outlet at parties in their neighborhood parks. Unorthodox DJs there wove a sound harder than the show-business boogie of disco bands such as Chic and Fatback. These rebel crews rocked the block with power that was siphoned from the city of New York by tapping into a transformer box at the base of a light pole. The performers reinvented themselves as grandiose street superheroes with flashy uniforms and spectacular names that suggested power, prestige, and respect. There were plenty of players on the scene, but three men permanently sculpted the revolution: Kool Herc, Grandmaster Flash, and Afrika Bambaataa.

Kool Herc, born Clive Campbell on the island of Jamaica, was the first to link the instrumental drum breaks in a song. He sewed together hard funk, connecting James Brown and the Average White Band and sought out obscure records with hot instrumental breaks to extend the jam. He called it "break spinning." It was the first sound of hip-hop. Herc spun in Bronx nightclubs and outdoor parks with his "masters of ceremony" or "mike controllers" (MCs), Coke La Rock, Luv Bug Starski, and Busy Bee, who kept the party moving like the Jamaican toaster emcees in the dance halls of Kingston. They'd hype the songs, commend the DJ's skills, and keep people on the floor with phrases that are still hip-hop staples, like "Ya rock and ya don't stop" and "To the beat, y'all."

Bambaataa, born Kevin Donovan, broadened hip-hop's sonic horizons and social image. Bambaataa, known for his sharp tongue and bold community politics, was the leader of the Black Spades, the city's biggest, toughest street gang. Using their influence, Bambaataa formed the Organization, a coalition that helped keep drugs and violence at bay in his home, the Bronx River Projects. Spinning breaks like Herc, Bambaataa brought a multicultural strain to the party, courtesy of the eclectic tastes and diverse record collection he picked up from his mother, which ran the gamut from Sly Stone to Led Zeppelin to Latin soul. He would scour secondhand stores to score diverse vinyl, adding everything from African, jazz, and Caribbean breaks to the Euro-synth of Kraftwerk's "Trans-Europe Express" to his mix. In 1974, as Bronx gangs imploded over turf wars, drugs, and police crackdowns, Bambaataa founded the Zulu Nation, a collective of DJs, breakers, rappers, and graffiti artists, plus some friends from the Black Spades, that still thrives today. The Zulu Nation strove to de-escalate gang violence by creating a hub for the various groups involved in hip-hop. Over the years Bambaataa and the Zulu Nation have become the U.N. of hip-hop, albeit with less red tape and more success stories. The Zulus were the first hip-hop artists to take the music to Europe (in 1981), while Bambaataa, with Soulsonic Force, scored as a recording artist with the 1982 robo-funk opus "Planet Rock," a genre-smashing classic, as influential for establishing Tommy Boy Records as it is for inspiring British dance DJs such as the Chemical Brothers, Fatboy Slim and the Prodigy more than a decade later.

Grandmaster Wizard Theodore is regarded as the first DJ who scratched a record backward against the needle while cuing up, forever loosing a shrill exclamatory tear into hip-hop's sonic vocabulary. But Grandmaster Flash, born Joseph Saddler, ran with the scratch. As a performer with the Furious Five, Flash expanded hip-hop's lyrical legacy of party-up jams into trenchant social commentary in one fell swoop with 1982's "The Message." But before that, Flash redefined DJ-ing. He used the electronics training he received at vocational high school to construct a homemade cue mixer, which allowed him to listen to one record while the other was playing. At the time, this was a feature found only on professional nightclub setups. With that advantage and the hand—eye coordination that earned him his DJ handle, Flash dexterously perfected back-spinning: winding back records on alternating turntables to repeat the same musical segment. He also invented punch-phrasing: quickly blasting bits of sound from one record into the mix while the other continues to play. Flash even integrated the original beat box—a customized Vox drum machine—into his performance. He made an acrobatic show out of DJ-ing as Jimi Hendrix had out of guitar-playing: using his elbows to mix and turning his back to his turntables while scratching and back-spinning. Flash was also the man who made MCs the main draw of the evening. Where other DJs had one or two MCs who improvised rhymes to keep spirits high and bodies moving, Flash performed with five. His group elevated the form with bounced rhymes, tandem flows, and back-to-back delivery that came off like one voice. They moved the attention off the recorded music onto the words, from the DJs to the rappers. Flash and the Furious Five were the first hip-hop juggernaut product—they had the skills, the outfits, and the sound, as well as the complete recording and performing package. And they defined the first wave of rap music.

Early hip-hop culture found its visual aesthetic in two non-musical scenes: graffiti artists and break-dancers. Not all graffiti kids were into hip-hop and not all of them were black (many of the best were Hispanic and some were white). In the Bronx, artists such as Dondi White and Lee Quinones covered the rotting buildings of the ghetto with ornate murals, testifying their tags, or pen names. They painted subway cars and broken walls, displaying the same DIY attitude as the crews throwing park parties. Many, such as the brilliant Jean-Michel Basquiat (who evolved soon beyond graffiti style), ended up selling canvases of graffiti to the downtown art crowd by the early eighties. Graffiti style permeated early hip-hop, from the logos of the groups to the flyers that advertised the shows. It is less revolutionary now; graffiti is hip-hop's calling card, expected everywhere there is hip-hop culture or the advertising aimed at the broad hip-hop market.

The other group making waves in hip-hop's early days were break-dancers. The dance style began as a trend among black gangs, devoid of the acrobatic tricks associated with it today. Like any novelty, it passed out of fashion, but when African-Americans moved on, Hispanic teens made it their own. In clubs and on street corners all over the city, "breakers" such as Crazy Legs (Richie Colon) elevated the style, integrating martial arts high kicks and spins. In the early eighties, break-dancing was as common as DJs at hip-hop parties, though the first glimpse many Americans got of it came through three peppy Hollywood treatments: *Beat Street, Breakin',* and *Breakin' 2: Electric Boogaloo.*

The first rap song widely sold on vinyl was the Sugarhill Gang's "Rapper's Delight" in 1979, the start of a four-year run for an independent label that included some of the most significant rap music made: Grandmaster Flash and the Furious Five's "The Message," "The Adventures of Grandmaster Flash on the Wheels of Steel," and "White Lines," as well as old-schoolers such as the "love rapper" Spoonie Gee and "Body Rock" by the Treacherous Three. "Rapper's Delight" sold more than two million copies worldwide, hit number four on the R&B charts and number thirty-six on the pop charts. It was rap's first commercial boom, all in one song; one that took many music execs, who were still pushing disco, by surprise.

The new and improved second wave of rap hit in the eighties. Kurtis Blow got the party started with a fantastic rap jam, "The Breaks," which sold gold as a twelve-inch in 1980. Kurtis's party-hearty vibe married to pointed lyrics slipped onto the radar of punk and New Wave fans to reach the Top 30 in the U.K. Kurtis, in turn, opened up for reggae legend Bob Marley at Madison Square Garden, and toured with New Wave giants Blondie in Britain.

But whereas Kurtis was barely known to pop audiences, Run-D.M.C. broke into the mainstream with their first twelve-inch, "It's Like That/Sucker MCs," in 1983. While the A-side is amazing in its own right, on the B-side rap evolved to a whole new level in just one song. "Sucker MCs" was a vision of rap to come; it is minimal, featuring only a drum machine and turntable scratches and the MCs' overlapping delivery in which they finished each other's sentences. Run-D.M.C.'s influence can't be overestimated: they were the first group to fully cross over to pop and rock audiences, the first to integrate guitar riffs into their music, and the first to forgo the funk superhero gear and hyperbolic ganglike names in favor of b-boy sportswear. The members of Run-D.M.C. were closer to the street in image and attitude; they were the first rappers to "keep it real." They were also middle-class kids who grew up in Hollis, Queens, and were managed by Joseph "Run"

Simmons's brother, mogul-in-the-making Russell. Run-D.M.C. ran with the rap ball, driving into the pop lane via the fledgling MTV. On the Music Television network, hip-hop had always played a bit part. Blondie's "Rapture" brought proto-rapping and Fab Five Freddy's name to the upper echelon (number one) of the pop charts, but true hip-hop culture first walked into the land of crossover on the robot legs of Herbie Hancock's electro-monster "Rockit" in 1983. The next year brought Chaka Khan's Prince-penned pop and R&B hit "I Feel for You," featuring the low, smooth stylings of Grandmaster Melle Mel (of the Furious Five). These were inklings, but Run-D.M.C. changed it all with "Rock Box" in 1984, the third single to drop before their gold-selling eponymous debut was released the same year. "Rock Box" was the first real rap video, and it set the low-fi production values that seemed to stick until late in that decade. It was also, like *Breakin'*, the first that many American suburban teens saw of this thing called hip-hop.

Run-D.M.C. may have opened the rap gates to the mainstream, but in the real world, eighties economics were laying waste to urban life in a way that would fuel the next wave of hip-hop. With more employment opportunities in post-Civil Rights corporate America, more African-Americans left for the suburbs, leaving what were once fully developed working-class urban com-munities behind. In Ronald Reagan's America, the urban landscape became a gangland of drugs. Crack epitomized the rampant capitalism of the times: the narcotic equivalent of the turn of the decade. Where cocaine's status symbol and social sniffing epitomized disco glamour, crack was its fast-food counterpart—a quick, intense high packaged for the masses. It was supremely capitalistic; it yielded more product from the drug dealer's initial investment, and its low price and highly addictive nature ensured lifetime customers. The ratio of man hours to wages paid found in the job market for high-school graduates couldn't compare to the money that could be made by crack, coke, and weed dealing, and there were plenty of openings in the inner city. Teenagers, even preteens, left school to work for gang corporations that produced, packaged, and sold drugs to a color-blind cross-section of society. It was common practice at that time, as it still is today in a variety of locales nationwide.

In a decade defined by conspicuous consumption, the division between rich and poor, addicts and dealers took on heaven-and-hell proportions in the cities. Profitable blocks—those with the most drug traffic—became war zones between rival dealing teams who would, as DMX put it in 1998's "Ruff Ryders Anthem": "Stop, drop, shut 'em down, open up shop / Oh, no, that's how Ruff Ryders roll." The dealers with the money bought more guns—big ones, such as the Israeli Uzi and the Austrian Glock, both designed for soldiers at war, which the drug game's players are.

Instead of a long-term path to a middle-management position, the drug trade is a shot at a moneyed life for those who can't make it in the system; a shot at the very dream in the heart of rap music. Selling drugs is in no way a viable alternative—there are two logical ends: one is a coffin and the other is jail, arguably just a different type of coffin. But for many enterprising young men who are marginalized by society for their race, death is a worthwhile risk for the power and riches to be gained, as well as the chance to flaunt them in a society that values them so much. As rap grew commercially viable, music became the alternative to the alternative—an equally competitive, legal occupation with the same spoils, a wider degree of respect, and less mortal risk. It is a shot at a different kind of independence.

"There's a hyperbolic individualism in rap that has to do with the mistrust in relationships," observes Shelby Steele, a research fellow at the Hoover Institute at Stanford University and author of the book *A Dream Deferred: The Second Betrayal of Black Freedom in America.* "All the central relationships of one's life, with one's single parent or whatever, are sources of pain, so therefore there's a self-sufficiency that meshes with the kind of simplistic capitalism of 'every man for himself.' It's all a fabric of the alienation, the inability to make lasting, meaningful connections with human beings. Therefore, there's a focus on things, on money, and a commodification of women, so their value to you is monetary. All of that kind of ugliness has to do with an underlying alienation. I don't think the music is an informed embrace of capitalism, it's an impulsive embrace of the self-sufficiency it seems to offer. Having said that, hip-hop has become this multi-billion-dollar industry and produced the first generation of black entrepreneurs who really have access to the American main-stream, like Puff Daddy. So, in an ironic sense, that's good."

The crack boom of the eighties also equaled more jailed young men. In the African-American communities, close to 20 percent of the male population was in jail or on probation by the end of that decade, leaving fewer male role models outside the prison system and far too many with lessons to teach inside. In the music that came out of this era, the street reportage of Run-D.M.C. that opened so many doors was bowled over by groups with an even grittier broadcast to air. Whether it was the agitprop genius of Public Enemy, the proto-gangsta philosophies of Boogie Down Productions, the unapologetic sex and violence of N.W.A, the ghetto storytelling of Slick Rick, the pulp-fiction pimpin' of Ice-T, or the sublime boast and groove of Eric B. and Rakim, rap's message had hardened. These groups dove deep into the realities of poverty, drugs, racism, and American hypocrisy while hip-hop producers such as the Bomb Squad (Public Enemy) and Dr. Dre (N.W.A) turned beats into barrage. The new age of hip-hop MCs came with social commentary, from the contradictory theories of former homeless teen KRS-One to the middle-class, university-educated Chuck D's literary sonic treatises with Public Enemy that forever changed what hip-hop could be. In an alternate take on the same issue, N.W.A shot their way into the depths of murder, mayhem, and sexism. In short, these are the groups that made hip-hop, as most consumers know, matter.

The East Coast acts, from Public Enemy to De La Soul, made huge inroads with white American teens, feeding the interest Run-D.M.C. had sparked. The sociopolitical agenda and hard edge of Public Enemy and Boogie Down Productions in particular dovetailed with the tastes of white punk-rock fans hooked on the Clash, and of those suburban rebels looking for a more extreme expression of anti-authoritarianism. By the release of their second album, 1988's *It Takes a Nation of Millions to Hold Us Back*, Public Enemy's bombastic sonics and Chuck D's lyrical rhetoric had set African-American pride to a revolutionary beat. They combined the social consciousness of Martin Luther King Jr., the stoic call for change of Malcolm X and the Nation of Islam, and the military imagery of the Black Panther Party. The group's dense musical collage, Chuck D's forceful baritone, and Flavor Flav's comic foil coalesced the entirety of hip-hop: its roots, the conditions of its present, and the possibilities of its future. In the same late-eighties "golden age," avant-garde groups such as De La Soul, the Jungle Brothers, and A Tribe Called Quest—three groups who collaborated with other artists and collectively dubbed themselves the Native Tongues—expressed Afrocentricity through a bohemian perspective. The Tongues' intellectual cynicism and humor took center stage, backed by a musical palette that integrated everything from jazz to Steely Dan. The Native Tongues and the artists like them who followed (Brand Nubian, the Disposable Heroes of Hiphoprisy, Arrested Development, and Digable Planets) crossed over with white college audiences. Literary-minded music fans of all ages and backgrounds dove deep into De La Soul's *3 Feet High and Rising*, a frog-hopping masterwork of pop music snippets and wit made in the brief age before music-publishing lawyers realized the profit potential in sample clearances. Whether it was the smooth, soulful storytelling of A Tribe Called Quest or the blood sport of N.W.A, in the late eighties and early nineties rap won a tremendous number of fans, mostly male, in white American suburbs. It was an obvious match. At a time when more young black men were convicted of crimes in America than any other demographic group, even rap that wasn't overtly violent sounded like black men shouting, a sound that scared parents and peers more than the fastest punk rock or heavy metal. At the same time that rap appealed to its new fans for its message, it spoke of real American issues—poverty, crime, racism—that hadn't quite filtered out to many suburbs. Compared to rap music, the rock-and-roll rebellion of Metallica and Guns N' Roses safely basked in its own excess.

Public Enemy wound down after member Professor Griff's anti-Semitic remarks in 1989 (Jews were "responsible for the majority of wickedness around the globe") did irreparable damage to the group creatively and publicly. The thirst for shocking, hardcore rap was soon to be quenched by West Coast gangsta rap. Over party-hearty James Brown and Parliament/Funkadelic samples, gangland storytelling equated social consciousness with a glorified view of the outlaw reality that has dominated hip-hop since the nineties.

Gangsta rap celebrated ghetto outlaw tales, both real and imagined, stories of men thriving by their own design in the face of every conceivable obstacle. In the early eighties, Kool G Rap, Too $hort, and Ice-T personified the stance that would become gangsta, but it was André "Dr. Dre" Young's musicality that perfected it and like Run-D.M.C., connected with the masses. Whereas East Coast acts such as Public Enemy and Boogie Down Productions relied on a dense, pounding musical backdrop, Dr. Dre melded his noise collages to a deep, rolling funk. Dr. Dre's earlier work, on tracks like "Express Yourself," from N.W.A's landmark *Straight Outta Compton*, followed producer Eric B.'s (of Eric B. and Rakim) style of mining James Brown for a new generation, yet to an altogether different end. Dr. Dre and his associates in N.W.A—Ice Cube, Eazy-E, MC Ren, and DJ Yella—upped the ante on scaring the system. Chuck D had called for revolution and had criticized society, but N.W.A stood for chaos. Without reflection or talk of consequence, their songs celebrated the harassment of women, drunk driving, drug selling, and shoot-outs with cops and rivals. In 1988, *Straight Outta Compton*, largely driven by the megaphone-blast shock value of the single "Fuck Tha Police," went platinum with absolutely no major radio airplay or support from MTV. The FBI deemed the group's image as threatening as terrorism: as sales of *Straight Outta Compton* added up, N.W.A's record company, Ruthless, and their parent company, Priority Records, were sent letters from the Bureau that warned that the group should tone down their act. At the same time, N.W.A's runaway sales perked the ears of corporate music executives who would soon craft stars in their image, as the group launched a legacy that defined popular rap music into the next century. It was a sign of things to come, and a reminder to any who hadn't noticed, that an excess of sex, violence, and money in entertainment connects with Americans.

When Dr. Dre formed Death Row Records with notorious executive Suge Knight in 1992, the West Coast "G-Funk" style became an empire. Death Row artists such as Snoop Dogg and Tupac Shakur dominated the hip-hop and pop charts in the early and mid-nineties with the hedonistic, romanticized nihilism of gang life, drug dealing, misogyny, and murder. Images of West Coast house parties, vintage low-rider cars and gang-banging "homeboys" who ruled the neighborhood from the comfort of their mom's house flooded MTV, at which point it was absorbed by teens in suburbs all over the country. White kids in the Midwest and elsewhere connected with the rebellion even if they didn't understand its roots, musically or socially. What they did was imitate its style and dance to its groove immediately. Across the country, suburban teens of all races, and a greater majority of young whites than ever, relished the music's tantalizing danger; they soon dressed, spoke, and attempted to party like gang members from Compton, California. Hollywood reflected the gangsta takeover, too, producing films that depicted the treacherous reality of West Coast ghetto life, like *Boyz 'N the Hood* (1991) and *Menace II Society* (1993), as well as those that made light of it, such as *Friday* (1995), the weed-fogged comedy starring Ice Cube, and the ghetto-themed horror movie *Tales from the Hood* (1995). As the decade tipped toward its second half, "thug life," like the motto tattooed across Tupac Shakur's torso, became an institution, a vision of living above the law without consequences; a vision shattered when art spilled into reality and the nineties' two brightest stars, Tupac Shakur and Christopher Wallace (a.k.a. the Notorious B.I.G.), were gunned down in separate incidents that remain unsolved mysteries. But gangsta rap as it is most commonly known began with Dr. Dre, who drove mainstream hip-hop—some say for the worse, some say for the better—into lewd, visceral territory: a cross between the insane reality comedy of Richard Pryor and the violent decadence of Brian De Palma's *Scarface*.

The *Chicago Sun-Times* writer Jim DeRogatis regards Dr. Dre as responsible for a decade of mediocre rap that has stifled the art form. "I think Dre is perhaps the most overrated producer in rock history," he says. "I don't think that musically Dre has ever been the genius people say he is. I think it's bubblegum—big, stupid, dumb, simple hooks. And that's okay, but I listen to De la Soul, Gang Starr, and Eric B. and Rakim and the innovations that were inherent in hip-hop pre-N.W.A's *Niggaz 4 Life*. I chart it all back to that album in 1991. Every single element of the Eminem formula—the same formula Dre has used to sell a billion records since 1991—were all there in *Niggaz 4 Life*. That record had memorable ditties like 'find 'em fuck 'em and flee,' 'she swallowed it,' 'to kill a whore,' and 'yo bitch, hop in my pickup and suck my dick up until you hiccup.' Hip-hop, to me, has betrayed the boundless artistic possibilities in the music and been mired in a gangsta rut ever since. It's a shame."

"There is certainly innocent hip-hop and then there's gangsta—and there's a whole range of expression included there," says author Shelby Steele. "Gangsta rap has something to do with the fracturing of the black family that began to be very serious in the seventies and eighties and has continued. It has something to do with the attitudes, it has something to do with life in the underclass. There seems to be a painful alienation there, between men and women, individuals and society. It's an anti-innocent culture. It does not allow for innocent expressions of love back and forth, you know, the way Motown did with all the 'ooh baby baby.' It suggests that innocence will get you hurt, get you wounded. So it seems to me to be in many ways emotionally defensive, and there's an undercurrent of alienation. You have to remember that seventy percent of black kids are illegitimate.

Black women get married at half the rate of white women, and get divorced at twice the rate of white women. That suggests an adolescence that is much, much more alienated than the one I knew. To me it's ridiculous to criticize hip-hop because it is an outgrowth of a very real change in the culture. It's just telling us what is there, whether we like it or not, and it's not a very attractive picture."

The deaths of the Notorious B.I.G. and Tupac Shakur (or 2Pac) brought another picture into focus: the side effects of mythologizing thug life and death. Their murders marked the decline of gangsta rap: Dr. Dre had left Death Row Records to form his own label, Aftermath Entertainment, in 1996, and Suge Knight's criminal management tactics landed him in jail. Countless rappers have borrowed from 2Pac and the Notorious B.I.G.; many, such as Ja Rule, profited more, as Eminem says in "Marshall Mathers" on *The Marshall Mathers LP*, and have all of the dollars that belong to Biggie and 2Pac, as if they had switched wallets. Violence, gunplay, and the drug game never disappeared from rap, but the flagrant celebration of them took a backseat as if rappers learned from 2Pac and Biggie that boasting could turn bloody and lyrically obsessing about your death could deliver it to your door. At the same time other hardcore rappers were eager to fill the void, they were also careful not to follow in Biggie's and 2Pac's footsteps too closely.

Toward the end of the century, the Wu-Tang Clan, DMX, and Jay-Z took the helm of what came next: a diverse range of hardcore viewpoints—from the Five-Percent-Nation-of-Islam-inflected, martial arts and mathematics-obsessed rap of the

Wu-Tang Clan to the spiritual gangster tales of DMX. The upside of gangsta rap—high living—became the focus, mythologized and exaggerated as guns and murder had been. On MTV and BET, for all intents and purposes the strongest outlets for nonurban youth to access popular culture, the hedonistic spoils of the game were celebrated to the fullest. Gangsta became synonymous with ostentatious consumption, the be-all and end-all of rap life. Violence, guns, and death were never far behind, in lyrics and reality, but it was as if rappers chose to accentuate the positive and reiterate what it was all for: the money. A display of power was no longer made by a street soldier's lyrical cold-blooded killing, it was asserted through boasts of popularity, wealth, and style befitting a kingpin. Puff Daddy epitomized the new gangsta, who preferred to be tough only in reputation, while dressing, rapping, and playing for success with mainstream America. Rappers spit rhymes that tied Chanel to Prada while hubcap-size diamond pendants hung around their necks; they sipped Cristal champagne like they once drank malt liquor, or mixed it with Kool-Aid like Mannie Fresh of the Cash Money Records crew does; block parties moved down to Miami's Ocean Drive as rappers opined about freaky sex on ecstasy, hot tubs, motorboats, motorcycles, Mercedes, and more words for money than ever before.

At the same time that hip-hop dominated late-nineties pop music with diamonds, parties, and accessible dance-floor anthems, independent record labels such as Rawkus and Quannum fostered an alternative to this overt materialism: back-to-basics innovation. Rap fans gravitated to their artists' simple, decidedly low-fidelity production aesthetics and diverse sensibilities. There is the raw, rugged stomp of Pharoahe Monch, who scored a hit in 1999 with "Simon Says," to the versatile, soulful production and remix work of DJ Spinna. Rawkus and the "backpacker scene" (dubbed for the casual, no-frills backpack, sweatshirt and baseball-hat attire that was typical of the fans and artists) were the antithesis of Bentleys and Cristal, an alternative that in 1999 and 2000 seemed on the verge of changing millennial hip-hop. In New York, Rawkus Records dominated the East Coast wing of the scene on the strength of a string of influential releases. Rawkus was a struggling label with no clear identity until it signed Company Flow, a three-man rap collective from Queens. Backed by the production work of El-P, short for El-Producto (born Jaime Meline), Company Flow revitalized the hip-hop underground with a series of twelve-inch releases, starting in 1992. Their dense abstract lyrics, irregular yet funky beats, and spacey ambiance brought experimentalism back to the genre that in 2002 made its way into the mainstream, echoed in the herky-jerky syncopation of songs like Missy Elliott's "Work It." But in 1995, the members of Company Flow worked day jobs to fund an EP on double vinyl, *Funcrusher* (1996), which sold a successful thirty thousand copies. The group was soon courted by several record labels, but the fledgling Rawkus was the only one to accept their demands: Company Flow maintained ownership of their recordings, received 50 percent of the net royalties, and were not tied to a multi-album contract. Company Flow kept their freedom, Rawkus earned credibility. The label signed Mos Def (born Dante Terrell Smith), Talib Kweli (born Talib Greene), and Cincinnati, Ohio's Hi-Tek (born Tony Cottrell) as the collaborative Black Star in 1997, a trio that preached a halt to the negativity in rap by echoing the self-awareness and freedom of mind in the teachings of legendary black activist Marcus Garvey. Black Star similarly harped on Afrocentric unity, reviving the style and consciousness of the Native Tongues collective in the eighties. When Black Star's eponymous debut was released in 1998, they were lauded by critics and fans as the next coming of hip-hop.

On the West Coast, a group of artists, most of whom met at the student radio station of the University of California at Davis, formed the Solesides–Quannum collective. Solesides began as DJ Shadow (Josh Davis), Blackalicious (includes Gift of Gab, a.k.a. T.J. Parker, and Chief Xcel, born Xavier Mosley), Lateef the Truth Speaker (Lateef Daumont), and Lyrics Born (Tom Shimura); Lateef and Lyrics Born also recorded as Latyrx. The Solesides crew, like some of the bright lights in the Rawkus family, were a mix of a fractured, funky, stream-of-consciousness aesthetics and rich, old-school rap. Through the nineties, first on Solesides Records, then on Quannum Projects, these artists made eclectic, quality hip-hop music that, like that of their East Coast counterparts in Company Flow, did not catch on until the decade headed to a close.

At the time, artists on labels like No Limit, Cash Money, and Puff Daddy's Bad Boy Records would sell a million records on the reputation of the label and the sound the label was known for, which often eclipsed the performers' abilities. At the height of No Limit Records' popularity, kingpin Master P could literally have put out an album by your mother and watched it sell one million copies. By contrast, underground acts with limited means relied on talent. Eminem came up with a solid class of battle MCs in the late nineties: Juice, Supernatural, Chino XL, Xzibit, Thirstin Howl III, as well as Detroit's Royce Da 5'9" and Proof. Some of these names have made it. Some, like Supernatural, are more the stuff of legend.

But the late-nineties underground hip-hop scene, even at its most innovative, focused on a return to basic, straightforward rap: looped grooves and MC skills first and foremost. Rap battles and ciphers—lyricists passing the mike from one to the other—hadn't disappeared, but had become a staple of underground parties. An MC's credibility depended on how well he could captivate a room on the spur of the moment, not on his clothes, clique, or cash. Competitions where MCs would take each other down with prepared and improvised verses, as in the final scenes of *8 Mile*, were the building blocks of a rapper's reputation.

The golden age of gangsta rap and the late-nineties underground are the two influences at play in Eminem, a convergence of the hardcore sensibility with a rhyme style born of a diverse, MC-centric scene. Eminem first heard rap music when his uncle Ronnie Polkingham, who was just a few months older than Eminem, played him Ice-T's "Reckless" from the soundtrack to the 1984 film *Breakin'*. Eminem grew up break-dancing, listening to LL Cool J, Run-D.M.C., and the Beastie Boys, and began writing his own rhymes in his early teens. He performed at local talent shows and at school functions in groups with names like the New Jacks and Sole Intent. As he continued writing, performing, and consuming, Eminem found his way into the heart of Detroit hip-hop and, when he turned his skill to a different end, accomplished locally what performances alone could not.

"Eminem started out just doing shows," Proof says. "He was doing local little high-school shows, like at Center Line, the high school in Center Line, Michigan. They had a lot of them there. He wasn't really a battle-rapper. That was more my forte. I did it because I enjoyed it. I clung to it because I was more of a freestyle artist. Em was focusing on constructing songs. He was a genius at it then and he still is now. But what he had to battle for was credibility. Battling solidifies your street credibility as an MC. You don't go talking about killing motherfuckers in your songs to gain credibility in the street. Most people are homing in on your skills, 'Can he rap? Can he flow?' Em is an extraordinary rapper and he was doing extraordinary things with his songs then, too. But it didn't matter; he had to earn that credibility in battles. Now everybody is doing battles, dropping verses about each other the way Jay-Z and Nas have been doing. Back then it wasn't really happening that much with that level of artists."

There is a well-documented history of popular artists battling for supreme boasting rights on record, with songs aimed at each other and popular opinion as the judge, that has come in and out of vogue. LL Cool J and Kool Moe Dee (formerly of the Treacherous Three) went at each other ceaselessly in the late eighties over who stole whose rap style. 2Pac and the Notorious B.I.G. taunted and accused each other over a series of songs and, though the tradition cooled following their deaths, it has returned with gusto: Jay-Z and Nas have lobbed lyrical shots at each other since 2001, and an animosity between Dr. Dre and

Eminem's Shady Records and Aftermath camps and the Murder Inc. family of Ja Rule and Irv Gotti, in part inspired by 50 Cent, grew into another theater of conflict in 2003. These recorded battle tracks and their renewed popularity bring the tradition to the radio waves—literally. New York's Hot 97 set up a battle of the beats during which Nas and Jay-Z's tracks were played back to back and listeners phoned and faxed in their votes for the winner (Nas was victorious, with 52 percent of the vote over Jay-Z's 48 percent). Battle competitions are more popular than ever, occupying more time on MTV and BET as well as inspiring more regional and national events sponsored by a variety of hip-hop entities, from magazines to coalitions of labels and promoters, than just a few years ago. The verbal warfare so well captured in *8 Mile* will do nothing but further the trend.

"Em's worked really hard to get where he is," Bizzare, of D-12, says. "He went everywhere back in the day — battles, conventions. I was one of the first to take him out of town, actually. He had never been nowhere besides Kansas City and Cedar Point in Michigan. Around '94, I think it was, me and him drove down to the How Can I Be Down? conference in Miami. There was like five of us in a Honda Accord, driving all the way down there. We didn't do too good, we passed out a couple tapes, we didn't get no respect whatever. We had to leave early because all this bad shit was happening back home with Kim at the house Em had with her. They was getting broken into and they was getting evicted. Me and him had to get back to Detroit right away, so we tried to catch a bus, and they wouldn't let him on it because he had his clothes in a garbage bag. He had to, like, put the clothes on and put shit in my bag."

It is impossible to relate the history of hip-hop and understand Eminem's place in it without including the white people who have affected the scene for better and worse. In hip-hop's early years, punk and New Wave artists such as the Clash and Blondie were early supporters: Grandmaster Flash and the Furious Five opened for the Clash on all seven nights of concerts that they played in Bond's International Casino Times Square in 1981, in front of sets painted by graffiti artists such as Phase 2. Blondie was, in truth, the first group to land a proto-rap on the pop charts with "Rapture," in 1980. Former Sex Pistol John Lydon and Afrika Bambaataa teamed up in 1984 for the cutting-edge dance hit "World Destruction," and it's impossible to think that plenty of the half a million copies of Kurtis Blow's "The Breaks" sold didn't go to white fans. In the early days of the music, white executives such as Tom Silverman (Tommy Boy), publicist Bill Adler, producer Rick Rubin and Lyor Cohen (Def Jam) and Barry Weiss (Jive) supported rap when black execs at the black-music divisions of major record labels regarded rap as a novelty, opting to develop R&B divas and funk bands. *The Source*, the self-proclaimed "bible of hip-hop," was started by two white guys, Jonathan Schecter and David Mays, out of a Harvard dorm room in 1988. From visionary believers like producer and Def Jam cofounder Rick Rubin to charlatans like N.W.A's manager Jerry Hibbert, whites have been involved in hip-hop from the start; they're as old-school of a feature as the rapper who never got paid—and the record company entrenched in white corporate America that didn't pay him.

The only unquestionably supportive role that whites have

played in nurturing the music is as members of the record-buying public and the select critical media. Grandmaster Flash and the Furious Five's landmark single "The Message" was heralded by white rock outlets such as the *Village Voice* and *Rolling Stone* back in 1979. The groups who have had the most universal appeal—Run-D.M.C., Public Enemy, N.W.A, Naughty by Nature, Snoop, Tupac, Biggie Smalls, Eminem—have drawn fans from the same well.

Of course, there *is* white rap. When Eminem debuted in the hip-hop press, each magazine, in one form or another, ran articles such as *The Source*'s "Other White Rappers Who Don't Suck," as a remembrance. All those articles were duly short. The Beastie Boys were the first significant white rap group; they weren't the only one to be nationally known before Eminem, although it may have been better if they were. Most white MCs have done more damage to white hip-hop credibility than C. Dolores Tucker, the staunchly conservative, antirap black activist has done to black free expression. Most white rap exemplifies cultural imperialism and inspires justified nonexpectations. It is a walking list of ways white men can't jump. In the past, white MCs who "made it" won short-term victories then fell out of favor, not by losing their edge, but, after revealing their one trick, by staying the same. The most commercially successful white acts before Eminem were hokey, safe, poplike visions of hip-hop, with a shtick that crossed over with young audiences: Marky Mark and the Funky Bunch (rap with one foot in the "urban" dance music of the early nineties), Vanilla Ice (the white MC Hammer), and House of Pain (Cypress Hill with pot leaves and bongs traded for shamrocks and beer), who, to their credit, released not one but two hit singles. There is the terribly awful *One Stop Carnival*, by *Beverly Hills 90210* star Brian Austin Green, that despite production work by Tré Hardson (Slim Kid 3 of the Pharcyde) remains an art-imitating-life caveat: Green's character on the show, David Silver, was also signed to a record deal for his gangsta rap stylings and didn't succeed. There is the Insane Clown Posse, a sorely undertalented Detroit rap-schlock hybrid act known more for their Kiss-style makeup and a taste for spraying audiences with Faygo cola than for their music; regionally, they enjoy a devoted cult following.

Only two white rap groups before Eminem enjoyed credibility; only one can be called widely successful. The Beastie Boys were a white group managed by a black man, Russell Simmons, who nurtured these upper-middle-class, well-educated punks into rap brats. The Beastie Boys were a punk rock band for two years, until 1983, when they became taken with the emerging sampling technology of hip-hop and released the *Cookie Puss* EP named for an ice cream cake by Carvel. The Beastie Boys showed that defiant beer-can nihilism and inept punk rock proved far more creative in hip-hop: the Beastie Boys' debut album, *Licensed to Ill*, went to number one on the U.S. pop charts in 1986. It was the first rap album to do so. *Licensed to Ill* was a collusion of Led Zeppelin riffs, an odd television-theme sample (from the *Mister Ed* show), and irony-free lyrical references from Picasso to porno. Their fuck-it-all formula embraced the machismo of heavy metal (caged strippers onstage), the aimless rebellion of white teens ("[You Gotta] Fight for Your Right [to Party]"), the anti-authority street style of hip-hop (huge gold chains with a Volkswagen hood ornament), and the anthemic rock-flavored dynamics that characterized the early days of Def Jam Records, a style proved successful by Run-D.M.C. (particularly on *Raising Hell*, in 1986) and LL Cool J (on *Radio*, in 1985). But neither of those acts sold as many records as quickly as the Beastie Boys' *Licensed to Ill*, which sold 750,000 copies in six weeks; at the time, it was the fastest-selling debut album in the history of Def Jam's distributor, Columbia Records. In light of the volume of their success, the Beastie Boys faced a controversy similar to the one that met Eminem fourteen years later. Hip-hop purists were horrified at the Beastie Boys' exaggerated, overly Caucasian delivery and excessive bad behavior, wondering if there was a line between an overenthusiasm for rap and a parody of the culture. The main-stream media protested the Beastie Boys' stage show, which was laden with strippers and an inflatable thirty-foot penis. But the Beastie Boys, like Eminem, played their role properly, pretending to be nothing but white boys, educated at that, though in inter-views their behavior and commentary indicated otherwise. "You know why I could fuck with them?" said Beastie Boys collabora-tor Q-Tip (of A Tribe Called Quest) to writer Matt Diehl in *The Vibe History of Hip Hop*. "They're just themselves, not trying to be something they're not." Culture-stealers or not, the Beastie Boys introduced a tremendous number of white music fans to hip-hop and received a tremendous amount of attention from whites in general, stirring an interest that other rap groups, from Public Enemy to N.W.A, filled in the years to come. For their part, the Beastie Boys followed their success by temporarily taking themselves out of the game. After an infamous tour for *Licensed to Ill*, during which they were accused of, among many things, deriding terminally ill children while abroad, they quarreled with their label over money and parted ways for a few years, eventually relocating to L.A. In 1989, the Beastie Boys proved themselves truly innovative, pushing the boundaries of sampling culture and predicting the prismatic genre-mixing of nineties pop music with the stunning but somewhat commercially unsuccessful *Paul's Boutique*, produced by the up-and-coming duo the Dust Brothers in 1989. The group has since defined modern white b-boy "alternative" style, the eclectic state in which hip-hop, punk rock, funk, and skateboarder culture resides. The band's fan base, despite the lengthy breaks between record releases, had not forgotten them: after four years away, the Beastie Boys' *Hello Nasty* debuted at number one on the Top 200 Albums charts in 1998.

A less commercially viable but more traditional white rap group was 3rd Bass, a trio of two white rappers, including Prime Minister Pete Nice (Pete Nash) and MC Serch (Michael Berrin), plus a black DJ, Richie Rich (Richard Lawson). White hip-hop artists like Marky Mark and Vanilla Ice fabricated or embellished tough upbringings and paid the price with their loss of popularity, but 3rd Bass did not: both rappers were from Queens and spent the eighties winning respect and taking their share of boos at club shows. 3rd Bass was the first white rap group with street-style rhymes and attitude; they lambasted the Beastie Boys for their rich-kid backgrounds, ridiculed MC Hammer, and recorded a Vanilla Ice parody, "Pop Goes the Weasel," which, ironically, became their biggest hit, in 1991. In the video for that song, 3rd

Bass even beat up a Vanilla Ice impersonator, played by punk-rock icon Henry Rollins. "Pop Goes the Weasel" was an interesting twist in the white rap credibility war, because 3rd Bass's parody hit was based on the same formula that Puff Daddy would use in the nineties and that Vanilla Ice had used for "Ice Ice Baby"—lifting a recognizable refrain from a hit song almost in its entirety. Ice borrowed from Queen/David Bowie's "Under Pressure", while 3rd Bass did the same from Peter Gabriel's "Sledgehammer." Nonetheless, whereas the Beastie Boys created their own talent pool after their debut album, 3rd Bass worked with some of the most proven, respected hip-hop producers of the day, such as the Bomb Squad and Prince Paul. 3rd Bass disbanded in 1992, and MC Serch worked as a solo artist while Pete Nice and DJ Richie Rich worked as a group, releasing albums that failed to equal the sum of their parts. MC Serch has remained devoted to hip-hop, as a spokesman against payola in radio and as head of artist development at the short-lived, highly respected record label Wild Pitch; Pete Nice retired from the game to open a baseball memorabilia store. Though 3rd Bass's public profile was not as high as that of the Beastie Boys, 3rd Bass proved, perhaps more so than the Beastie Boys, that every white rapper isn't a sham.

The litmus test for past white rappers remains the same for those today: authenticity and devotion to the culture. White teens brought up on rap and turned on to rhyme appeared in greater numbers than ever before in the nineties, with names like Miilkbone, Cage, Eminem, R.A. the Rugged Man, and Remedy, all of whom have had tough upbringings, the backing of hip-hop royalty, or both. Rappers such as Eminem and Cage detail revenge fantasies and the damage of troubled childhoods in their music—Eminem's broken home and Cage's time as a teenager in a mental institution, where he was placed by his stepfather. Miilkbone was brought up in New Jersey projects; Remedy, a rapper from a wealthy family who boasts the backing of the Wu-Tang Clan, writes rhymes about his Jewish ancestors who died in the Holocaust. Not quite fitting in is a blessing *and* a curse to whites in hip-hop, placing them on the periphery, where they may innovate wildly, or prove their way onto the main stage. Whichever path a white hip-hop artist walks, inauthenticity at any step will be their last.

Eminem is the white rapper who integrated mainstream accolades and credibility most successfully; he's raised the bar on white rappers immeasurably, and on all rappers significantly. He has proved himself to be the highest form of white rapper: an authentic innovator in traditional hip-hop terms.

"The top two rappers right now, as far as skill, writing, and delivery, are my partner Big Boi and Eminem," says André of OutKast. "That's truly how I feel about it. I mean I can tell that it's real for Eminem. It's a passion for him, you know. It ain't just like fly by night, he's jumping to it."

"What Eminem does particularly well among many other things," says music critic Soren Baker, "is that he actually makes you care about him. A lot of the whole 'keep it real' mandate that rappers purportedly adhere to is obviously totally false because there's not enough time in the day to kill as many people, have sex with as many women, and sell as many drugs as these guys claim to, and still have a recording career and national tours."

Eminem's rhyme style has also evolved while remaining true to the battle tradition that weaned him. He's met the challenges of other MCs and has always responded, even to less-than-stellar lyrical opponents, with battle rhymes as intricate and fresh as the verses he pores over for his albums. "Being in battles keeps Eminem grounded, I think," says Sway Calloway. "Back in the day, that's what helped develop and shape who he is. The only thing that was at all good about his whole 'beef' with Benzino is that it reminded Eminem where he came from. This is still rap, and guys like Cannabis or Benzino or whoever are still gonna come for you and you gotta prove that you're still a warrior, a gladiator, no matter how many millions you sold. That's what keeps a rapper's arrogance, his spirit, his edge, going." In addition, Eminem has moved into production, helming tracks for Jay-Z and Nas, proof enough that he is a rare talent, one who is authentic, passionate, different, and gifted enough to communicate his reality so universally that fans of all ages, colors, and musical preferences can feel it—every single time.

"Eminem came out of the box with this surreal violent thing going on. It wasn't just that, it was also really funny, even more because he aimed so much of it at himself," says the *Village Voice*'s Sasha Frere-Jones. "That was the huge difference. Everyone in rap has shot everyone else a hundred times, and everyone's done mean things to people, and I really don't need to hear that again. But, like, suicide and self-mutilation analogizes a useful state of mind—which is, 'okay, I feel bad about myself.' That's a huge, not very well explored part of hip-hop. I know people who think even that part of Eminem is a moral force for bad. But, you know, I don't know anyone who thinks he's not a good MC. He's like Biggie, and I've never heard anyone say that Biggie wasn't dope. Nobody didn't love Biggie—and it was the same thing when Eminem first came out; everyone's running around with the same look on their face like, 'Did you hear this shit?!' *When Ready to Die* came out, it was the same thing—you couldn't open the door without somebody quoting Biggie."

On *The Eminem Show*, the rapper makes reference to retiring his jersey at thirty. He knows that hip-hop isn't a forgiving medium: fans move quickly, and a weak album may be a rapper's last—as a white rapper of his stature, the pressure is double. "I'm gonna stop when I've got nothing left to say," Eminem says. "As soon as I don't feel it, that's it, it's over." If that happens tomorrow, history has dictated that, statistically, another skilled Caucasian will hit it big in hip-hop in nine years. Those who have followed in Eminem's wake, such as Bubba Sparxxx, Haystack, Poverty, and Stagga Lee, have not enjoyed instant success. None of them approach the level of Eminem's talent, but if they were close it still would not be enough. Eminem's skills and success may have opened new doors for white rappers, but his legacy has set the standard forever higher, making their burden of proving themselves that much more difficult. The next great white MC will have to be better than Eminem, a quality that escapes 95 percent of the MCs of any race today. Even if a new white rapper doesn't emerge in the near future, Eminem is wise enough to know the dangers of being a white rap also-ran; that parking lot is well populated. House of Pain's Everlast had to switch to acoustic guitar in a kind of rock-rap-blues to hit the charts again in 1998

(*Whitey Ford Sings the Blues*), eight years after his solo rap album flunked. Vanilla Ice, after being exposed for inventing a gang-life past, fell into pop culture's footnotes, despite a film, a live album, and a second album of rap in 1994 that aped the pot-and-gun-smoke vibe of Dr. Dre and Cypress Hill. He then, still aping the tastes of the day in 1998, reinvented himself as a rap-rock artist caught somewhere between the sound of Marilyn Manson and Limp Bizkit.

The Beastie Boys, Everlast, and Vanilla Ice (as well as every musician Eminem has ever criticized) all turned down (or rendered ridiculous) my requests to interview them for this book, perhaps afraid that, like Mark Wahlberg may have been on *TRL* with Eminem, they would be ridiculed by comparison. The goal of my query was made clear: nothing but to learn of their experiences as white artists in hip-hop and to find out if they felt times had changed. It couldn't have been easy, as it wasn't for Eminem. Perhaps the only answer worth noting is the only one that was given, in an e-mail response from Vanilla Ice's manager. His e-mail followed a phone conversation in which the subject of "compensation" was brought up—in light of an author's publishing advance for a book. I have no regrets that this work suffered for the lack of insight that Robert Van Winkle, a.k.a. Vanilla Ice, would have provided in the twenty minutes of phone conversation I could have purchased for $5,000. My apologies to readers who disagree.

In post-Eminem times, the fate of white rappers will be brighter if their talent and credibility are in the right place. More than any other pop music form, rap is supremely Darwinian;

freestyle panache or connections (though this could be argued) are not all it takes. There is promising talent coming out of the Midwest, like the young Asian rapper Jin and nineteen-year-old Eyedea, the winner of *Blaze* magazine's 2002 Freestyle Battle, a white rapper who, despite offers from major record labels, has chosen to remain true to his roots on an independent, local label.

"For white rappers, there's such a fine line between shit you can and can't do," Eminem says. "The main thing is to be yourself. A lot of white rappers—look at Vanilla Ice. Yo, he got exposed. You can only put up a front for so long before people start coming out of the woodwork like, 'Yo, you didn't grow up here, you didn't do this. You talk about guns in your rhymes and you never shot a gun! Talkin' about shit you never lived, you've never even seen.' If you ain't got the balls to walk up and sock somebody in the mouth, don't write it down, because if you say that shit on wax you're gonna get tested. If you're not that type of person, don't say it! Don't talk about growing up in hard times in the city if you grew up in the fucking suburbs. White rappers, if they grew up in the suburbs, should play off it, like, 'Hi! I'm white.'"

It's because I'm w-h-i-t-e

5. Caucasian persuasion: flipping the race rap

"At first it confuses people. It's like seeing a black guy do country music."
DR. DRE, 1999

The West Side Highway hums like radio static. The light poles and parking signs lining Forty-sixth Street are plastered with stickers, some still bright but advertising a faded product. The newest ones have posters to match, all red and white, like name tags, with black scrawl in the box: "Hi! My name is Slim Shady!" Fifty yards of dressed-up hip-hop—clean jeans, sneakers, and many skimpy skirts—trails from the door of the Sound Factory. Heels tap and bodies bounce in the midnight March air.

A white limousine slithers up the block. It waits across the street, in front of the door. Four young men stroll up and look in the window. When nothing happens, they lean on a nearby wall. The door opens ten minutes later and a large black man leads out a pack of white men. The men against the wall are perplexed.

"Who y'all with?" one asks. No one seems to have heard him.

"Yo, man, who y'all with?" he asks again, walking over.

"Eminem," I tell him.

"Who?"

"Eminem. He's signed to Dr. Dre's label."

"Oh yeah?" he says, skeptical, surveying the pack of whiteys. "He performing?"

"Yeah, three songs."

"I'm gonna have to see that," he says. "Hey, yo, can I come in wit you?"

Eminem, buried in an XXXL hooded sweatshirt, emerges from the car and we move to the door. We wait in a cluster, while the eyes on line scan us for a clue as to why we made it to the front so quickly. The answer hangs along the block, but no one shouts out. They look on, Manhattan unimpressed; but it could be disbelief. It is Friday, March 5, 1999, at a large weekly hip-hop party. A pack of nonfamous white guys and their black security guard just cruised up in a king-size white stretch and entered the building.

Inside the entrance, three guards much bigger than Eminem's guard pat people down and trace them with metal detectors. Pockets are emptied, arms are uplifted, and shoes are scrutinized. On a chair sit a few knives, a box cutter, and a pair of brass knuckles.

"You had any problems in here?" someone behind me asks a guard.

"Somebody was poppin' shots outside a couple of weeks ago,"

the guard says. "They was driving by and shootin' in the air like cowboys. We knew who they was and we saw 'em, so we don't let 'em in no more. They're not too happy about that, but it's all good."

Downstairs is a lounge, hot and crowded. The patrons are drinking, jostling for room to stand or dance or smoke, to turn away or make headway with a member of the opposite sex. Some people are flossy, sporting jewels and new clothes; others are in sweatshirts and big jackets, holding Heinekens. It is a predominantly mainstream crowd, turned out at the week's end to hear the hip-hop hits of the moment and the classics that never get old. The DJ and dance floor are upstairs; here, the bumping is muffled. A few underground MCs, record-industry people, and journalists sip cocktails in the booths or stand shoulder to shoulder. We in Eminem's entourage fill a small dressing room too easily, and the guard closes the door. As soon as he does, there's a knock on it—a sound that won't stop for the half hour we're in here. Most will be turned away, but this knock is warranted: it's Jonathan "Shecky Green" Schecter, cofounder of the magazine *The Source* and founder of Game Recordings, the hip-hop record label/softcore-porn video production house that celebrates, in image more than in music, the fruits of gangsta fantasy: money, rap, and curvaceous ethnic ladies. Earlier this year Game made themselves known with their second twelve-inch release: *Bad Meets Evil/Nuttin' to Do*, by Royce Da 5'9". Featuring Eminem, it was released just as Eminem's buzz took off. Schecter is armed with the spoils of Game: champagne and a pair of video house talents—sexy, nearly naked black women in leather bikini tops.

His Eminence presiding over a mock Senate at the 2002 MTV Video Music Awards on August 29, 2002, just as he has presided, lyrically, over the national debate about his lyrics.

Photo by Kevin Kane

Believe it or not, his lyrics say that if he weren't rapping, he'd be raping in a Jason mask: Eminem flips off Sydney, Australia, on July 27, 2001. Photo by Dave Morgan

Eminem don't give a fuck it's not his birthday.

Photo by Andrew Hobbs, 2001

Image reconfiguration, phase one: Elton John and Eminem play what the rapper called career Russian roulette at the 43rd annual Grammy Awards in Los Angeles on February 21, 2001. Photo by Frank Micelotta

TOP RIGHT

Shady's consequences: Eminem and his attorneys during his sentencing hearing on weapons charges at Oakland County Circuit Court in Pontiac, Michigan, on June 28, 2001. Photo by Bill Pugliano

MIDDLE RIGHT

I don't care what you say, unless it is about me: Eminem scares his chronic critic Moby at the 2002 MTV Video Music Awards, August 29, 2002. Photo by Gary Hershorn

No more fightin' with Dad: Kimberly Anne Scott outside the 37th District Court in Warren, Michigan, after her hearing on charges of disturbing the peace, October 2, 2001. Photo by Bill Pugliano

RIGHT

Blue-collar balladeers: Eminem and his fan Bruce Springsteen backstage at the 45th annual Grammy Awards on February 23, 2003.

Photo by Kevin Mazur

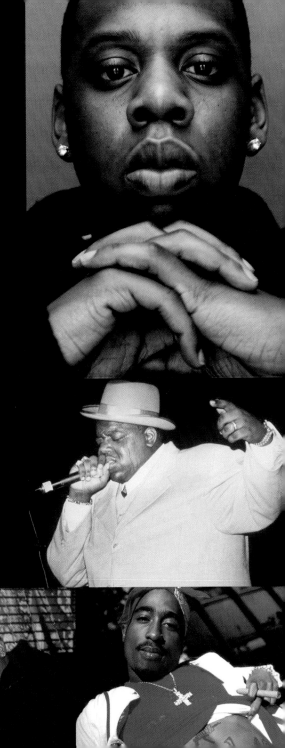

OPPOSITE,CLOCKWISE, STARTING FROM TOP LEFT: **Grandmaster Flash, Run D.M.C., N.W.A, the Beastie Boys, Rick Rubin and LL Cool J, Eminem.** Photos by David Corio, Chris Vooren, Howard Taylor, Rick Rubin, Cindi Palmano, Estevan Oriol

RIGHT, FROM TOP **You can't knock the hustle: Jay-Z in 2000.** Photo by Phil Knott

I got techniques dripping out my buttcheeks: Christopher Wallace, a.k.a. Notorious B.I.G. Photo by David Corio

A young G, gettin' paid: 2Pac in 1995. Photo by Michael Benabib

I'm on a mission and my mission won't stop. Snoop Dogg and Dr. Dre. Photo by Michael Benabib

Past and present masters: Eminem with Rakim.

Photo by Estevan Oriol

ABOVE LEFT

It's less how you look than how you do it: Eminem and Nas shake hands while Russell Simmons looks on at the Detroit Hip-Hop Summit on April 26, 2003.

Photo by Paul Warner

ABOVE RIGHT

That was then: Eminem when he was M&M, performing on the Detroit talent show circuit in 1996.

Photo courtesy of WENN

RIGHT

A white man in a black man's game: Eminem at *The Source* Awards in Pasadena, California, September 15, 2000.

Photo by Ron Wolfson

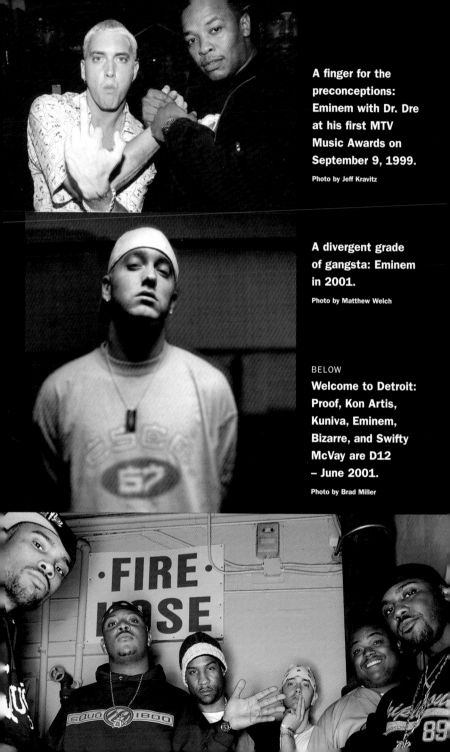

A finger for the preconceptions: Eminem with Dr. Dre at his first MTV Music Awards on September 9, 1999.

Photo by Jeff Kravitz

A divergent grade of gangsta: Eminem in 2001.

Photo by Matthew Welch

BELOW

Welcome to Detroit: Proof, Kon Artis, Kuniva, Eminem, Bizarre, and Swifty McVay are D12 – June 2001.

Photo by Brad Miller

Crossing this full room is like playing a game of checkers; only diagonal moves to any open space are possible. Schecter and the Game girls map a path to Eminem, Royce passes out Heinekens, and someone fills the room with blunt smoke.

Eminem sits on the dressing-room counter, leaning against the mirror, a Game girl at each leg. The security guard plays bouncer, quizzing the crowd at the door. He turns away a group of girls who just want to say hello, then a pair of dudes who are not who they claim to be. The door closes. There's a knock again: MC Serch, one-third of the well-respected early-nineties white rap group 3rd Bass. The rapper comes in and gives Eminem a hug. Three years from now, Serch will leave his native New York to host a morning radio show in Detroit for WJLB, the station that Eminem mentions in "Rock Bottom" (*The Slim Shady LP*) to criticize them for their lip-service-only support of local hip-hop. Two knocks later, West Coast rapper Ras Kass slides in; the room is now past full and Ras must leave his boys outside. Well-wishers work their way toward Eminem, who holds court with his two newest fans.

"Can I get an autograph?" one Game girl asks.

"Yeah, I can give you an autograph," he says, pulling a Sharpie marker from his pocket. "You got something you want me to sign?"

"Yeah," she says and pulls one breast from her bikini.

"Yo, you want me to sign *you*?" he says, smirking.

"Yeah, right there."

The scrawl matches the posters, angular and racy, and stretches across her breast and cleavage: SLIM SHADY. She giggles.

Insistent knocks go unanswered; Eminem's security guard just leans against the door now. After a few minutes, he opens it a crack to see who is pounding. Standing there is a guy who says he manages Miilkbone, the white rapper whose anti-Eminem track, "Presenting Miilkbone," will be released next month on the ill-conceived (produced from his prison cell) Death Row Records compilation *Suge Knight Represents: Chronic 2000*. On the rap, Miilkbone responds to a line he heard in Eminem's "Just Don't Give a Fuck," from *The Slim Shady LP*. On his track, Eminem laced together the names of white rappers past, including Everlast and 3rd Bass, not so much on a mission to insult them as to proclaim his mission to defy the white-rap stereotype as a "quest to crush a Miilkbone." Miilkbone didn't see it that way. Miilkbone's manager is denied entrance. Next there is a trio of white girls who squeeze by the manager, attempting to pass Eminem's security guard while he is talking. They've tried three times so far. Patience failed to get them in; flirting, too. This time, they try sympathy.

The guard is holding the door open, blocking traffic, allowing smoke and heat out of the room and only air in.

"We just want to say hi. We've come all the way from New Jersey," one of the girls says.

"Oh, yeah, all the way from New Jersey?" the guard responds.

"Yeah!" another says, hopeful. "We came all the way just to see him. We love him. We promise we won't bother anybody. We just want to say hi and we'll leave."

"Can't do it. Too many bodies in here."

"But we came all the way here just to see him," the first insists. "We're small, we can fit. You won't even know we're in there."

"You're gonna see him onstage in a minute. Ladies, you gotta move back."

A smallish guy in a baggy leather jacket tries to slip through the door.

"Hey, who you with?" Eminem's security guard asks.

"I was just in there, dog. I'm with all of them, yo."

"What's your name?"

"I'm K, man. KG." The guy looks past the guard into the room at one of Royce's crew facing him. "Yo, dog, what's up, man? How you feelin'?"

"Aiight."

"He wit you?" the guard asks.

"Nah. I don't know him."

"Who you with?" the guard asks the guy.

"I was just in there, man. I know the guy at the label."

"What label?"

"Shady's label, man. Dre's label," the guy says. "I'm KG, man."

"There's no one here from the label tonight," the guard says. "Keep it moving."

KG steps back but doesn't leave. The girls move in for another round. "Sir, I promise, we'll just say hi and leave," two say, almost at the same time. "We promise, we just want to say hi."

We in the room move toward the door when it opens, breathing in the cooler air as the smoke escapes.

The guard has had it. "Everybody! Get away from this door right now. Do not block it. Move outside unless you were invited in here. I am closing this door!"

A line of people wring themselves out of the room, Game girls included, then the door again seals in the bong-water humidity. In the confusion, to the Jersey girls' dismay, two different teenage white girls have pushed themselves in and now sidle over to Eminem.

"Hey, Slim Shady," one of them says, "I like your song."

"Oh, yeah?" Eminem says. "Which one?"

"The one with the video," she says. "It's really good."

"Yeah, when you dress up like Marilyn Manson," the other says. "That shit's really funny."

"Thanks a lot." He looks unimpressed. "Hey, have you met Paul?" he says, looking at his manager. "He's a fuckin' fuck. His life is over."

"You're too late," Paul Rosenberg says, bemused. "I already quit."

"Oh, yeah? Well, you're so fired then that you're rehired, you fuckin' fuck. You know why? Because you're fat, bald, and Jewish."

The girls smile awkwardly.

"Can I get a beer?" one asks someone next to the cooler. He doesn't notice.

"So you're from Detroit?" her friend asks Eminem. "What's it like?"

I predict to myself that this will end her interview.

"It's aiight," Eminem says, a mischievous glint in his eye. "Hey, you two know Dee, right? You've met Dee?"

The girl crinkles her nose. "Dee who?" she says.

"Deez nuts!" Eminem shouts in her face. The joke is a hip-hop test and it looks like these girls have failed. "Deez Nuts" is a classic gangsta rap track featuring Snoop Dogg, Nate Dogg, Warren G, and Daz from Dr. Dre's *The Chronic* (1992); it starts with a phone-call skit much like the joke Eminem just played. "Deez nuts" is big in Eminem's crew right now; anyone answering a "who" or "what" often gets "deez nuts" as the response. "Deez Nuts" are tough to avoid even if you know the joke; as the newest hanger-on, I myself am served plenty of "deez nuts," the loudest set coming in the middle of Minneapolis–St. Paul International Airport. I didn't stand a chance, anyway; interviewing is a minefield of "who" and "what" questions. Before I was finished, though, I doled out "deez nuts" myself. Once. I'm not sure, but I think it signaled the end of that joke's run in Eminem's crew.

Everyone in the room is laughing, including the two young women, but it's clear they don't quite know why. Eminem stares at them with a toothy, he-crazy grin.

One of them pokes him. "You're funny!" she says.

"Am I funny? Paul, am I funny?" Eminem asks.

An authoritative knock at the door reveals a man in a headset. "You're good to go," he says. "They're all ready up there."

The crowd in the lounge has grown and is now pressing up against the dressing-room door. Eminem's security guard and the club staffer back us all up, and we file out in a line, Eminem in the middle. I hear drive-by comments from the VIP peanut gallery:

"Who's that?"

"Yo, that's him?"

"He's a little guy."

"He is so cute. He doesn't look that good on TV."

"Oh my God, I have to meet him."

"Yo, Shady, mushrooms, dawg!"

"Why he rollin' like dat?"

"Dre got a white Snoop, yo."

The dance floor is full of grinding bodies, so is the balcony overlooking it. The DJ fades the music and announces Aftermath/Interscope-recording-artist Eminem's performance as we enter the room. DJ Stretch Armstrong waits on a platform in front of us. He drops the needle onto the groove of "Scary Movies," juggling and winding it back and forth between the turntables. Heads peer from the balcony. I sidle onto the platform, between two people on the back edge. Eminem and Royce hop onto the platform and pick up their mikes.

Royce strides from side to side, loosing his verse, while Eminem, loose from his dinner of more substances than sustenance, paces stage right, pointing and punctuating Royce's lines with shouted *whats*. The two are raw, tight hip-hop; the song, two long serrated battle raps bound by the chorus "Y'all want drama? Wanna make a scary movie?"

This isn't the kind of jiggy anthem that was rocking the room minutes ago. The audience stands still; the expressions are hard to read, but I place them between intrigued and unsure—and stuck at "What the fuck?" The three white Jersey girls whom I recognize from the doorway of the dressing room are in front of the stage, bobbing with enthusiasm, though they don't seem to know the song. Eminem stands, eyes closed, his beat hand—the right—keeping time with definitive gestures, as it does when he scribbles rhymes on a pad. The song ends fast on his last word.

"OK," he says, gathering his pants, which are baggy and prone to falling down. "I'm gonna take it back for a minute." Eminem joins Royce center stage as Armstrong rolls out Dr. Dre's "Nuthin' but a 'G' Thang." Royce throws his hands in the air. "C'mon!" he shouts. "Put 'em up, yo! Sing that shit!!"

Bodies start to sway and arms are raised in allegiance. All eyes are on Eminem. He will prove himself now or lose them forever; by the end of this song, he'll be either an MC with skill or a Caucasian karaoke casualty.

Eminem commences his performance, his delivery laid back, a mix of his wacky modulated monotone and Snoop Dogg's silky drawl. The room awakens again as the crowd begins to move; the energy is tangible, spreading, and palpably warm.

"Ain't nuthin' but a 'G' thang . . ." Eminem sings. Armstrong cuts the music.

"Baaby!" the crowd shouts.

"Two loc'd-out Gs goin' . . ." Eminem raps, avoiding, as he always does, the word *niggaz*.

"Craaazay!" they shout.

Eminem scampers herky-jerky across the stage, bobbing his head and with one hand holding his pants. The crowd is won. They're dancing while watching the action; people hang over the balcony railing to see. Royce and Eminem meet at the front of the stage, chanting the song's chorus. On the last beat, Armstrong cuts from mentor to apprentice, splicing "'G' Thang" into "My Name Is."

Anyone who didn't know, knows now. Of the four times I see Eminem perform "My Name Is" tonight, this one will be the best. Earlier, on Staten Island, he faced teeny-bopper reality. Later, he will do his thing for the beautiful people. But *this* crowd is home to him: skeptics, haters, new fans, devotees, and indifferents. He loses himself in the song, running out ahead of the beat, then falling back into it. His eyes are closed and he nearly falls from the stage, throwing himself back from the edge just in time. A formidable black woman in front has been watching his performance with a wrinkled brow. She gives it up finally, cracking a huge grin at the line "My English teacher wanted to flunk me in junior high. / Thanks a lot, next semester I'll be thirty-five." She dances in place and raises her hands at the chorus, singing the loopy hook like the white teen girls next to her.

Armstrong cuts the music during the last chorus to initiate an audience call-and-response, which grows to a loud crescendo, then the music stops.

"Good night," Eminem says. The mike thuds when he drops it, unlike his pants when he drops them, flashing bright geometric-print boxer shorts. The audience cheers. Eminem jumps off the back of the stage, dragging a human wake behind him. There is a mad rush to the dressing room and the knocking begins anew, more insistent than ever. The air in the room is dank. Eminem sits, sweaty, lit with adrenaline and slaps from his crew. A new line of well-wishers trail from the door.

I leave the room to catch a breath. A white girl who is jockeying for door position tells her friend, "I love him and you know I don't love hip-hop."

"I know," the friend answers. "He's, like, so original! And he's so cute. He's perfect. I want to marry him."

Her friend nods.

"And I will, too," the other continues. "I know when he sees me, we'll be together forever. He's perfect for me."

When I return to the room, I squeeze into my place by the door. Eminem is surrounded by friends and strangers, drinking water, and not really smiling. He doesn't look mad or glad, or under siege. I critique his game face, and though I've only been with the camp for eight hours and he hasn't directly said a word to me yet, in that moment I see everything. He is raw star quality, fuming with the entitlement of deep, broad, untapped talent. He's not the extrovert I thought he was, but he can play the part. I watch him scan the room, his vision attuned to the details, yet focused far, far beyond here.

Before our flight to Detroit, we sit in a booth at the food court in Terminal B of Newark Liberty International Airport. Pizza Hut Personal Pan Pizzas, Philly cheese steak sandwiches, orange curly fries, withered salads in domed plastic cups, and oily cookies are lined up. We've missed three flights already after last night's shows, which actually ended this morning. My headache is finally gone, faded by medication.

"You have to ask yourself how hungry you are," Paul Rosenberg says, sliding into the next booth with a tray of dubious snacks. I see marbleized pizza in a triangular paper dish and a basket of amorphous breaded blobs.

"What *is* that shit?" Eminem asks.

"They're calling it fried chicken," Paul says.

"Nah, I can't fuck with that."

Behind him, three girls in a pack try to determine if Eminem is Eminem. He doesn't notice.

"So, like, I was telling you about JLB, the radio station in Detroit," he says. "I dissed them on the record because when I was coming up, those motherfuckers showed me no love. They had two local favorite rappers. One was the cousin/niece of the program director and shit. They got airplay for, like, three years and never fucking got a record deal or nothing. I got friends who work at the station, and one of them told me when I had *Infinite* out that one of the DJs played it and Frankie Darcell, the program director, when he found out I was white said, 'We ain't playing this record. What the fuck is a white person doing with this?' And that was it—he took my record off. Believe me, I had my boys begging to get it played. I ain't just mad at them for that. There were so many dope MCs when I was coming up, and they would never fucking play them. Their saying is 'Where hip-hop lives.' I told them in the Detroit papers: If JLB is playing my song now, fuck them. As soon as I get home, I'm telling the motherfuckers to take my shit off the air. I don't want them to play it. Fuck those fuckin' ragged-ass fucks. No help from them at all, motherfuckers."

Eminem stretches out sideways in the booth, with his legs on the bench. Last night, he won over a doubtful black crowd; fended off a rabid, mostly white one; and today is heading to his racially divided hometown, which has an underground that knows him and a mainstream that didn't want to.

"Man," he says, looking sidelong at me, "the respect level I get now, I never got before. I couldn't play at or even get into a club like the one last night just being Eminem before all this shit with my video being out. It's fucking bananas. It's some scary shit because you can fall just as quick as you get to the top."

A black food-court employee walks by our booth to pick up two trays from the top of the closest garbage can. He eyeballs us on his way back to the kitchen and returns a minute later.

"Uh, what's up?" he says.

Eminem turns to look. "Nothing man, how you doin'?" he says.

"Um, are you . . . ? Uh, I was just wondering . . ."

"Eminem?"

"Yeah! What's up, nigga! Yo, your shit's tight, yo. All about the mushrooms and shit!"

Eminem sits up and laughs in short snare-drum blasts, "Ha-ha."

"Hey, can you sign this?" the guy asks, holding out a paper plate. "It's to George Ito and Wah, that's W-A-H."

Above his signature, Eminem writes "Do you like violence?"

The group of teen girls are convinced now; they're in conference to choose a plan of action. Another uniformed employee walks over.

"Can I get a signature, too?" he says.

"No problem, what's your name?"

"Daniel."

To show his appreciation, Daniel gives handshakes and hip-hop half hugs to everyone in the two booths around Shady, almost including a third booth of two men who aren't with us.

"Man, Paul waking me up this morning was my worst nightmare," Eminem says. He looks alert enough, but washed out. "Him waking me felt like somebody crushed my back. It was daylight when we left the club. I got two hours' sleep, if that. Paul, he gets home, he goes into instant snore mode. Paul, your life is over."

203

Paul nods from behind *Blaze* magazine. Beyond him is another autograph-hunter, this one from Pizza Hut, and judging by the piece of pizza she's biting into, she's on break.

"I think we've been discovered," Eminem says.

"Which one of you is Slim Shady?" she asks, chewing and looking at us.

"Uh, that would be me," Eminem says.

"Can I get a signed picture?" she asks.

"I don't got any pictures," he says.

"Where you from?"

"Detroit."

"Where you goin'?"

"Back to Detroit."

"Will you sign this for me?" she asks, holding out an unused, unfolded slice-to-go box.

"That's a bugged-out song you made," she says.

"You should get the album," he says. "What's your name?"

She extends her name tag.

"Rashida," he says.

"What are you writing? Here, will you sign this one for Jimmy?" She holds out another box.

On both, Eminem writes "High, my name is Slim Shady."

It is time to leave, just in time—the fans and the curious are growing. We pass the three white girls, still huddled near the doorway.

"Are you a singer?" a brown-haired one asks.

"Nah," Eminem says.

"Slim Shady?" another asks.

"How you doin'?" he says to them, smiling wide. "I should just have cards ready to give out," he says as an aside to me.

I'm not sure if the variations in race, sex, age, and background of the curious he has met today alone have registered with Eminem. They've approached him, mobbed him, sought verification of his identity, or solicited him on this trip in ways he has only seen, perhaps, in his dreams. I think that the encounters I've witnessed must be more amazing to me right now than they are to him, not only because I've never seen anything quite like this, let alone at such close range, but more because he is too busy living for every second of right now to analyze it. I have a feeling that he wouldn't notice anyway. The vision of music Eminem is tapped into, and the hip-hop creed he believes in, doesn't see differences. It sees only people, and that makes anything possible.

RACE PLAYS INTO EMINEM'S STORY JUST AS IT DOES THROUGHOUT AMERICAN history in the post-Civil Rights era. The divide of, the struggle of, and the prevailing opinion on both sides were more clear when patriots like Martin Luther King Jr. stood up to be counted; now, more subtle differentiations between the races exist, overlapped by subdivisions of class and the practices of the ruling hegemony—our national government and the corporate institutions that run America. Eminem is the product of a white background as well as of a black culture, and he was alienated from both groups when he was growing up. He was picked on for "acting black" by white kids in the trailer-park suburbs; he was jumped for simply being a white kid on the streets of the city. In hip-hop, his talent triumphed over stereotype, and as he gained national recognition, the handicap of his color became an asset beyond his estimation. Eminem personifies city and suburb, archetypes of black and white culture, and the common ground where they have met for fifty years: pop music. He also represents the current paradigm of race consciousness in America, whereby skin color is almost of secondary consequence to one's racial identity.

It cannot be said that Eminem is a white musician poorly imitating black music. He represents a synergy of black and white styles so completely that he destroys convention by transcending it, as only a few artists in pop music have done. In 1956 America, just two years after state legislatures were ordered to end segregated schooling, Elvis Presley brought black music into American homes with "Heartbreak Hotel," the song that remained number one on the pop charts for eight weeks, and his explosive stage presence stamped the music with an image. Presley was censored on his infamous television appearance on *The Ed Sullivan Show*, during which his sexually suggestive swiveling hips were kept out of the camera's eye. Much has been made of Presley as an American icon, more for the pop-star excess that killed him than for his talent, but also regarding the debate whether or not and to what degree he stole, supported, or assisted black culture for his own gain. The racial implications of Elvis as a pop-culture symbol often overshadow, particularly today, his early musical innovations born of the racial overlap in Southern folk music as well as his talent and charisma. Like Eminem, Presley possessed a deep gift. He had a rich, versatile voice. The fact is that he did not choose to be born white, though he surely benefited from it. Presley's early era was innovative, combining black and white, country and western, and R&B into the vibrant rockabilly that touched a nation of teenagers while a nation of parents feared the immorality of it all. Elvis wasn't alone in blending musical styles across racial lines. Chuck Berry, truly the father of rock and roll, developed the style in St. Louis blues clubs by adding a black flavor to white hillbilly music: "Maybellene," essentially the first rock-and-roll song ever recorded (1955), was Berry's interpretation of a hillbilly folk tune called "Ida Red." The true legacy of Elvis Presley seems to be that he made the boundaries between black blues, white pop, and country and western irrelevant.

By the late sixties, rock and roll had become psychedelic folk music, the soundtrack of American dissent. Against the backdrop of the Vietnam War, there was racially motivated violence following the Civil Rights Act of 1964. This act prohibited states from denying black citizens the right to vote, among other injustices. During that time, Sly Stone, a Texas-born Bay Area DJ who sang soul and doo-wop, formed Sly and the Family Stone. At the height of the hippie era, the group was an idyllic rainbow coalition, blending psychedelic rock, soul, R&B, and pop without pause. Their members were black and white, men and women; and Sly's lyrics set a revolutionary precedent of social awareness and commentary, a vision as utopian as it was realistic. Sly and the Family Stone redirected the message of soul, R&B, and funk music forever. Sly Stone, like James Brown, brought hard funk to the mainstream and infused it with an agenda of social commentary followed through in the seventies by Marvin Gaye, Curtis

Mayfield, and countless others. In a tumultuous societal climate, Sly and the Family Stone's very membership challenged Americans on both sides of the race issue, as well as the lip-service equality laid out by our Constitution. In the late sixties, when the Family Stone's white players took the stage at Harlem's legendary Apollo Theater, they were greeted with boos, and although Sly calmed the crowd, a near-riot followed the band into the street. When the Family Stone were inadvertently caught in the Detroit riots of 1967, while gassing up their tour van, the black members were held at gunpoint by the National Guard. Sly's rumored affair with Doris Day, which circulated after he covered her hit "Que Sera, Sera," as well as his marriage to a white woman in front of a sold-out Madison Square Garden crowd in 1974 brought the reality of racial integration to the mainstream in bold strokes.

In the eighties, Prince redefined pop music with his third album, 1980's *Dirty Mind*. Playing nearly every instrument himself and recording it in his home studio, the Minneapolis native blended funk and soul with the New Wave and dance-pop styles of the white artists of his day. Prince's sound dominated the decade: in his own work; the songs he wrote for other artists; covers such as Sinead O'Connor's rendition of "Nothing Compares 2 U"; and the spectrum of acts, from Madonna to Terence Trent D'Arby, who learned from Prince's template. Prince also toyed with gender preconception with an overtly sexual, androgynous image and stage gear that ranged from motorcycle jackets to high-heeled boots and skintight lace jumpsuits. Prince as a black man fronting a mostly white band, giving white music a black angle—and enjoying critical acclaim and commercial success—must have affected a young Eminem in the early eighties as much as the Beastie Boys did a few years later.

Elvis, Sly Stone, and Prince, like Eminem, are not your average artists or individuals. They are driven to express in their own terms, in spite of convention; to stand up and be heard apart from the pack. They were unique among the popular music and entertainers of their day, truly gifted innovators with the versatility and vision to challenge and alter perceptions in music—and, by extension, society—and to set a new precedent. Artists of this caliber are signposts in American culture, reflections of their times, even if they, as Elvis did once he went Hollywood, change their musical trajectory. They were not the only artists to bring together black and white music the way they did, but each of them possessed the talent and a unique point of view realized enough to inform their image. All of them bore, from the start, performance personas that powerfully communicated the confluence of influences in their music. Elvis was a dreamboat rebel, a white-pop outlaw with the pompadour of black rock and rollers. Sly and the Family Stone were flamboyant urban hippies, combining the garb and ideals of the middle-class kids who "turned on, tuned in, and dropped out" with a physical manifestation of what those ideals meant. Prince's feminized, overtly sexual ladies'-man image was as complex and liberated as his musical scope, turning New Wave black with his racially and sexually mixed backing band.

Eminem is hip-hop's signpost artist, the one gifted enough to blend black and white musical and cultural elements without compromising the integrity of the music. We are at a time in

America in which blacks and whites and all races have culturally met on a wide patch of shared ground, where white rock acts freely appropriate rap and where black artists front an image of capitalism reminiscent of Donald Trump. Eminem stands squarely in the middle: accepted—and debated—by both sides. At the same time, his "meaning" is deeper. His achievement is doubly significant in spite of the cultural overlap of the times, because of the ingrained race identity inherent in hip-hop. In the thirty years of the music's history, and in spite of a few respectable white MCs, hip-hop remained uniquely black in image until Eminem.

"My feeling about hip-hop was, and I mean this as a white rock critic, 'Oh good, finally something white people can't steal,'" says Dave Marsh, one of the founding fathers of pop-music criticism, who has written books on Elvis Presley and Michael Jackson, among others, including two best-sellers on Bruce Springsteen. "I never wrote that about hip-hop because I didn't want to sound fake, but I thought it. Beyond whatever the nuances of the music are, which are hard enough to know if you didn't grow up in that culture, there was the authenticity of race involved. As much as I hate the identity politics of it, it's very valuable in hip-hop because it puts white people at the disadvantage they need to be at. Eminem has now shown that authenticity has very little to do with what you look like."

The threat to this racial identity in hip-hop—the only arena aside from sports in which young black men dominate—will be problematic in the years to come. Eminem's success, while undisputed in terms of his musical abilities, will surely raise issues of resentment for some black fans and may spark opposition to other white rappers (if any emerge that are on par with Eminem's song craft) and even to the participation of white hip-hop fans in the culture. It is an understandable, perhaps unavoidable predicament. Eminem is the first white rapper of true skill who is worthy, beyond his commercial success, of a place in the hip-hop hall of fame, alongside the game's great black lyricists. He has managed to be hardcore, confessional, and humorous in songs with articulated structure. In contrast, most of today's black MCs revel in a commercially successful formulaic bling-bling or thug aesthetic. Those who complain that, because of his color, Eminem is allowed to release rap that black artists could not are generally right. While such statements negate Eminem's truly gifted way with melody and song construction, focusing instead on his often taboo subject matter, they touch upon the fact that rap has fallen into a rut and that innovation is not rewarded by fans or embraced by the record industry. Then again, tradition also holds that a white rapper should do nothing but suck, so perhaps a change is not far off.

It isn't Eminem the person or artist whom the artists (for the most part), executives, and pundits of the black hip-hop community oppose; it is Eminem as a symbol of institutionalized, corporate white domination in a genre reserved for blacks that is hard to accept. In this light, Eminem's popularity is a product of the white system. Denying that Eminem enjoys greater commercial success and a more diverse fan base because of his color is ridiculous; Eminem himself has made the point repeatedly in song ("Without Me," "The Way I Am," "Square Dance") and in print. His popularity with white fans who don't usually listen to hip-hop is, it can be argued, ethnocentrism, or the preference toward members of your own group. Ethnocentrism isn't synonymous with the negative implications of racial prejudice, but isn't terrifically far from them. While true to the hip-hop art form, Eminem is more accessible to his peers because his stories of white angst don't pass them by; they're told in Eminem's distinctive voice with less slang than most black rap. Holding a white fan's preference for a white rapper against Eminem is as ridiculous as claiming that he does not sell more records because of his color.

"The thing that still bothers me most about the ascension of Eminem is that we live in a country that is obviously majority white," says Farai Chideya, journalist, founder of popandpolitics.com, and author of *The Color of Our Future*. "White people, in general, react better to white people as role models and public figures. And there was a long wait for the great white hope of rap. When he did appear the problem for me was that he received all this analysis and psychoanalysis that black rappers never got. If you look at somebody like Tupac who now has been given this kind of psychoanalysis posthumously, when he was alive he was a 'bad boy', that's all people thought of him. There was no effort in the media to deconstruct who he is or where he comes from. But as soon as Marshall Mathers appeared they all said 'Oh, this troubled white youth. May we lay you down on the couch? What is your problem?' To me it really highlighted the issue that nobody gave a rat's ass about why young black men felt like expressing themselves in this way, but as soon as a white guy did it then there was an effort to understand."

If anything, Eminem downplays his race advantage, out of respect for hip-hop and to maintain his credibility. If he chose to, Eminem could be everywhere. There isn't a media outlet in the country that would refuse an interview with Eminem, and this has been so since 2000. Eminem is careful about the kinds of media projects he participates in, and most of the magazines and TV shows that feature him do so without his cooperation. The number of corporations willing to pay Eminem millions for product endorsements is even greater. Whereas the average fan doesn't hold it against Jay-Z for doing a Heineken commercial, or Method Man and Redman for hocking deodorant, Eminem would not be judged as kindly as another rapper trying to get paid in full. To his credit and to his credibility, Eminem has done virtually nothing to cash in on his popularity that wasn't directly tied to the music: aside from a DVD release of an animated series and two limited-edition action figures, Eminem's clothing line, Shady, will be the rapper's first nonartistic merchandising venture beyond T-shirts and hats. Still, the idea of a popular and consistently genuine white rapper does not sit well with many rap fans.

"It almost seems as if the black folks who love Eminem want to love him more than any of the white people who love Eminem," says *Village Voice* critic Sasha Frere-Jones. "It's like some kind of anti-recapturing. It's a game in which there have been so many moves at this point. There have been white people fucking with hip-hop and black culture before, but I don't think anyone has ever gotten the one hundred percent stamp of approval. I think that gold stamp has been in the box for fifty years. And he is the first dude to get it. The Beastie Boys got it for a minute, but they took themselves out of the game. Eminem wants to be in hip-hop, right in that tradition. And he got the full-on go-ahead."

"He's the great white hope," Snoop Dogg says. "He's the first one that's really solid, hardcore, really committed."

In 2002, when Eminem's commercial gain and artistic breadth expanded further than that of any rapper in history, his achievements sparked new concern and dialogue in the hip-hop community, including a roundtable organized by *The Source* magazine for their March 2003 issue. In their online journals, Bay Area radio DJ and hip-hop archivist Davey D (www.daveyd.com) and rap icon Chuck D of Public Enemy (www.publicenemy.com), in very informative columns, praised Eminem's take on hip-hop but also highlighted, as both have been doing for years, the conditions inside and outside the black hip-hop community that have reduced the art of rapping to a commerce of detrimental imagery. Chuck D pointed out what was true when he wrote "Don't Believe the Hype" in 1988: the thug imagery of rappers sensationalized by the media and beloved of the sex-and-violence-hungry American public has eroded hip-hop culture by turning a negative image of blacks into profit, and blacks eager to cash in have willingly participated. Davey D, in an entry titled "Is Eminem the New Elvis?," related that the debate about whites in hip-hop is not new but is more heated now that hip-hop has become a multibillion-dollar industry and a viable career choice for so many minority Americans. He related his experience in the radio industry over the past decade, which was that as white tastes turned to hip-hop and it became more profitable for radio stations, minorities often played the role of puppets of authenticity for the white corporations that were actually in control. With the option to put a white face on hip-hop, Davey D wrote, white advertisers will, and that is the danger. He compared Eminem not to Elvis but to Larry Byrd, the one great white basketball player in the NBA throughout the eighties.

"Like Byrd, [Eminem] respects the game and has paid his dues. There's no denying that. Cats in hip-hop know that Eminem was out there getting dirty like everyone else. Like Byrd, he's good. He's frustratingly good ... Because Larry Byrd was this iconic figure that could do no wrong in the media, as a result he became the scorn of a lot of cats in the 'hood while simultaneously garnering throngs of enthusiastic fans—mostly white—who now had someone running up and down the court who they could identify with. Byrd was the man you loved to hate but had to respect because there was no denying his skills. Byrd maintained his own style of play. If you recall, everyone in the NBA at that time was colorful. They were flashy. They personified the bling bling of their day. Byrd was the exact opposite. He wasn't as colorful, he wasn't as flashy, but he was always in the winner's circle ... At the end of the day, whether you like him or not, Larry Byrd was someone who you had to give it up to. Eminem is someone you have to give it up to. He plays the game. He plays the game well and will be around for a while. But Eminem being who he is does not change the racial dynamics that are always at work in America. Let's keep our eye on the prize and really direct our rage at the machine."

American culture (and society for that matter) on a mass scale is corporate owned, defined, and controlled; a symbiotic interplay between advertising and product, from politicians to Pop Tarts. The influence of race on the public's acceptance of an artist or art form is subtle, tied up with economics and played as such by those in power, who remain very much behind the scenes. In the music industry, including MTV and BET, radio holds the reins, dictating to a large degree how and if an artist will blow up commercially, by how much they are heard. Exposure to a mass audience who have become accustomed to accepting what they are fed equals success in today's market. And the scope of what that audience is exposed to in rap has continued to narrow, over the past five years particularly. Record labels take little risk today, promoting or, likely, adapting artists to fit a successful marketing strategy. The same practices occur in other genres, but rap's meaning is greater than just entertainment, and the power play of white corporations over black artists is that much more significant.

"Eminem is not really the best example of what I would consider the white appropriation of hip-hop," Chideya says. "I think the issue is so much larger. It's not the appropriation by an individual, it's the market choices that get made to appease what is essentially now a majority white audience. I'm much more interested in finding out what black artists are asked to do in the studio and how their labels treat them and how they're positioned in a market that's 70 percent white than I am in Eminem, who *is* white. The market forces that come to bear on black female artists I'm particularly interested in. Missy Elliot is the only one who has gotten away without showing T&A and it's partly because she doesn't look like a cover model, but she has to do some kind of music jujitsu to keep her place. That's the real issue—how do black artists make the music they want to make? Nobody's told that story from the perspective of somebody who's been forced to make tough choices. Chuck D talks about it happening, but that's only because he's not in the same position he was before."

The history of hip-hop on the radio is a clear-cut story between perception and profit and a good barometer of how race, rap, and the music industry have arrived at their present state. In the late eighties and early nineties, when hip-hop proved itself a commercially viable format, the industry fell into a racial quandary. Black "urban" stations at the time were formatted as predominantly R&B, reserving hip-hop mix shows for a few hours late at night on the weekends. There were maybe a handful of rap stations in the entire country. While advertisers paid top dollar for spots on Top 40 stations (dubbed "contemporary hits radio"), at urban stations, even those that were first in their regional marketplace, ads cost less.

In the late eighties, the term *urban* was adopted to distance a station's image from the rebellious, violent image of rap; and many stations further distanced themselves by opting to draw an older audience, moving to a black adult contemporary format of mostly soul, funk, and R&B. It was a message to advertisers that a station's listeners were older, affluent black men and women— the target consumer in marketing plans aimed at African-Americans. Regardless of these efforts, advertisers were willing to pay more to reach Top 40 listeners, who were mostly white or

Asian. When hip-hop truly exploded in the nineties, its multi-cultural appeal changed the marketplace. A few stations, like KMEL in San Francisco, where Davey D was a DJ, abandoned pop for rap, as did New York's Hot 97, losing their high-energy pop-dance format. These stations discovered that not only did their audience remain but the station outdrew their local urban competition. Advertisers that were hesitant to hawk their products on urban stations strangely had no issue with a station classified as pop that played rap.

To the hip-hop community, urban stations that were careful with rap in order to still pay the bills looked like conservatives pitted against the spirit of the black community. It indicated a generational divide consistent with hip-hop's acceptance in America. Urban radio programmers similarly felt that they were being robbed. The efforts they'd made to integrate rap into their stations' playlists while balancing their image were useless in the face of the pop stations that had coopted their culture.

The transformation of stations was never a high and mighty revolution, nor was it particularly noted or debated outside of the industry. It was, as is most human history, about Darwinism and money. Pop stations saw an opportunity and they took it; the multimedia corporations who determine the images and art in major media channels have done the same with hip-hop. The trend that dictated a change in format from pop to rap radio in the nineties has spread across advertising and media. As the hip-hop generation came of age, more hip-hop-related art, ads, and other media have spread. Call it a revolution, but don't be disappointed when you don't see the system come down; hip-hop is a part of the American marketplace because it is meaningful to a large enough sector of the country to be profitable. Corporations of all kinds, like the pop stations that became rap stations, are integrating hip-hop where they can in order to increase their profits.

Artists in this scheme are the face people, the pawns in a larger scheme. To recognize the fact that Eminem sells hip-hop better to mainstream white audiences is to get at the underlying structure of image-making in America. He graced more magazine covers in 2003 than any other artist, and many of the magazines, like the January 2003 issue of *Rolling Stone*, were issues in which Eminem was used as consumer bait—he wasn't even interviewed. Eminem makes corporate advertisers comfortable, and for that reason the black hip-hop community has something to worry about. In America, mainstream media is targeted at the most desirable consumer group: whites, ages eighteen to thirty-four, particularly females. Eminem is authentic, Eminem is good-looking, gifted, popular, and Eminem is white. He is a marketing man's dream figure.

"When you have people in the mainstream, à la white publications and outlets, caring about this guy, that would never care about the average black rapper, then obviously he's doing something right," says writer Soren Baker. "Being white has at least a substantial part to do with that, but it's not like he's not talented, he's immensely talented. The fact that he's white just makes it all the more compelling. The rules of rap dictate that he shouldn't be that good. We have come to expect that white rappers aren't that good. Since he is and he makes good music and he has great production and he presents himself well and his videos are entertaining, he is fully, completely embraced."

Whether Eminem's success will launch a tide of white hip-hop artists pushed by major labels—a condition he parodied in the chorus of "The Real Slim Shady"—remains to be seen but isn't likely. Greed Corporate machinations have played a major part in the development of hip-hop, though the quality control of the audience, to some degree, has kept the product in check, as they have also dictated prevalent aesthetics. Artists signed to major labels in any genre are allowed little room for development. They are rushed to churn out second albums quickly, particularly if they've just scored a hit, before their audience moves on, often at the expense of the music. Public taste and profit have dictated that rap artists with lyrics promoting a bling-bling thug lifestyle, real or imagined, from Ja Rule to Fabolous to Lil' Kim to Ludacris, sell the most records and earn the most time on MTV and BET (Black Entertainment Television)—which, not coincidentally, are both owned by the same corporation, Viacom. Such corporate relationships allow for more exposure and synergy if an artist makes their cut. For many rappers who see rap as their one shot at a better life, making more money by following a template is a more important motive than promoting the greater integrity of the hip-hop community. At the same time, artists concerned with social issues in the black community (like the great and unknown female rapper Jean Grae, Mos Def, or Mr. Lif) might have fans but do not get major exposure—even in the black hip-hop media, where, like everywhere else, sex and violence is the big sell.

It isn't a new situation in hip-hop, but the emergence of a white rapper with undeniable skill and the embrace of the mainstream

has brought the debate to a head. Of late, as the American go...
ment becomes increasingly right wing, opting for Big Broth...
security over civil liberties, hip-hop seems to be more of a target,
even at the business level, as both the law offices of So So Def
Records and Tha Row Records were raided by the FBI as part of an
investigation into whether these legitimate businesses were once
funded in part by drug dealers' money. In an industry in which far
too much media ink has been spilled over rappers' arrests for
everything from speeding tickets to unregistered firearms
possession to rape accusations, the hip-hop community's worry
that a white, "safer" version of hip-hop is more attractive to white
corporate advertisers, and may dictate future artist signings,
development, and promotion, may be thoroughly warranted.

In the article that resulted from *The Source*'s March 2003
roundtable—those assembled included CEOs such as Roc-a-
Fella's Damon Dash and So So Def's Jermaine Dupri, and artists
such as Fabolous, Eve, and Talib Kweli—the conversation ranged
from how major-label moneymakers like Dash give back to the
community to how little the younger artists, like Fabolous,
actually know about the system that is paying them, from the
materialistic mentality among younger fans to what kind of
responsibility the artists and labels have as role models and
creators of the culture. Given the nature of the subject matter, pat
solutions are impossible, but the conversation has begun.

A more visceral, less-informed reaction to Eminem is the
racially charged view of *The Source* coowner and rapper Ray
Benzino, born Ray Scott, who, while he protested Eminem's
embrace by a mainstream media of America that does not afford

blacks the same treatment, essentially questioned Eminem's right as a white man to be a rapper. Benzino, a half-white Boston native, had spent a decade in hip-hop in two groups, the Almighty RSO and Made Men, and as a solo artist, producing and performing with little success despite elaborate marketing campaigns that ranged from expensively outfitting a truck to drive through Boston playing RSO's album, to Made Men's monthly three-page advertising spreads in *The Source*, an endeavor, before it became known that Benzino was secretly a co-owner of the magazine, that would consume most of the promotional budget for a major artist. Benzino befriended *The Source* cofounder David Mays some time in the mid-nineties, but the details of their business arrangement and friendship were not made public so much as exposed in 2001, when Benzino prepared to launch his solo career and began to be listed in the magazine's masthead. In 1994, however, after Mays inserted an article praising the Almighty RSO into the magazine without the consent of his editors, his top-tier staff quit and his cofounder Jonathan Schecter thereafter sold his interest in the magazine. Benzino's albums, *The Benzino Project* and *Redemption*, are littered with cameos by artists who had enjoyed major *Source* coverage or did shortly afterward: Pink, Puff Daddy, Scarface, Foxy Brown, Snoop Dogg, Mobb Deep. Benzino himself was granted the December 2001 cover, later declared a "collectors' cover" in a *Source* retrospective. In the months leading up to Benzino's second solo release (excluding a remix album) Benzino made disparaging comments about Eminem and dropped a bootleg single on which he called Eminem "Vanilla Ice 2003." In an MTV News interview, he maintained that the controversy was not racial, but in subsequent bootleg singles he proved otherwise. He questioned Eminem's legitimacy, falsely claiming that Eminem portrays a gangsta image in his music that doesn't jibe with reality. Benzino claimed to be singling out Eminem as the "hood ornament" of the white corporate machine he wished to call attention to. He feels that the machine won't allow black artists to cover the same lyrical ground as Eminem, and that black artists only get airplay for party jams while white artists and businessmen live off hip-hop and coopting the culture.

Eminem responded with the mixtape singles "Nail in the Coffin" and "The Sauce," which shed light on Benzino's relationship with *The Source* and the biased critical praise Benzino has received in their pages. "Put me on your fucking cover just to sell your little sell-out mag. I ain't mad, I feel bad," Eminem raps in "The Sauce." He also criticizes Benzino for "eating off his own son" in the same song, a reference to a group of child rappers called 3 Down that includes Scott's nine-year-old son, Ray Ray. Eminem then went for the jugular, including Benzino's own verses on his mixtape, followed by Eminem's response cuts, allowing, like any battle MC worth his weight, the listener to judge. Benzino responded by sabotaging any legitimacy in his argument with increasingly personal, race-based slurs against Eminem, tagging Eminem "the rap David Duke, the rap Hitler." Benzino attacked Eminem's credibility by defining hip-hop as a storytelling tradition, represented by true-life gangsters who come from the harsh streets of the drug-dealing life, something Eminem has never claimed. Benzino's series of anti-Eminem singles, which, for all of the magazine's purported objectivity, were posted on *The Source*'s website while Eminem's rebuttal tracks were not, translated into only fourteen thousand copies of his album *Redemption* being sold the first week of its release, despite a cross-promotion that included a free three-month subscription to the magazine. The sales figure was approximately four thousand more copies than Benzino's last two albums' first-week average.

"One of Benzino's issues with Eminem is that Eminem acts like he's a street guy, a hard gangsta, and that he's not, he's a fraud," says Sway Calloway. "In rap, who doesn't? Everybody's been gangstered out or else they rap about stories that haven't always happened. From the beginning, people have made themselves into superheroes in their raps. But the thing is, Eminem has never tried to say he was a gangsta growing up, just that he grew up hard. The only point Benzino has is that Eminem was accepted in the industry and the world easier for doing the same things that black rappers have done over the years—and Eminem's had more success doing it. There is validity to that because Eminem reaches new fans who probably grew up like him and look like him a little bit and can relate to him better than they'll relate to DMX. To those fans, Eminem's like a rock star, like Nirvana was. They can relate to him, and it's just cool and hip to be down with the guy who's antiestablishment."

Benzino is a representative of the problem he wishes to assail, the pressure of greed in an increasingly lucrative industry. Rumors have surrounded his involvement in *The Source*, from the influence he must wield to have warranted repeated coverage of a solo career of which sales have barely broken the 100,000 mark and of which the greatest sales numbers to date (with his former group, Made Men) top off at about 125,000. In addition, for all his talk of racial impropriety, Benzino is half white, the son of a white mother and black father. While Benzino's attack did not damage Eminem's career, it did alter the public perception of what was once the bastion of hip-hop music criticism. In this way, perhaps, Benzino achieved his goal, managing to damage a white-owned media corporation that profits from hip-hop: *The Source*, founded by two whites, one of whom, David Mays, remains at the helm.

"*The Source* is part of the same system Benzino is talking about, to be honest with you," says Calloway. "It's confusing, but everything they're saying the system is guilty of, they've been guilty of, too. They had Eminem on the cover just as many times as *Rolling Stone* has to sell issues. And *Rolling Stone* is pretty clear about the fact that they don't put too many black artists on their cover. Eminem isn't lying to himself or his audience about selling more because he's white. But he's also saying, 'Let's be real, I'm one of the best that's doing it right now, hands down.' And he is."

Race is the newest debate in the ever-evolving identity of hip-hop, and likely will be for some time as the effects of Eminem's success are felt throughout the industry. Hopefully the discussion will bring to light the industry standards and expectations that limit what hip-hop can be. Eminem is, in this arena, as much of a lightning rod for conflicting views as he is a symbol of cultural trends. His talent, however, transcends the issues and will hopefully leave the most lasting impression on hip-hop, whether it is a public demand for a less materialistic brand of rap or a move toward more complex song-craft and unique confessional storytelling.

"To me," says author Shelby Steele, "the thing to do is not call Eminem Elvis, it's to compete. If he sets a new bar, meet it. That's how music forms evolve. It has not a thing on earth to do with race. Because he is white, it is an invitation to misread the situation and talk about Elvis and the music being ripped off. You can't put a 1955 pattern on something happening in 2002. Eminem has shown considerable respect for rap as an art form. He's not taking it, as they did in the fifties, into some bubblegum form. He respects and identifies with it. What more can you ask? There is homophobia in his lyrics but there's certainly no racism. Is it somehow against the law for whites to practice this? Playing the race card on Eminem will get attention and plenty of ink. People will take it seriously and anguish over it. But playing to race isn't going to change Eminem's standing with anyone. You can't just call him a white boy. You have to be better than he is, you have to have a larger audience, a greater appeal—in short, you have to compete. You have to win Eminem's audience away from him if you really want to do him damage. And you can't do that with the race card."

In an essay titled "State of the Art 2003," posted on his website in December 2002, Chuck D decried the lack of wordsmanship in mainstream hip-hop, proclaiming that the newest generation of rappers care little for language and wit, the foundations of rap's greatest lyrics. Chuck blamed the get-rich-quick attitude of rap's support system (the major record labels) and the artists themselves—in short, the success of capitalism over art.

Many successful rappers other than the Jay-Zs and Nasirs [Nas] have shunned the basic artillery. Today we literally have rappers who simply cannot speak, much less have a limited vocabulary of 50 to 100 words ... Right now some cats have rejected the notion of using wit in words, which in "rap" certainly leads to an oxymoron ... Eminem has gained the throne of hip-hop consciousness, if you can call it that, by default. The hip-hop nation slides into settling for "dumbassification" while the opinion, wit, and words come from a white kid from the suburbs of Detroit. There's nothing wrong with Eminem being brilliant, the kid is like a rap Roy Jones Jr. It's just that his black peers have settled for not working as hard on the elements or skills of rap and hip-hop, choosing to dwell instead on dumb shit. This is Elvisification in a different manner ... Here, in rap, the tenants treat the condo like the projects, giving it away in the sloppy process of it all.

Rap success today, more than ever, is judged by everyone—the artists, labels, media, and fans—in terms of units sold. This attitude has grown beyond the mission of self-improvement, betterment, and the freedom to flaunt that was inherent in early hip-hop; instead, the aesthetic of mainstream hip-hop is a glorified accumulation of goods and the necessary toughness to keep them. Rappers are hardly bashful about the pursuit: Method Man told MTV News in a February 2003 interview that if he did three movies for $5 million each, he'd drop out of music and never be heard from again. His view is entirely understandable from the social context of someone wanting to work hard, earn enough to take care of their family, and then retire comfortably, but it is problematic to the identity and quality of hip-hop music as a black American expression.

"Hip-hop is so different now," says André of OutKast, whose first record came out in 1994 when the duo were still in their late teens. "Rap is kind of dead to me because it *is* the mainstream now. People are saying 'We're keeping it underground. We're keeping it underground.' But really, that's bullshit. Because, shit, once they start putting rap songs in commercials and rap is outselling country music and all this type of shit, it's not the same any more. It's a different type of white kid that listens to it now. It used to be kids listened to it for the same reason they liked punk—it was a rebellious thing your parents didn't like. To those kids, it was cool to listen to N.W.A say 'fuck the police.' That was like your music while you're skipping school and partying and drinking shit like that. Rap was something those white kids discovered, it wasn't just there in front of them. Now, it's everywhere, it's not a novelty to anybody."

If anything, and perhaps fittingly, the materialistic vision of hip-hop at the early part of the new millennium is more an expression of "white" America than the music has ever been. As the first generation of hip-hop entrepreneurs—CEOs like Puff Daddy, Russell Simmons, Jermaine Dupri, and Damon Dash—take their place as power players within the system of our society, from summering in the Hamptons with New York City's upper class to establishing a hip-hop political lobby group (the Hip-Hop Action Summit Network), the leaders of the culture are living a life closer to the white American dream of luxury homes, expensive clothes, and upper-crust influence than to the street style that got them there. This current hip-hop aesthetic as it plays out in the music seems to be searching for a middle ground, pulled by roots in a lifestyle that success seems to necessitate leaving behind. Today, the most successful mainstream rappers and businessmen find a way to promote a black image without a true sense of identity politics—the opposite of what defined success for late-eighties groups such as Public Enemy. As he has through the history of hip-hop, Russell Simmons has set a wise, commercially viable example of the new hip-hop identity. Through his many ventures, from the Tony Award-winning Broadway show *Def Poetry Jam* to the HBO series *Def Comedy Jam* and from his clothing label, Phat Farm, to his wildly influential record label, Def Jam, Simmons espouses an all-inclusive philosophy. His take reflects the origins of hip-hop, in which races and musical styles mingled freely under the leadership of black DJs and MCs, but he wisely also adopts the attitude of all of America's youth as hip-hop's own.

"Kids of all colors, all over the world, instinctively seek to change the world," Simmons said in his autobiography, *Life and Def.* "They usually have this desire because they don't want to buy into the dominant values of the mainstream. Rappers want to change the world to suit their vision and to create a place for themselves in it. So kids can find a way into hip-hop by staying true to their instinct toward rebellion and change." In his book and in interviews, Simmons places hip-hop into terms that the white mainstream can understand, drawing parallels to the Woodstock generation and the Baby Boomers' faith in the power of music to change the world. Simmons is accepted because he does not equate hip-hop with black America, he equates it with youth, a stance more true every day. We live in a time when race-identity politics, regardless of this country's social conditions, are simply not popular and, in many ways, are no longer relevant. Hip-hop, a musical form that existed and thrived in spite of the system, even when it includes images as anti-authority as those of N.W.A, Ice-T, and Public Enemy, has become part of the system.

"The most benign version of what's happened between white and black music in the past fifty years is that white people took the part that applied to them," says Dave Marsh. "There is, obviously, a much less benign and equally accurate version of that story. I think Eminem has destroyed that framework and I think it's going to be a problem for black people and white people now. If you want to see some of the results of it, go listen to that second Nelly album, *Nellyville*. The vision he's talking about ain't got nothing to do with being black. There's no identity politics what-soever, and there really isn't anybody who is terribly popular in hip-hop right now that does have that angle going on. Public Enemy [was] a very intelligent version of it, but I don't even think Chuck D is running the identity side of it anymore. Because it is over."

In hip-hop, the most successful artists of the last few years, from Nelly to Nas to Jay-Z, have not overtly or exclusively flown the flag of black consciousness that once defined hip-hop identity. Nas comes closest, particularly with the single "I Can," from *God's Son* (2002), an empowerment call to young black fans that includes a verse about the earliest origins of slavery. "The Nas song 'I Can' is so, sort of, classic KRS-One," Farai Chideya says. "It's really cute and has a great social message. But it's been, what, like ten years since a song like that came out? I'm not saying that every song should be that, and I'm not saying that hip-hop can't still be angry and complicated, but I'm pretty sure that there's a market bias against songs like that, songs you actually could play for an eight-year-old." But Nas is the exception to the norm, and although he's a far superior lyricist, he's not as hot a seller as Nelly, who has sold about thirteen million copies of his two albums. Nelly's 2002 album, *Nellyville*, is, as Marsh asserts, an album with values traditionally associated with white America. On the title track, "Nellyville," the St. Louis rapper envisions a bling-bling version of what sounds like a post-World War II suburb, complete with paperboys doing their rounds in Range Rovers and half a million dollars given to every newborn. It is a rap redefinition of the white American dream: a house, marriage, and a community without crime, poverty, or strife in which to raise children, complete with a sunny sky above. Nelly filters this image through hip-hop aesthetics, but the only reference to the history of black Americans comes in his recasting of reparations from "forty acres and a mule" to "forty acres and a pool." When Nelly appeared in a 2002 "Got Milk?" print-ad campaign, it was true symbiosis: he is the first black musician to be in such an ad, joining the ranks of everyone from the Backstreet Boys, the Dixie Chicks, Steven Tyler, Alex and Eddie Van Halen, Britney Spears, Tony Bennett, Hanson, Elton John, Billy Ray Cyrus, and other artists deemed appropriate to hock dairy. Nelly's take is clearly connecting with fans; his single "Hot in Herre" hit the top of more *Billboard* charts, from pop to R&B, than any other song in 2002, while his album ranked second for overall sales with 4.8 million, second only to The *Eminem Show*'s 7.5 million.

Eminem, more than Nelly or any other pop-culture artist at the moment, personifies American society's present racial awareness, one no longer based solely on skin color. This trend is easy to see in music, and representative of the greater change. Today it isn't unusual to see an Asian MC lead an alternative rock band, as in Linkin Park, or a mixed-race guitar player be one of the best in the business, as is Tom Morello of Audioslave and Rage Against the Machine, or a band where a dazzling range of traits come together, as in P.O.D., a group of dreadlocked rap-rockers, including three Hispanics and one black Born Again Christian. So too are racial "norms" open for reinterpretation. "Today, race is performative," says Farai Chideya. "You can be a white guy who acts black; you can be a black guy that acts white; you can be a Chinese person that acts Latino. To a great degree, Eminem does come from a place where this kind of black performative identity was not unnatural to him, but it's also performative in how he chooses to do it and how, as a performer, he directs it to appeal to not just the white crossover audience, but particularly to a black audience. What Eminem demonstrates clearly is that race now is not just about the color of your skin, it's also about your psychology. It's about you positioning yourself. It is a mix of conscious and unconscious factors that situate you in a demographic which your skin color might even deny. It's a fact today and it took hip-hop to make this face manifest. There have always been people who have had cross-racial identities, not because they are mixed-race, but because of how they grew up. But hip-hop laid it on the table that people were choosing an identity. Because of hip-hop, kids of all races and from different countries buy into what hip-hop says about their lives. These people's life circumstances help dictate that they are different from what their skin color might say they are."

America's move toward this new racial reality has accelerated in the years following hip-hop's mainstream takeover and Eminem's ascension to prominence. In researching her book *The Color of Our Future* just a few years ago, Chideya interviewed teens of all races across the country and encountered a different sensibility. "I met black teens who seemed 'black', classically black, and black teens who seemed 'white', and every cross-hatch. This was in 1997 and one guy I interviewed was a white 'black' guy, a 'wigger.' At the time everyone was using that term and people were still freaked out that white kids listened to hip-hop if those white kids lived in Iowa or Indiana, and the guy I interviewed insisted that I not call him a 'wigger.'"

Cross-race musical hybridization, pre-Eminem, was often regarded as a faux-pas. When the eclectic electric folk singer Beck released *Midnite Vultures* in 1999 (his quirky tribute to soul, funk, Prince, and R&B), it was taken by some critics as an elitist hipster parody of black culture. Somehow, Beck's stream-of-consciousness humor, the same that informed the line "Drive-by body pierce!" in "Loser," the hit that introduced him to the world in 1994, was seen as pointed and judgmental. Some people particularly harped on "Debra," an R&B ode sung in falsetto by a guy who would like to "get with" the subject of the song, a girl named Jenny, as well as with Jenny's sister, Debra. The vocals and the music are as earnest as the lyrics are hilarious, with the narrator asking Jenny to step inside his Hyundai after comparing her to ripe fruit and impressing her with a fresh pack of gum.

"My whole intention with that record was to tap into the kind of energy you see at a hip-hop show or an R&B show," Beck told me in 2002. "It came out of a love for the music, but people think I'm making fun of it because I'm not afraid of humor. Particularly the song 'Debra.' I didn't want to put it out at first because I knew people would think I was lampooning. 'Debra' wasn't really meant to be funny. If you take the subject matter of one of these contemporary songs, it's amazing what they get away with. I didn't want to do a real white, soul, Al Green-influenced thing, because then I'd be in Steve Winwood territory, which is fine, but I wanted to duplicate where people were at in the R&B world. It's funny because when I'd meet people in R&B and hip-hop people like Timbaland, they really loved it, they totally got it. The only people that looked at it sideways weren't involved in that world at all."

Within this era's shifting musical and cultural scene, Eminem is riding, and virtually *is*, the zeitgeist. His music is played on BET, MTV, rock and rap and Top 40 radio stations, and his fans range from the age of fifteen to fifty. Hip-hop is the language that erased many of these borders and is the common denominator upon which all racial influences mix freely, whether or not the roots or pathology of hip-hop culture are understood by more casual consumers. A generation of kids who grew up with hip-hop's flavor in pop culture has come of age, inspiring a deeper degree of hybridization even in traditionally white schools of music, such as heavy metal. Angsty bands like Korn, Limp Bizkit, and Linkin Park, whose music has loosely been labeled everything from rap-rock to neu metal, may be predominantly white acts (with some Hispanic and Asian members), but their singers rap their verses and wail their choruses over minor-key melodies while the bands' DJs (in Linkin Park's and Limp Bizkit's cases) scratch out solos. The imagery of the bands is even more cross-racial. Korn spent a good deal of their early career in Adidas tracksuits, like Run-D.M.C., and were photographed with pit bulls and on low-rider bicycles, two symbols associated with West Coast Hispanic gangs. Limp Bizkit front man Fred Durst wears baggy hip-hop gear and a backward baseball hat, which in the past signified a break-dancer who was ready to compete. Korn and Limp Bizkit were the first rock outfits to openly adopt hip-hop posturing in the late nineties, inspiring one writer in the alternative paper *The Boston Phoenix* to proclaim them "blackface metal." The writer, Carly Carioli, found Korn's "racial transgression" to be the expression of youth who choose, in the face of the complicated issues of race in this country, to express themselves in knuckle-headed gestures on a par with fart jokes. Carioli might have felt the same about the simultaneous emergence of Kid Rock, a Detroit native who fuses classic rock with a pimp image and an old-school rap delivery and has been doing so since 1990.

In the face of these white hybrids Eminem more fully and organically expresses the state of race and hip-hop today.

"The problem for white artists is that there are very few people who are even near as good as Eminem," Dave Marsh says. "But I think they should keep on keeping on. The future doesn't lie in segregation, it lies in integration. What integration meant in the sixties, it might mean now: How about we let black people lead for a while. That's how it plays out in Eminem's story. Everybody knows Dr. Dre is there and is crucial to his process. At the same time, everybody knows Eminem is not Dr. Dre's puppet."

Like his integrated racial identity, Eminem's music is an organic fusion of black and white: white as seen through a black lens and black as seen through a white lens. He is as proficient in a black art form as he is at finding a sugary melody. Like the best subversive pop of any variety, Eminem's music manages to relate complex realities—from celebrity worship ("Stan," "Superman") to self-loathing and nihilism ("My Name Is," "Role Model," "The Real Slim Shady")—to pop radio. Eminem tells stories, like his most talented black counterparts, yet from recorded freestyle raps such as "Greg," about a kid with a wooden leg, to *8 Mile*'s epic "Lose Yourself," his output illustrates a confessional voice and a constructed, cinematic songwriting eye that are more typical of rock and roll and R&B than of hip-hop. Eminem has evolved musically as well, particularly on *The Eminem Show*, into a more guitar-laden, anthemic production style that is a unique, powerful amalgam of both traditions.

"What white rappers bring," says André of OutKast, "is a fuck-it attitude. The Beastie Boys brought a fuck-it attitude, but it was more or less a party fuck-it attitude. Eminem's attitude is 'Fuck it, I'll say anything, to anyone, anywhere, fuck it, fuck it all. Who's the hottest pop group on MTV right now? Fuck them. What did the president do? Fuck him, too.' I think that's what's lovely about it. It ain't like he's trying to wear gold chains and shit and playin' like he's from my neighborhood. And people respect him for it. They can identify with all of it because it's real. That's all that people will identify with—what's real to them."

In this free-form climate in music and "racial performance", the only true test is one of the oldest: Does the artist's formula work? More important, is it credible? On this front, Eminem, as a talented white man, had to, and still has to, work twice as hard. Hip-hop might be changing its face, but to many young black Americans, it is still the forum for their group's identity in the post-Civil Rights era, and although a white man on the mike might be compelling, in order to endure, he had better consistently be very, very good.

"I never asked Dre if he knew I was white when he heard my tape," Eminem says. "I had met one of his A&Rs at the Rap Olympics, so I guess he knew. I don't think it really mattered much. It's because I'm dope. It sounds corny coming out of my mouth and I don't want to sound prima donna or nothin', but if somebody takes it to a certain level, it doesn't matter. A few people who work with Dre told me at first when they heard about him wanting to work with me, they were like, 'no white rappers.' Dre told them he didn't give a fuck if I was green or yellow or whatever color, he was working with me as his next project."

"To be real with you," Dr. Dre says, "usually white MCs aren't good—it's as simple as that. It's not a racial issue, you just have to be good and most of them aren't. Someone like Eminem is rare. A white MC is like seeing a black person in a hockey rink—it's gonna get some attention, but you know he'd only be playing if he was real good. Eminem is one of the best MCs I've worked with and one of the best out there, period. I didn't think twice. To me, I don't give a fuck if you're purple; if you can kick it, I'm workin' with you."

Another key to Eminem's unassailable identity is his fundamental honesty about his position in hip-hop; a quality he learned
when writing battle raps: by dissecting himself, he left his
opponent little ammunition. His timing doesn't hurt, either: as
Eminem's success reached unprecedented levels for a white
rapper, in a type of prediction of the fact, the rapper addressed the
commercial advantage of his color just before *The Eminem Show*
took off. "It's just an obvious fact to me that I probably sold double
the records because I'm white," Eminem says. "I'm not saying that
if I'd been a rapper of another race I wouldn't have sold records. In
my heart, I truly believe that I have talent, but at the same time I'm
not stupid. I know that when I first came out, especially because I
was produced by Dre, he gave me that foundation to stand on.
That made it cool and acceptable for white kids to like it. In the
suburbs, the white kids have to see that the black kids like it
before they do." On the album he made his point even more
clearly with lines such as "if I were black, I would have sold half,"
"hip-hop wasn't a problem in Harlem, only in Boston," and "I'm
not the first king of controversy, I am the worst thing since Elvis
Presley to do black music so selfishly and use it to get myself
wealthy." Clearly, this is a man who knows how race has played for
and against him; it's proof that he knows the score—and so should
everyone else.

Eminem personifies the sub-divisions of America—black,
white, city, suburb—and the cultural convergence of limber race
identity in America. Above and beyond his gifts as a musician,
Eminem is a lightning rod for debate, for projection, and for con-
jecture, because he is an embodiment of what is happening, the

most visible, most complete example of a complex evolution. Like so many significant artists who come to represent their times, Eminem did not campaign for the job, he is merely reflecting the influences that formed him and the times in which he lives. Hip-hop to Eminem was an escape from his life—literally and figuratively—as it is to so many others; more every day. It bonds inner-city kids who hear their reality reflected in the lyrics of the same black rappers that spell out to suburban kids, both affluent and poor, how to escape from whatever real or imagined prison holds them. Alienation from society, each other, and ourselves knows no boundaries, and neither does the art that reflects it. In that trait, it offers some salvation.

"There's always going to be assholes," Eminem told writer Matt Diehl in 1998, "but if there's one music that could break down racist barriers, it's hip-hop. When I do shows, I look out into the crowd and see black, white, Chinese, Korean people—I see all these nationalities there for one thing. You don't see that shit at a country show, you don't see it at a rock show. It's hip-hop that's doin' it."

We call it amityville

6. That's the mentality here, that's the reality here: to live and thrive in detroit

It is squat, with a wide roof that hangs low over synthetic log walls. There are moose aplenty here; horned heads hang from plaques, and dark eyes stare from all directions. Chandeliers of antlers cut the headroom in half. The image of one moose, in sunglasses, appears everywhere: on the sign outside, on the staff's chests, on the menus, on the hats for sale. Gilbert's Lodge, where "sportsmen, sportswomen, and regular folk alike enjoy delicious home-cooked meals, famous pizza, and big-screen TV in a rustic lodge setting," is open for business tonight. Gilbert's Lodge is open 364 days a year.

Inside, worn wood furnishings humid with years of human traffic are lit in the chilly radiation of television and neon. A sign advertises a trophy room, where jerseys remember the past glory of softball games and bowling tournaments.

A few of the wait-staff in green aprons chat at one end of the bar.

LEFT

A tale of two Marshalls: Marshall Mathers II holding Marshall Mathers III during the two years he was in Eminem's life (1972).

Photo courtesy of WENN

BOTTOM LEFT

I never meant to hurt you: Debbie Mathers holding her infant son, Marshall (1972).

Photo courtesy of WENN

ABOVE

Wee Shady in 1974: as a toddler Eminem was shuttled across the Midwest, eventually landing in Detroit.

Photo courtesy of WENN

Eminem as a teen in the car his mother gave him (1992). Proof called it "the stinkin' Lincoln," and it was depicted as less than reliable in *8 Mile*.

I'm reminiscing on your tenderness: Eminem and Kim Scott at their non-denominational wedding ceremony in St. Joseph, Missouri, on June 14, 1999.

Photo courtesy of WENN

OPPOSITE

The only lady he adores, Hailie: Eminem displays his daughter's portrait on his upper right arm, 2002.

Photo by Estevan Oriol

ABOVE

The Bassment: the building that housed the Bass Brothers' former recording studio on West 8 Mile Road in Ferndale, Michigan. Eminem's *Slim Shady EP* was recorded there in 1997.

Photo by Danny Moloshok, October 19, 2002

BELOW

It means "I love you" in southeast Michigan: Eminem and Kid Rock at the opening of the Experience Music Project in Seattle, Washington, June 23, 2000.

Photo by Kevin Mazur

A million young men who act, look and feel like him: Eminem and his phalanx of look-alikes rehearsing for the MTV Video Music Awards on September 6, 2000.

Photo by Frank Micelotta

Kim came by to say hi: Eminem and his inflatable wife on stage in Seattle, Washington, June 23, 2000.

Photo by Kevin Mazur

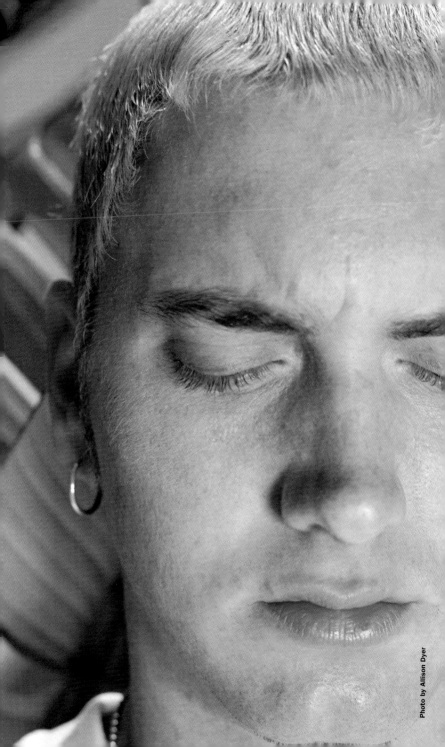

Photo by Allison Dyer

Near them, two men drink beer and watch football in silence. A party of five, waiting to be seated, goes unnoticed. After a few minutes, one of them walks into the kitchen.

"Yo, Pete, wassup?" he says to a mustached man who is surveying the cooks.

"Hi, Marshall," he says, with a slight smile. "Coming in to buy the place?"

"Yeah, Pete, you're fired," the blond guy says. "Nah. We're coming in to eat."

"Well, sit anywhere you like, you know the place. We'll get ya set up."

A woman bustles through the door and attaches an order ticket to the line.

"Oh, hi, Marshall, good to see ya!" she says. "I saw your video on MTV."

"Oh, yeah?" Eminem says. "Thanks."

The cooks look up and say hello. As Eminem leaves the kitchen, a waitress in her forties stops him.

"Hi, Marshall!" she says, in a cotton-candy Midwestern accent. "You know, I heard you were on MTV all the time, that's what they're telling me, but I watch it and I never see you."

"Oh, yeah?" he replies.

"Yeah," she says. "I watch it all the time and I never see you. Am I missing it? When is your video on? Is it on late at night when I'm sleeping?"

"You know, I don't know," Eminem says, his smile static, his eyes glinting. "It's on a lot. I don't know why you haven't seen it."

"I don't know, either. I turn on MTV all the time and I look for you, but I never see you on there. I'm starting to think they're all joking me about you being on MTV!"

"Well," he says, "keep watching and you'll see it. Nice to see you, we're gonna go sit down."

"OK, Marshall," she calls as he's walking away. "I'll look for you on MTV, maybe I'll see you sometime!"

He leads his party past the bar, toward the wide tables and barrel-backed chairs. Televisions box the area, broadcasting sports in visual stereo, while Sugar Ray's lazy ballad "Every Morning" blares from unseen speakers. We sit, five at a table for six, in silence.

Ten minutes later, our table is still devoid of silverware, water, menus, and conversation. I watch a man and woman dig into a pizza not far away. A waitress refills their water glasses. Eminem stops her as she passes our table.

"Can we get some beers here?"

"Yeah, sure," she says, "but I need to see some ID."

"I don't have my wallet," he answers flatly. "I used to work here. Ask Pete, I'm over twenty-one."

"OK, I'll have to do that," she says. "I'll be right back."

Eminem is a bit wild-eyed but civil, like an unbelieving host whose guests never arrived. He doesn't look crushed, more ready to crush something.

"Don't worry about it," Paul Rosenberg says. "She must be new."

"Yeah," Eminem says, leaning back in his chair. The silence is filled by more pop music, now Eagle-Eye Cherry's "Save Tonight." The waitress delivers a beer and a shot of Bacardi for Eminem. He swallows it before she leaves the table and he orders another. I talk to Paul until we run out of steam. Eminem stares at the televisions.

"Why did that bitch have to say that?" he says, turning back toward us. "Fucking bitch, I never liked her. Always watching MTV. She probably doesn't even have a TV." He pauses. "Bitch."

Paul looks at Eminem, scanning him. "Well, she's still here and you're not," he says. "She's jealous."

"Ahh, yeah," Eminem says. "I'm getting another shot."

He ambles to the bar and shakes the bartender's hand. He downs the liquor and brings a refill with him to the end of the bar, where some of his former coworkers chat.

"Man, everything can be going right," Paul says, eyeing Eminem, "but a comment like that will stick with him for days. She's seen the video, you know she's seen the video." He sips his pint.

"This is his reality," Paul continues. "He came from this. And after everything is over, this is the reality he has to go back to."

Eminem lopes back to the table, his spirits lifted by Bacardi and Kathleen, a coworker who always believed in him.

"You know, Paulie, a lot of the shit that's happened to me," he says, dropping into his chair, "is because you're fat."

He stares at Paul. He laughs, two quick chops. "Heh-ha!"

Eminem knocks back some beer. "I can't wait to do my second album. That shit is gonna be fucking bananas. Every time I make music, I know more and more what I'm doing, so it's gonna get hotter and hotter."

He looks at us and then at the waitress by the bar. "Lots of drugs and lots of fuzz," he says, throwing his hand in the air. "Hey! Can we get some more beers over here?"

Eminem surveys the room, the backdrop to a past too recent for nostalgia but just far enough away for examination. "You don't even know how much at home I felt here," he says to me, leaning in a little. "My home away from home. Dog, I fucking lived here, man. I worked forty-eight hours a week. Sometimes I pulled sixty-hour weeks and still wasn't making shit. I started off at five-fifty. That's not a lot of money."

He isn't proud or ashamed of the details of his life, even the darkest; his mood is bittersweet. Sitting here, watching his old co-workers react to him, warmly, coolly, mockingly, or not at all, I see Detroit's mixed message in his life. Eminem endured here in an isolated rap scene, rejected by the radio stations that now play his song; in New York and L.A. he is a celebrity already, but his former coworkers at home don't come to his table. There is a territorial pride in Detroit; it doesn't allow its own to grow an ego. I will watch this play out as Eminem's fame grows. When Eminem buys his first house, fans will swim in his pool, flip him off, take his mailbox, and wait in his driveway until he resorts to guns as a deterrent. In 2000, after the same guns get him in trouble with the law, he will return to his hometown with Dr. Dre's Up in Smoke Tour for two concerts. City officials will successfully pressure promoters not to screen a pre-show video in which Snoop Dogg and Dr. Dre hold up a liquor store and sit in a hot tub with semi-naked women. The mayor's office will ask to preview and edit the video to their approval; they will be refused. Hours before the show, city officials will threaten to cut the power to the stage if the video is shown. They will also strongly recommend that Eminem not bring an inflatable sex doll onstage. He has been using it to represent his wife, Kim. Eminem will comply; he will have been in court already that day, for the initial proceedings of one of his two trials. Dr. Dre will be ticketed for promoting pornography for screening the video at the first night's concert. Detroit will be the only city in the country to censure the tour, one of the most high-quality, incident-free, and professionally run (from sets to security) hip-hop tours ever. Dr. Dre will sue Detroit for violating his First Amendment rights and will win $25,000. It will hardly be a homecoming for Eminem. I understand now why he thrives in the face of adversity; it is a way of life here.

"Hey, Marshall, how you doin'?" Pete Karagiauris, manager at Gilbert's Lodge, asks. "How about we make you guys a special garlic chicken pie?"

"All right, Pete," Eminem says. "We're going to be sitting here awhile. We plan on getting drunk."

"OK, drink up," Pete says.

"Pete's cool," Eminem says. "But the owner, Louie, he ain't here. That motherfucker was a fuckin' dick. I worked here for three years, cooking, washing dishes, I was a busboy, all that. And the whole time I kept saying I was going to be a fucking rapper. Louie used to always come in when I was cooking and be like, 'Oh shit, Marshall, you're here. I thought you'd be gone, blowing up as a rapper by now.' That guy always fucked with me. When I got fired right before Christmas, he was the one who OK'd it. It was like a week before Christmas, and then they hired me back eight months later."

The waitress is more friendly now. "How are you doing over here!" she says.

"I'm wasted and good!" Eminem says.

"This shot is from Kathleen, she wanted to get you drunk."

"Well, OK," he says. "Tell her she's too late."

Pete and two waiters return with plates and a sizzling pizza, preceded by roasted garlic aroma. "Here's the special," he says.

"Marshall here was a good worker," Pete tells me, sitting down in the empty chair, "but I always knew his music mattered the most. I had to stay on top of him sometimes. He'd be in the back rapping all the orders! I had to tell him to tone it down sometimes. But he was good about that."

"He'd rap the orders?" I ask.

"Yeah," he says. "Everything that came out of his mouth was a rap. Every once in a while, I had to check on him and make sure he wasn't fooling around back there too much. No matter how much he was joking around, he always took his music very seriously. We were all really surprised when we saw he really did it."

"Did you think he sounded like a good rapper?" I ask.

"Oh, I don't know anything about it," Pete responds, chuckling. "I wouldn't know at all. I listen to Greek music. Call me next time you guys are coming in, I'll bring my bouzouki."

"And I'll bring my bazooka," Eminem says, in a mobbed-up Italian accent. "And, ah, I'll blow up the place. Then we're good."

The pizza is eaten and the beer is drunk. The plates are cleared and a round of shots arrive from the bartender.

"OK!" Eminem says. "You gonna drink that, Paul?"

Later, TLC's "No Scrubs" plays as we walk to the door.

"Hey, Marshall," says a smiling lady, "I see your video all the time."

"Hi, Holly," Eminem says.

"I'm so fucking proud of you!"

"Thanks a lot, Holly."

"How's your daughter doing?"

"She's good," he says. "Real good."

"You take care of yourself, Marshall. Be careful."

Eminem walks across the parking lot, crunching snow underfoot. He strides along an invisible path he knows well, but he doesn't go to the Dumpster this time; or around the back to where he's parked his worn Ford Tracer. He opens the door to the chauffeured van that is billowing smoke, and he disappears inside.

DETROIT IS AND IS NOT A TYPICAL AMERICAN CITY. IT IS A MIDWESTERN metropolis with all that entails: the full spectrum of neighborhoods, from no-frills, working-class life to suburbs as plush as executive pay can buy. But Midwestern small-town quaint resides next to burned-out factory wasteland; country clubs and crack houses lie within short miles of each other. As a great flat bastion of conservatism, the Midwest screams organized homogeneity lacking in character, while Detroit flies the bird.

It is the fuck-you cousin of the Midwest, if not of the country. Safety after dark in metropolitan Detroit is a legitimate concern; a trip to a downtown club can be on a par with taking your life in your hands. People raised in Detroit have their stories involving random acts of violence or scenes taut with threat. They relate them with a mix of pride, nonchalance, and Midwestern economy. There's a tactile air to Detroit, like New Orleans or

New York—a permeating mood. Detroit feels dead yet electric, animated in rigor mortis. Like New Orleans's mausoleums, the decay is above ground, among the living. There's regret in Detroit, a tangible loss echoed by the vacant fortresses of industry. The city feels closed, resentful, unconventional, and conservative. There is an unstable yet exciting energy to Detroit, too, perhaps born of listlessness, lawlessness, and the overlap of dreams and decrepit memories.

Detroit has proved itself to be America's most racially divided city despite an all-encompassing business that blurred the barriers. Auto-industry economics made the factory line color-blind, but the county lines within the city have been painted black and white for centuries. Detroit celebrated its three hundredth birthday in 2001, with little but hope to celebrate, even though times have improved: it is a stagnated city that hasn't seen a population increase for most of a decade. The city's fortunes have peaked and dipped with that of the auto industry since 1908; it is an American dream that did not come with a warranty.

Detroit's juxtaposed soulfulness and divisive delineations have, however, made for unique cultural crossbreeding. In its rifts, self-hate, and innovation, it is our most American city. It is a city founded by French fur traders, where freed Southern blacks migrated to stake their claim next to whites; a city where unions made equality a question of class and racial prejudice ignited more upheaval than in any other city in the nation. Detroit is a city divided from within and in identity is divided from the rest of the country. But more American cities become like Detroit each year, eroded by economic downturn, the loss of manufacturing dollars to overseas vendors, the high cost of living, and in some cases an influx of immigrants and state governments that are more sympathetic to the suburbs. The poverty gap between rich and poor is growing steadily wider in America, as income has shown growth only in the richest ranks of the private sector. Many more American metropolises, like Detroit, are being stratified further along racial lines: poor minorities generally remain in the cities while poor whites are able to move to affordable outlying areas. It has been so in Detroit since the sixties, if not earlier; now cities such as Newark, New Jersey; Miami, Florida; Milwaukee, Wisconsin; Cleveland, Ohio; and New Orleans, Louisiana, are facing similar circumstances. No state exemplifies America's increasing class divide better than Connecticut: according to the 2002 census, that state was ranked richest in the union, but its capital city, Hartford, was ranked the poorest.

The government's 1990 census ranked Detroit as the ninth-largest city in our country, home to more than two million residents. It was also ranked first in poverty: one-third of the population in the metropolitan area lived below the poverty line. In 1990, there were more single-parent households and more residents on public assistance there than in any other major urban area. Detroit adults were second to last in the top seventy-seven cities for the percentage who had earned college diplomas. The average worth of a home in metropolitan Detroit was about $25,000, whereas similar homes in Boston were worth close to $160,000, or in Los Angeles $240,000. The year 1990 was a low point not seen in the Motor City for twenty years.

The history of Detroit reflects the history of the auto industry— and the river running through its rifts. Henry Ford put Detroit and the mass-produced motor car on the map in 1908, and the automobile has remained, aside from housing, Americans' primary expenditure (consider the number of auto ads shown during an average hour of network TV compared with those of other products). In one fell swoop, Ford's production-line system gave the city of Detroit a purpose.

The two World Wars established Detroit as the throne of vehicular industry. When World War I broke out in 1914, Detroit's factories churned out trucks and honed their production capabilities. In the years between the wars (1919 to 1938), America expanded its roadway system and drove it like mad. In the twenties, the auto industry grew faster than any other industry in the country, and Detroit swelled to meet the needed output. But the city did not grow organically as it should have; it became a residential auto plant. No other industries moved in, no colleges or cultural centers were built. It was the equivalent of an Old West mining town for the motor age.

In the twenties, the largest wave of Italian and Eastern European immigrants came to America, but very few moved to Detroit. Immigration laws kept most of them out of the auto industry, leaving Southern workers to man the lines. In these years, the black majority moved into Detroit—and remained: African-Americans account for 23 percent of the city's population today, almost double the national average.

In the thirties Detroit redefined the life of the American worker. The establishment of auto unions to defend workers' rights laid the groundwork for what we now call the middle class. The auto unions were well organized and became, at the time, the country's most powerful, able to halt production at a factory successfully enough to send profits into the basement if their demands were not met. The unions broke down barriers for black workers, more out of necessity than due to any moral stance: union leaders realized that if the black labor majority was left out of the unions, it would be called upon to replace the white workers if a strike were declared. The auto unions ensured equal pay and equal rights for black members, an unprecedented move at the time, securing Detroit the most integrated industrial work-force in the country.

During World War II, Detroit was dubbed the "Arsenal of Democracy"—its factories provided the Allies with a massive supply advantage. The war necessitated high-volume production and forced industry into the suburbs in order to churn out planes, tanks, and trucks at larger, newer factory sites. After the war, returning soldiers moved to Detroit in search of a fair, blue-collar slice of the American dream. The modern plants located in the suburbs eclipsed the older ones in the city when production reverted to automobiles, and gradually the nexus of the industry moved out of the urban hub. The older factories, like the neighborhoods around them, began to decay.

White workers followed the newer facilities and management positions in a flight out of the city and into the outlying town-ships, closer to the new factories. For a while, the unions kept wage rates high and the quality of life stable for their members, but when the market began to slow with the onset of the

Vietnam War in the sixties, many auto manufacturers cut costs by subcontracting work to factories in other states or overseas, out of union jurisdiction. In the seventies, the industry took a major downturn, crushed by efficient, well-made imports from Germany and Japan, and an oil and gas crunch that did not bode well for gas-guzzling American luxury cars. The auto manufacturers further trimmed operating costs by automating production and eliminating employees. Automated assembly lines translated into more management positions, however, to oversee operations, while unskilled laborers, a major percentage of urban Detroit's workforce, became unemployed. The move to automation favored white workers, who, on average, had attained a higher degree of education, and management-level jobs were more accessible to them.

These changes in the auto industry deepened the existing racial divide and doubled it along economic lines. Blacks who moved up the economic ladder encountered prejudiced opposition when they tried to move into the better, predominantly white neighborhoods. Open conflicts were common in the fifties, as black and white city neighborhoods began to overlap. Whites yielded, moving out of the city to take advantage of federal development grants, while the black population, for the most part, remained. The line along 8 Mile Road, metropolitan Detroit's east–west artery, was permanently drawn. To the north side of 8 Mile Road is Warren County, the city's first suburb; on the other side is the city of Detroit. Warren runs the gamut from run-down trailer parks to middle-class homes, and it is overwhelmingly white. The city side of 8 Mile Road, or at least sections of it, looks identical to its counterpart to the north, but it is predominantly black and lower class. The surrounding neighborhoods closest to 8 Mile on both sides are poor and crime-ridden. Still, if the road manifested its symbolism to Detroiters, instead of a road it would be a wall. It is a true divide between the classes and the races, and the two sides do not mingle much. Residents in Warren, for example, removed basketball hoops from the township's public parks to discourage Detroit kids from crossing the road to play there. Predictably, suburban police are more plentiful than city cops along 8 Mile Road. Though the statistics were worse a decade ago, the reputation of what lies south of 8 Mile Road in the Motor City—and the communal suburban anxiety about it—remains: lawlessness, robbery, and murder. In the film *8 Mile*, the road was a metaphor to the same effect: dividing black from white and rich from poor, it symbolized the hurdles between Eminem's character Jimmy Smith Jr. and his dream, the border he must find a way to cross.

Since this country was founded, federal guards have been called to Detroit four times to quash black–white violence: twice in the twentieth century, twice in the nineteenth. A telling statement on Detroit race relations came from George Edwards, a liberal police commissioner in the sixties who tried to increase sensitivity to the racial divide among the city's police force. Edwards concluded that a "river of hatred" ran between the city's whites and blacks.

The Civil Rights Movement slicked that river with oil and torched it. The Movement was zealously supported by Detroiters and the Detroit United Auto Workers Union. Prior to the March on Washington, Detroit sponsored what was at the time the largest public display of support for Dr. Martin Luther King Jr.: a 1963 parade down Woodward Avenue. Nonetheless, in 1967, a four-day racial riot occurred that claimed forty-three lives.

Today, Detroit attracts few new residents, even among the country's newest immigrants. The U.S. Department of Commerce estimated in 1998 that only one in a hundred Detroit residents were new to the city. The population of Detroit's suburbs has dropped as well. These towns, however, are still not poor. There is a ring of mostly white counties in which the yearly income ranks seventh in the country out of cities of similar size. In a study done in 1997, the income of Detroit households in the well-to-do suburbs averaged about $56,000 a year, about $10,000 more than metropolitan families in New York and L.A.

While the suburbs are generally white and rich, the central city majority is black and poor. The 2000 census states that the city was 76 percent African-American, with only a 5 percent representation living in the suburbs. Of the 76 percent in the city, nearly half of those African-Americans are under the age of eighteen, living in impoverished homes, compared to just 10 percent of kids in the same straits in the suburbs.

This degree of racial and economic division is as close as a major American city gets to the kind of class imbalance found in Third World countries. During the years of the auto industry's decline, particularly in the seventies, African-Americans were unable to find better housing, steady employment, and good schools. The tense undercurrent in Detroit today is a product of the decline of labor economics, definite unflinching patterns of residential segregation, and a tradition of racial upheaval and mistrust.

As the economics of the seventies and eighties wreaked havoc on Detroit, racial tensions eased a bit as blacks and whites found themselves walking the same poor middle ground. However, negative racial attitudes still prevail. In their 2000 book *Detroit Divided*, professors Reynolds Farley, Sheldon Danziger, and Harry J. Holzer conclude from an array of interviews that most African-Americans in Detroit feel that they miss out on better jobs, promotions, and better neighborhoods because of systematic discrimination, regardless of their level of achievement or education. The whites who were interviewed recognize the same prejudice among residents of the city and surrounding areas but feel that it poses less of a practical problem for black Detroiters. They feel that blacks don't work hard enough or take advantage of the opportunities presented them. The authors concluded that, while blacks see discrimination everywhere, whites seem to doubt their neighbors' intelligence and feel that they are difficult to get along with, as neighbors or as employees.

In the nineties, Detroit along with other Midwestern manufacturing centers bounced back as the country enjoyed the boosted economy of the Clinton years. General Motors opened new plants, and the city built a new sports center and casinos that increased the number of unskilled labor positions. In 1992, the unemployment rate in Detroit was the highest in the country. Six years later, it had fallen faster than that of any other city in the country, but still remained well above the average.

Detroit has always been at the mercy of the hands of industry. The city was not developed with an eye toward infrastructure or culture, and in its bountiful times did little to change that. The auto trade's down years have left Detroit pocked with gaping holes—zones full of abandoned factories and rotting neighborhoods. In these craters, however, cultural flowers have bloomed. An architectural example, rendered more by cost-cutting necessity than by design, is the parking structure in downtown Detroit that was used as the setting in *8 Mile* for an impromptu rap battle between Jimmy Smith Jr. and Free World, his rap rivals. The garage was built in 1977 into the gutted remains of the Michigan Theater, which in 1926 was one of the city's largest, most ornate movie houses. The molding and intricate plasterwork of the theater were preserved within the new structure, not to save history but to avoid the costs of removal. The result is a unique, beautiful, and inadvertent statement on the true nature of the city itself.

In contrast to the lack of mainstream culture, a rich musical tradition well outside of the lines of the norm is Detroit's legacy. Though there is little evidence in the form of celebrated music festivals, such as New Orleans' Jazzfest, or large museums, such as Seattle's Experience Music Project, to reflect the fact, Detroit is one of the most influential and least appreciated cities in the history of American music. From the country-and-western music of plains-states workers who moved to the city in the twenties to the fertile jazz scene of Detroit in the fifties, local musicians consistently took new turns at developing their own sound. From MC5 to Motown to Kid Rock to Carl Craig—Detroit artists are the innovators in the music culture of their day, alien to the norm and free to create due to a geographical and cultural alienation from the mainstream.

Some of the richest music of the twentieth century was born in Detroit, nurtured in pockets of a city that has no outlets to support them, in the thick central industrial belt of a country ruled by its coasts. Blues legend John Lee Hooker followed the Southern black migration to Detroit, developing his eclectic take on the craft in the Paradise Valley and Black Bottom sections of the city in the forties. Singer Dinah Washington was raised in Detroit, peppering everything from R&B to blues to jazz with her critically disdained, distinctive, high-pitched grit. The Detroit jazz scene of the fifties gave us innovators such as jazz chanteuse Betty Carter, who shredded convention with radical tonal and time changes, while guitarist Kenny Burrell epitomized cool swing, gracing records by all the greats of his day (Stan Getz, Billie Holiday, Milt Jackson, John Coltrane, and Duke Ellington among them). Of course, Detroit is more known for Motown Records, the label that changed the music business in the sixties. Visionary Berry Gordy Jr. founded Motown Records in 1959 in a recording studio housed in a small two-storey home on West Grand Boulevard. Gordy made stars overnight—the Supremes, Martha and the Vandellas (all Detroit talent)—as well as launched Marvin Gaye, the Temptations, Stevie Wonder, and the Jackson 5. Gordy was the original hip-hop entrepreneur, nurturing and packaging black urban talent for mainstream consumption and cultural domination. He created the Motown sound: pop with soul, both precocious and innocent. The Motown sound spoke to teenagers because it reflected both sides of teenhood, and the operation became the most successful black-owned company in the nation.

In the late sixties and seventies, Detroit was duly dubbed

Detroit Rock City. During that time, it birthed Grand Funk Railroad, Ted Nugent, Bob Seger, ? and the Mysterians, and the original American punk rockers: MC5 and the Stooges. These last two bands eschewed hippie idealism to confront the dark realities of the times, such as the Vietnam War, the Watergate scandal, and nationwide racial unrest. These bands echoed acts from across the Atlantic, from Black Sabbath to the English punk-rock scene that emerged by the end of the seventies. As the image of the counterculture was sold into commercialism in that decade, from the shaggy fashions that became mainstream to the appropriation of the hedonistic side of hippie culture in the music scene at the expense of its egalitarian ideology, MC5 truly called for revolution, while the Stooges deflated the bloat of rock and roll and the idol worship begat at the dawn of the arena rock era. Iggy Pop and the MC5 did not become widely recognized for their influence for nearly two decades, when their experiments with feedback, distortion, and rhythm were celebrated by alternative rockers. In their day they remained fringe artists; MC5 played their final gig at Detroit's Grand Ballroom for just $500.

In the eighties, Juan Atkins sent dance music leagues ahead with just one song, 1982's "Clear," recorded with Rick Davis as Cybotron. The pair infused the hip-hop groove of the electro music blasted by break-dancers with a chilly expansive quality as wide and craggy as the bowels of the city. Under a host of names, Atkins and peers such as Kevin Saunderson and Derrick May established a scene that was *so* underground, early local fans had no clue that the music was even made in Detroit. Through Atkins's label, Metroplex, and a club, the Music Institute, the scene grew, nurturing techno's second wave: artists such as Richie Hawtin, Carl Craig, and Stacey Pullen, all top artists in dance music today.

Detroit seems as unaware of its groundbreaking cultural contributions as the rest of the country. There is little remnant of any of these creative microcosms left in the city, aside from the efforts of industrious citizens. Detroit seems to consume its relics with little ceremony, reflecting the city's roots as an industrial center where the production of goods takes precedence over the production or the development of anything else. The legendary Black Bottom neighborhood, where the city's rich blues and jazz tradition developed, was destroyed in the fifties to make way for a new interstate. It is now alive only in the re-creations of a museum exhibit, the memories of those still around to tell about it, and a short list of books. The Motown studio and headquarters on Woodward Avenue are boarded up and vacant, as they have been since Gordy moved the company's headquarters to L.A. in the eighties. The only echo of the mighty Motown is the Hitsville Museum, originally a very modest affair that opened in 1988 and comprised two houses on West Grand Boulevard where Gordy lived and worked in the early days of the label. Finally, in 1995, Ford Motor Company donated $2.7 million to renovate the Hitsville Museum and install a permanent Motown exhibit in the Henry Ford Museum—located in the rich and white suburb of Dearborn. Detroit techno thumps on, though much of it is recorded in Chicago and L.A. and is revered mostly overseas.

Detroit music's innovations are both born of and transcend the race demarcations of the city and the surrounding counties of the southern Michigan industrial complex. In a city where black and white remain separate, a different kind of racial honesty exists, one that only natives truly understand, yet one that is coming into play among a greater number of young Americans. There is a sense of awareness among Detroiters about the role of race in the sociopolitical context of American society, because it is so very visibly central to their geography. In Detroit music, there is a similar honesty, informed by the belief that artistic passion crosses all borders. This innate self-assessment is how Eminem knew he was right to be in rap, because he knew that even if Detroit fans didn't care for his subject matter, he had the skills, the honesty, and the heart to connect.

"I don't think you can imagine a single white performer from Detroit—from the era of McKinney's Cotton Pickers to today—who didn't want to sound like they were making some kind of African-American music," says legendary rock critic Dave Marsh. "I don't mean that they wanted to be black, whatever that would mean. I'm talking about the deepest influence for everyone from Mitch Ryder to Johnnie Ray, to Bob Seger, to the Romantics, to Iggy Pop, to the MC5—you name it, it was black music. Rob Tyner of the MC5 once told me, 'What all of us wanted was to sound like an R&B singer.' If you talk to the new garage bands like the Detroit Cobras, whom I know, and the White Stripes, whom I don't, but I would imagine, as dangerous as it is to imagine, that they would agree."

Marsh should know; he grew up in Pontiac, Michigan, in the fifties, an area due north of Detroit, dominated by the environmental pollution of the foundries in its midst. In a 1971 article,

Marsh wrote that the foundry grit on his family's windowsills is his earliest memory; no matter how quickly his mother would clean it off, it would reappear the next morning. Marsh refers to his part of Oakland County as "Klan country" and recalls that KKK members torched school buses to dissuade local government from busing in black students. "That's what 8 Mile really means," Marsh says. "But it means something different now. In one way, that division is much more extreme because the poverty in inner-city Detroit is so enormous. But on the other hand, from a race point of view, it means less, because there are towns like Oak Park, Southfield, and parts of Birmingham that are pretty middle class with very large black populations who fled the city, too."

The history of hip-hop in Detroit is like an episode of *Survivor*—a study in isolation, competition, and community among peers. A small scene began in the late eighties, with local versions of popular hip-hop styles and little else, but by the mid-nineties there was a rich underground, as there was in many cities, of young artists brought up on hip-hop. Dominated by the shadows of the East and West coasts, most Detroit rappers reached for a style that blended the two, flowing East Coast gritty over elastic West Coast beats—a formula that Eminem turned to gold. "I take a piece from everywhere," he said back in 1999. "A little from the east, a little from the west. The East Coast is mainly known for lyrics and style, while the West Coast is more known for beats and gangsta rap. I kinda blend it so east meets west halfway, which is the Midwest. To me, that's what it should sound like because that's where I am. I'm in the middle, so I'm getting shit from both angles."

Unlike the packed, amped club scenes in *8 Mile*, Detroit hip-hop in the mid-nineties was spartan. "In Detroit, if you were an underground MC," recalls Paul Rosenberg, "your crowd was mainly other MCs. Eminem would be rapping in front of a room basically of his competitors. But everybody knows who the best guys are and they still become fans of them. The best of that scene are like the rapper's rapper."

The scene roved around several spots, and in the tradition of Detroit cultural landmarks, they are almost all gone. Clothing designer Maurice Malone deserves a Detroit lifetime-achievement award for the Hip-Hop Shop, a boutique that turned into a hip-hop café on the weekends. "I used to run most of the open mikes and shit around 1993," says Proof, "because I was the battle king. The Hip-Hop Shop was a place where you could really get your skills off. Motherfuckers came from far and wide to come there because they heard about it. We had people like Fat Joe stop through, Miilkbone, he used to stop in back in the day. Big L fucked the shit out of the Shop one day, just came in there wrecking rhymes, just for no reason."

Around the same time, the Shelter, a room in the basement of St. Andrew's Hall (a church turned club), hosted hip-hop Fridays full of local talent. The Shelter was the arena for the rap battles in *8 Mile*; however, since it has been redecorated, it had to be re-created in a warehouse. There was also the Ebony Showcase, another local party. The rappers and fans on the scene supported one another, but no one else in Detroit did. It was easier for Detroit rappers to get airplay on the radio in other cities than it was at home. In a reaction against the city's hip-hop station WJLB, the Detroit Hip-Hop Coalition (a collective of hip-hop artists, managers, and local labels) picketed the station and in 2001 sent an open letter to Big Tigger, host of BET's *Rap City: Tha Bassment* and the nationally syndicated radio show *Live in the Den with Big Tigger*:

> We are quite sure that you've been made aware of the tensions between your new employer (JLB) and many members of the Michigan Hip-Hop community. The differences have now been well documented. For the past several years, your new employer has been very successful in the dual tasks of ignoring, snubbing, or refusing to give airplay to all but a few Detroit- or Michigan-based independent artists (regardless of requests) and offering nominal support to the metro Detroit Hip-Hop community that makes up its listening audience. This situation has become even more exasperating in recent years, chiefly because Det./Mich. artists have generated national and international acclaim . . . How can a self-proclaimed "urban music" station broadcast out of Detroit (Motown) yet ignore "significant" Detroit artists? We don't understand that one either.

In *8 Mile*, the characterization of JLB falls under the fiction column, where it was portrayed as a bastion of local support. "You know, that was pointed out," director Curtis Hanson told the *Detroit Free Press.* "There were mixed feelings about [the radio station], actually. Some felt that way, some didn't." The lack of support or curiosity may be a kind of unconscious Detroit self-hate, or just a test of its artists' mettle. "I busted my ass," Eminem says. "I didn't have any money to go anywhere. There was nothing in Detroit as far as labels and shit like that to get you recognized, unless you put some independent shit out and it happens to blow up, which is rarely the case."

"Motherfuckers don't know, man," Proof says. "Eminem's song 'Lose Yourself,' that line about having one shot—that's some of the best work he's done in his life. People don't understand, in this industry you really only do get one shot because out of sight, out of mind in this game. Detroit gave us that gusto times ten, man. It's so hard to get a foot in the door that when you do, you fucking *do* that shit. You know how many people's asses I had to whup? Niggas would not play your shit for nothin' in this town, man. I'm talking about for nothin', no matter what you do or say. They don't want to support you, they don't even act like they like you as a person. Now that I understand the music game, I see how radio is controlled by corporate shit, but I still see where they could help locals. They're doing it more now, because Detroit is like the third-biggest music market. The problem lies with Berry Gordy—when those motherfuckers left here, there was nothing to build on. Detroit was in the music industry then, we had radio. But after Motown left, everything here stagnated."

In the Detroit music hall of fame, Eminem is less of an anomaly than he is in a more mainstream view of pop-music history. Detroit artists from Diana Ross to Iggy Pop have cross-pollinated black and white music and performed across cultural stereotypes in order to express themselves. Like pop performers Diana Ross and the Supremes, Eminem has infiltrated middle America, essentially putting Detroit hip-hop on the map. In 2003, Eminem resembled Diana Ross in another way; the Supremes' runaway success in the sixties appealed to teenagers as much as it did to adults. But Eminem has more in common with the rebel faction of Detroit music, the vibrant rock and roll that informs his swagger and flavors his music, from his anthemic cadence to his burgeoning production sensibility. Of the icons of Detroit rock, Eminem is symbolically most like punk godfather Iggy Pop. Like the Stooges, Eminem defied the hip-hop mainstream he entered in 1999 in every way, from his content to his color, and was equally infamous before he was famous. Iggy and the Stooges, in all of their smutty glory, defied the prevailing mythology of rock-and-roll rebellion in the late sixties. Iggy eschewed the Dionysian love-god imagery of rock stars like Jim Morrison of the Doors, Mick Jagger of the Rolling Stones, and Roger Daltrey of the Who, instead smearing himself with peanut butter and blood and diving into the audience rather than remaining above them, enthroned on the stage. Iggy Pop baited his audience; he was reviled and was an anti-role model; he was a punk rock Slim Shady who distilled the paranoia, rage, and angst of his darkest recesses into lyrics and exorcized them onstage.

"It doesn't come so much out of the black music tradition in Detroit, but there's this business of attitude and in that respect, Eminem, whether he knows it, is inheriting Iggy Pop and the MC5," Dave Marsh says. "He is inheriting the whole 'fuck you' culture built here in the sixties." Eminem as Slim Shady embodies the angry-white-man stereotype, but in a manner very unlike Ted Nugent, the other Detroit musician who made a career of the same. Nugent, both with and without the Amboy Dukes, was one of the top live acts in the arena rock days of the seventies and is now infamous for his right-wing politics and his progun and pro-hunting advocacy. Unlike Eminem, Nugent is entirely devoid of irony or satire. "Both Ted Nugent and Eminem are angry white men," Marsh says. "Only one of them is the angry-white-man stereotype. It's not a generational difference, which some people might imagine it to be, it is a class difference. Ted Nugent is much more middle class. Ted don't come from factory workers, he don't come from poor people. Ted has pretty bourgeois political attitudes, probably as a direct result of his upbringing—there's a reason he acts like that. I'd say the most bourgeois rocker from Detroit after Ted is Iggy Pop, whose parents were both teachers and still live in a trailer park."

There is another, unlikely element of Detroit music history that Eminem embodies, and it may explain his brilliance at con-structing narrative raps such as "Stan," from *The Marshall Mathers LP*, or "'97 Bonnie and Clyde," from *The Slim Shady LP*. "Eminem is a great storyteller," Marsh says. "I think Eminem relates back to the best of the Detroit songwriters. There is Bob Seger, Del Shannon when he wanted to, Holland-Dozier-Holland, and Smokey Robinson—that really puts him up there with the giants. But it is there, you can hear it in the way he thinks to tell a story. I hear Patti Smith in there somewhere, too, both in his attitude and in his approach to narrative flow. Though I have to say that Patti's race politics are unclear where Eminem's are not. She's very confused about race. You can tell she's from here but she didn't live here. For white people, people from Detroit are relatively unconfused."

Debbie Mathers-Briggs raised her son, Marshall, in some of the worst years Detroit has seen. She moved frequently, either around the city or back to her family in St. Joseph, Missouri, requiring Eminem to change schools more than once a year, on average. By his mom's estimate, Marshall attended between fifteen and twenty schools before finally dropping out of Lincoln High School, located north of 8 Mile Road in Warren County, in 1989. In the years between 1995 and 1998, when Eminem tried to move out of his mother's house, sometimes with girlfriend Kim, he could only (and just barely) afford to rent a house off 8 Mile Road, in the city limits. At the time, Detroit's unemployment rate was about 4.5 percent, meaning roughly 100,000 people were out of work. There was an average of 450 reported murders and about 20,000 burglaries annually during those years. "There's nothing to do, so motherfuckers get bored," Eminem recalled in 2000. "All they got to do is shoot each other and rob. I was coming back from St. Andrew's club one time a few years back with my boy Denuan—Kon Artis, who's in D12. This must have been 1997, I think. We were in a White Castle parking lot at the drive-through right across from a gas station, and we saw this motherfucker get popped. He dropped right in the middle of the station. We didn't even see where the bullet came from."

Whatever Eminem has made of his family history, now mythologized in song lyrics and captured for perpetuity in court documents, it couldn't have been easy. The years he lived in Detroit were tough ones in his home and in the city around him. Before his daughter was born in 1995, the low wages available to him made it tough to afford rent; afterward, the added expenses made it nearly impossible. He lived, like so many young Americans, from paycheck to paycheck, trying to make ends meet in the kind of urban environment that is becoming the American norm.

"I grew up on the East Side of Detroit, but I don't like to give people a sob story," Eminem says. "I had a hard life, blah blah blah. A lot of people did and a lot of people do. I didn't have the greatest upbringing, that's why I turned to hip-hop and that's why I love it so much."

Detroit has served Eminem in the twofold, bisected way in which it exists, a place where division imparts an understanding in a fashion that is alien to outsiders, but becoming less so today. It is a place with very real, very visible racial and class lines and no misconceptions about what those factors mean in American society. The city itself is a constant reminder. In Detroit, abandoned neighborhoods and the ruins of its past industry are everywhere, as easy to eyeball as the relative wealth of a suburb's residents. Where more financially well-off American cities pave over, redevelop, or preserve their past, turning former factories into loft space and landmarks into museums, so, too, are the politics of race and class often given new costumes. But as more American cities have encountered hard times and economic stagnation, they're beginning to look a lot like Detroit. There is no denial in Detroit, only an honesty that demands the same, honed over years of economic hardship and fed by the hardiness, hope, and realism of its people. "*8 Mile* for me was such an affirmation," Dave Marsh says. "It all goes back to the race thing, and the R&B influence in the past. Times have changed, but it was everything that I thought about the place. Everybody had gotten poorer, but the essence of Detroit, the essence of how people continued to relate to one another didn't change. What you find out is that it isn't about ethnic authenticity, but emotional authenticity. It is the gospel message and to some extent the jazz message. It's not 'You are right,' it's 'Can you get it right?'"

Detroit has exercised a dual influence in Eminem's life. It both nurtured and hurt him; it provided hard times and material to mine from. It held him down creatively, forcing him to innovate to be noticed. He was alienated on both sides of the racial divide and then made race as it relates to his music irrelevant locally and nationally through his talent. Detroit taught Eminem to be humble, but it also fostered a fuck-it attitude. It is the place where he leases a Mercedes but owns a Ford, and where America's most controversial rapper is beloved by his neighbors in the upper-class gated community that he now calls home. Detroit is where, when he was arrested for weapons possession in 2000, Eminem found himself signing autographs in jail.

"I'm in the fucking precinct getting booked, and these cops are askin' me for autographs while they're fuckin' booking me," Eminem says. "I'm doing it, but I'm like, 'My life is in fucking shambles right now,' and they're looking at me, literally, like I am not a fucking person. I am a walking spectacle."

What's most telling about Detroit—and Eminem—is that for all the bad times, the probation, the boos, the marriage, the divorce, the whuppings, the tears, and the scars, he'll never leave. "I have a love-hate relationship with Detroit," he says, "but all my friends are here. I'm used to the pace here, it's so relaxed. There's no hustle and bustle. That whole city atmosphere in New York and L.A., I only like to visit it. This is where I'm from." Eminem can't leave Detroit; he isn't that kind. Detroit is *in* him; in many ways, it *is* him. Detroit is the creative well that feeds him—mud, blood, and all.

If I'm a criminal, how can I raise a little girl?

7. Moms, marriage, and the morals of marshall mathers

Ladies and gentlemen, their story has been told in many ways. In verse, in print, in film, on television, in government papers and judicial transcripts. The two parties adhere to opposing points of view. Through a series of events, I, Anthony Bozza, was privy to said testimony. I present it now to you. My opinion is of no consequence, let the following inform you as it will: bear witness to the statements and judge, convict, or dismiss as you see fit, governed only by the tenets of your individual law. The court is now in session. All rise. In the matter of *Mathers v. Mathers*, I enter into evidence exhibits A through D. It is for you to decide if he is a moral man or a monster, a perpetrator or a product.

Exhibit A: testimony of Marshall Mathers
DATED MARCH 1999:

I was born in Kansas City. My mother tells me I was six months old when my father left. He lives in L.A. now. He tried to get in touch with me when I first blew up. I told my mother to tell him to go fuck himself. Fuck that motherfucker, man. Not one letter. Not one, all these years. Nothing. I never even saw a picture of my father. I don't know what he looks like. I don't even think my mother has one. She probably has pictures, she probably just doesn't show me and shit. Actually, I saw one picture of him. He was about nineteen, but I couldn't really tell if I look like him or not. The picture was kinda cracked and fucked up.

My mother had a different boyfriend every day of the week. She used to get her fuckin' boyfriends to move in with her and bring all their shit. Then she'd kick them out and keep all their shit— couches, TVs, beds, everything. Hardly anything we ever had in our house was ours, ever. My mother never had a job. The only one I can remember her having was at some candy store when I was a little boy. And she was a nursing assistant for a week and a half. She said it hurt her fucking back too much. My mother was lawsuit-happy. She would say she slipped and fell in K-mart, then fake a neck injury and shit. She did whatever she could do to get money that way without fucking working. My mother never had a job, that's why we was always on welfare, ever since I can fucking remember. I'd hide the welfare cheese under some lettuce or shit when my friends would come over.

That's why I dropped out of school. As soon as I turned fifteen, my mother was like, "If you don't get a fucking job and help me out with these bills, your ass is out." I ended up getting a factory job while I was still enrolled in school. I wasn't old enough to drop out yet, so I stayed enrolled and never went. I worked at Gearse

Machinery, this little factory about a mile from where we lived. I swept floors and made $140 a week working full time. My mother would keep the hundred and give me the forty. Then she would fucking kick me out, half the time right after she took the money.

I stayed with my mom until I was eighteen, but I kept getting kicked out. I was only there full time really when I was thirteen and fourteen. My mother did a lot of fucking dope and shit, so she had mood swings. She took a lot of pills. She took two or three naps a day. She'd go to sleep cool and wake up and start yelling, "What the fuck's wrong with this fucking house? This house is a fucking mess! Motherfucker, get the fuck out!" My room was upstairs, so she'd come up and throw open the door and flip on me. I used to record her. I've got those tapes somewhere. I'd play them for my grandmother. She's actually my great-grandmother—my mother's grandmother. Those two never got along, but I liked her. I used to go over there when my mother would kick me out. She's real old now, like ninety-two, I think.

Exhibit B: testimony of Deborah Mathers-Briggs
DATED MARCH 1999:

I put a lot of effort into Marshall and a lot of time as a single parent. I'm over forty now and Marshall's twenty-four. I live in St. Joseph, Missouri, right outside of Kansas City. Jesse James is from here, and it was the home of the Pony Express. All of my friends from grade school call all the time, my doctor and lawyer friends all see the video, but they say they don't like the part where Marshall says, "I just found out that my mom does more dope than I do." Well, that's just a joke. At first I was really hurt, but then Marshall said, "Mom, it doesn't mean anything. Don't take it personally." I felt a little intimidated by it because Marshall was raised in a drug- and alcohol-free environment. If I were like that, he would have turned out to be a loser. I worked hard to raise him. I went through beauty school after high school and divorced his dad when Marshall was two. He's never even seen his real father, but he's got his name—he's the third. His father lives in L.A. When I had Marshall, I had toxemia poisoning and went into a coma. So his father named him after himself. We had talked about it, but while I was out, he signed all the papers. Then he had nothing to do with Marshall, even while we were together for those few years. He was very jealous of Marshall. I got married at fifteen and had Marsh at seventeen. Bruce, his dad's nickname was Bruce, was twenty-one or twenty-two. I left a message with Grandmother Mathers a few months ago about all of the stuff happening with Marshall's career and told her to tell his dad to give him a holler, and she asked me why. I said forget it. That's their mentality.

Me and his father were in a band, Robbing the Satellites and Daddy Warbucks. His dad was the drummer and I was the backup singer. Our management had a deal for us to play at every Ramada and Holiday Inn. We traveled over Montana and South Dakota for two years. Marshall was with us at the time, I knew he'd end up doing something musical.

I left Marshall's father because he became abusive. He drank and was heavily into drugs, and I didn't want to raise my son that way. In 1976, I left everything behind and headed to Missouri. I even had a Buick Skylark almost paid off. I haven't been in touch with Marshall's dad since. He never paid child support. Well, we saw one check but nothing else. He was a mommy's boy. He and his mom moved to California. He's been married five or six times.

Marshall used to write to him, and the letters would come back "return to sender." He got one letter in 1982 with two pictures, one of his dad with a surfboard and one at a birthday party with a note that said, "Call me sometime." It was too hard for Marshall at that point. He just shoved it away and said he didn't want anything to do with the guy.

His dad never affected Marshall because he didn't miss having a father. I was always there for him and we were very tight. I would just go to the Father's Day at school. He thought that was neat. Or one of my friends who was male might go with him. I was very selective about who I had my children around, as I am today. Marshall was always very sheltered.

Marshall called any men friends I had boyfriends. I would try to explain the difference between boyfriends and friends. Sometimes they might stay on the couch or something if they didn't want to drive all the way home. I'm an affectionate, huggy person, always have been, and he took that the wrong way. I give everybody a kiss. It was a jealousy thing—"How come you hugged him?" Marsh was the man of the house.

For a single parent, I did well. I'm tiny, five foot two, and ninety-eight pounds soaking wet. Everyone tells me I look like a blonde Cher. First it was Heather Locklear, now it's Cher. I like Cher.

*

Though he has not directly refuted these assertions, Eminem's father has responded in the tabloid press that Debbie's claims are lies.

Exhibit C: testimony of Marshall Mathers
DATED MARCH 1999:

I hated Kim so fucking bad for like a year because I thought she was fucking her boss at work. It devastated me. I had my deal! I got engaged to her, bought her a ring, went out on a limb for that girl. I took some of the advance and flew her and Hailie out to L.A., flew 'em back. I had bought us both, but really for her and Hailie, a car. I came back from L.A. a day earlier than I should've and I went to her house, and since she left the door unlocked, I went upstairs in her room and found my engagement ring in the box. I'm like, what the fuck is going on. I wait outside her house until four in the morning. She's gone with my car and never came back—she stayed the night somewhere. I go to her job the next day, to a pay phone right next to her job and call and say I'm in L.A. still. I'm like, so where were you at last night. She's like, "Oh, where did we go, Dawn?" That's her sister, they work in the same place. "What time did we come home?" She's like, oh, about 12:30. I was like, oh, that's cool because I waited until four o'clock in the fucking morning outside your house, you fucking bitch! You're fucking busted, I'm right next door, I want the keys to my fucking car! Walked one block, she came out of her work and just gave me the keys. Didn't say nothing. She still denies it to this day.

Exhibit D: testimony of Kim Mathers, as it appeared in the *Detroit Free Press*
DATED JUNE 2001:

To whom it may concern,

First and foremost, I would like to start off by saying that just because my husband is an entertainer, that does not mean that our personal business is for everyone's entertainment purposes, but since the press seems to think that it is, then they should get their story straight. My husband came up to Hot Rocks to check up on me, why is still unknown to me, because if I was to cheat on him it wouldn't be in a neighborhood bar where he knows I am. Had he asked any questions before he flew off the handle, he would have realized that everyone with me (both male and female) were only friends. The fact that he just jumped to conclusions has gotten him and myself in trouble.

I would also like to state, since my husband has had no problem trying to make me look like an unfaithful wife, that every time I find a picture of him with other women, or read in magazines that he's involved with "groupies," I don't go and show up where he is, making a huge scene and getting our faces put all over the TV and papers. I have always taken his word on things and stood by his side. Even after the whole situation up at Hot Rocks, I tried to defend him.

Sincerely, Kim Mathers

IN THE ALPHABETIC "DIRECTORY" OF EMINEM'S LYRICAL ISSUES, UNDER "W," after *weed* and *white*, the rest of the book is filled with entries on women. At the center of Eminem's lyrical drama are some of the more cinematic misogynistic fantasies ever plucked from the depths of the male psyche, yet today he is admired as an artist, sex symbol, or both, by women of all ages. It was just a few years ago that Eminem was a cause for protest by the National Organization for Women, and his onstage routine included battering an inflatable sex doll that represented his wife while arenas full of fans chanted "Kill Kim." In 2002, middle-aged women like Maureen Dowd of the *New York Times*, who are of the feminist generation, were as titillated by Eminem's new macho paradigm as pubescent girls at an *NSYNC concert. Perhaps Eminem's elevation to icon by the mainstream epitomizes the mood of both sexes in millennial America. Real-life issues like employment and independence have replaced more politicized goals, while antifeminist attitudes are tolerated because unbridled maleness is celebrated. But there is more to Eminem's significance than his having achieved the magic media formula: he is both the man whom men respect and whom women want. As a thirty-something-year-old product of a single-parent home, where his mother was supreme ruler, he resonates deeper as the product of this ongoing blight. The ongoing chronicle of his life in his lyrics, in addition to the lawsuits between them, leaves little doubt that Eminem and his mother have a difficult relationship, one that has been echoed in Eminem's marriage; and one that, in the examination of his music, illuminates the roots of a common pathology.

Eminem's attitude toward women in his canon is split between focused anger at specific women and unfocused disdain and distrust for women he doesn't know. Eminem's more general antifemale sentiments, regardless of their degree of truth, are standard in hardcore rap and are reflective of today's harshest popular music. Male mistrust of women or gleeful objectification of women is an age-old theme in music, and all art for that matter, from bluesmen done wrong by their lovers and country crooners driving lonely back roads, pining for the one that got away, to the Rolling Stones' dissection of the pros and cons of their female admirers in 1978's "Some Girls." Both Jay-Z and Mötley Crüe offered similar dissertations, both in songs called "Girls, Girls, Girls." American culture is in a state in which objectification of women is an accepted aesthetic. The feminist-identity politics of the late eighties and early nineties that drove the issues of date rape and sexual harassment into the national dialogue are gone. But the antifeminist attitudes popular today are not new, either. In the eighties, as the efforts of politicized feminists of the seventies began to pay off, women enjoyed more power in the workforce than ever before, and pop stars like Madonna and Cyndi Lauper embodied a young, vibrant, sexy brand of self-aware woman. But by the second half of the decade, a popular male-driven backlash began to color pop culture.

"The angry white male became a sort of emblem of a new Republican party that integrated sexual issues into their politics in the eighties which really helped them a lot," says Richard Goldstein, executive editor of the *Village Voice*, and political and cultural critic since 1966. "All of these pop-cultural changes are very related to political issues. At the same time that the angry white male arose as an icon in politics, it arose in heavy metal, hip-hop, and comedy, too. It was a backlash against feminism and a male paranoia that was an issue in culture at the time. Sam

Kinison and Andrew Dice Clay spewed the most violent misogyny on television, *Saturday Night Live* was another bastion of it—it was what you might call 'hip macho.' Shock-jocks did the same thing; Howard Stern did it with a more bohemian edge."

Perhaps in reaction to the growth of the "angry white male" figure in the first half of the nineties, women's issues were center stage in national awareness, culturally and legally. Women's rights were hotly debated in the national media, as the legality of date rape as well as sexual harassment in the workplace, following Anita Hill's allegations against Clarence Thomas during his 1991 Supreme Court confirmation hearings, were navigated. An overriding mood of identity politics pushed America into the mores of political correctness that changed the policies of corporations, universities, and the government. During the Clinton administration's eight years in office, women held more positions on Capitol Hill than ever before and celebrated a still higher profile in corporate America. In music, led by the success of Sarah McLachlan's ethereal folk-pop smash *Fumbling Towards Ecstasy* in 1993, women such as Jewel, Joan Osborne, Shania Twain, and even one-hit wonders like Meredith Brooks began a run on the pop charts. The all-female Lilith Fair was one of the summer's top-grossing outings for three years running, from 1996 to 1999, until a desire for and corporate push toward more dance-oriented and harder-edged pop squelched the popularity of these sensitive and introspective female singer-songwriters. Then sassier women like Pink, Britney Spears, and Destiny's Child came into vogue, personifying a liberated and sexually aggressive woman, while Lilith Fair figures such as Tori Amos represented as outdated a paradigm as traditionalist feminist theory. The male response to this cultural estrogen surge was immediate and compensatory, buoyed by the oppression of an increasingly middle-class economy: the transfer of wealth into the hands of a smaller percentage of the population ensured that generations coming of age would not reach the same level of success as their parents had. The angry white male of the late eighties was back, this time in a whole new incarnation.

In 1997, *Maxim*, the American version of a British magazine for men, opened its doors and in one year tripled its number of readers with a combination of soft-core porn and adolescent sex-obsessed humor. The magazine captured the mood of young American men who, in the face of women flaunting their femininity, were proud to consume the cultural opposite: male boorishness. *Maxim*'s runaway success inspired a slew of copycat, British-based or -flavored titles. *FHM* and *Gear* coach young men in the pursuit of the opposite sex through "proper" lifestyle and cultural choices, while justifying the objectification of women with a celebration of adolescent humor. According to statistics, men's magazines of this variety attract male readers who are in their mid-twenties with incomes of $60,000 or higher, generally in the corporate world. This is the boys-behaving-badly school of men's magazines. In the hip-hop press, regular columns such as *XXL*'s "Eye Candy" or those in the magazine *King* feature pictorials of beautiful women next to reviews of the freshest materialistic expressions of hip-hop success: custom cars, expensive clothes and jewelry, liquor, and the latest technology. Magazine newsstand sales are always a good indication of what an impulse-purchase public wants to see, which, from fashion to music to general-interest magazines, is clearly as much female skin as possible. Pornography, too, seems to have lost its taboo, as documentaries, national magazine features, books, and even a cable-TV reality series, *Family Business* (Showtime, 2003), expose the workings of an industry with viable careers for young women and men, an industry in which the women earn more than the men for enacting male-driven fantasies. Younger women, less affected by feminism than by the tolerance of antifeminist sentiment, joyously engage in blatant objectification, from the "Girls Gone Wild" series to the resurgence of breast-flashing at rock shows—hardly the rage in the more socially conscious and more intellectual heyday of the nineties alternative-rock sensitive male.

The embrace and celebration of women as sex objects in mainstream media did not fully express, however, male anger and power in the face of female equality. Nowhere was it more apparent than in the change in popular rock music starting around 1997. In the absence—by death, breakup, or break-down—of alternative-rock talents such as Nirvana, Soundgarden, Rage Against the Machine, the Smashing Pumpkins, and Pearl Jam, a host of watered-down copycats and dull, introspective substitutes like Bush, Matchbox 20, and Creed held sway until a new wave of hard-rock jocks drowned them out. Bands such as Limp Bizkit, Korn, and the Deftones ushered in an aggressive, testosterone-addled soundtrack of frustrated male nihilism. It was self-loathing in the guise of directionless, unilateral destruction, driven by, to cull from Fred Durst's vocabulary, a love of "the nookie" and the need to "break stuff" when you're "just having one of those days." Sexuality in the Korn—Limp Bizkit view was male-dominated service sex, best summed up by the line "I don't know your fucking name / So what? Let's fuck," from Korn's "A.D.I.D.A.S.", an ode not to the clothing company but to the schoolboy acronym for "All Day I Dream About Sex."

The apex of male aggression and ritualized domination of women was reached in the music world in a new incarnation of Woodstock, the hippie generation's greatest communal achievement. At the 1999 festival, love wasn't free, it was forcefully seized. Held on a former military base, one hundred miles away from the original site, Woodstock '99 featured Korn, Limp Bizkit, Kid Rock, the Red Hot Chili Peppers, and many other acts. In a poorly organized, painfully overpriced event in the blistering July heat, young men sexually harassed hundreds of females, according to the reports filed (let alone those unfiled), and four rapes were reported, one of which occurred when a female fan who was crowd-surfing over the audience was pulled down and gang-raped while Limp Bizkit played. In the days following the festival, more victims came forward, many claiming they were raped in the campgrounds, others in the mosh pit, and one woman claimed that a state trooper whom she approached for help after an assault demanded that she first show him her breasts. Hundreds of stories eventually surfaced, from assaults and rapes in Porta-Johns to the encouragement by police officers for women to remove their tops for photos, some of which were posted, briefly, on a government-run law-enforcement website. But few allegations could be proven, and they were given little exposure in the mainstream media. Limp Bizkit front-man Fred Durst, who had encouraged the crowd into a frenzy during his set, later apologized in light of pending prosecution for the charge that he incited a riot. The three-day festival ended in flames, as crowds burned trash and pulled down light rigging. In the media follow-up to the events at Woodstock '99, more ink would be spilled over property damage, the capitalistic greed of the concert's vendors, the promoters' ineptitude, and the irony of peace, love, and rioting than on discussion or investigation of the incidents of sexual assault.

Eminem certainly profited from the angry male, antifemale mood of American music fans in 1999. Though he was initially lumped in with one-dimensional testosterone-rockers like Limp Bizkit and Korn (again signalling a bias that white rap must really be rock), Eminem proved to be a more complex entity, one who is far more talented and insightful than those one-trick ponies. Eminem rode the macho wave, for sure, but not only was it much more common to his genre, he also superseded it with a deeper, multifaceted portrayal of the male psyche in a more compelling and communicable form than the abused-animal vocals of Korn, the knuckleheaded rebellion of Limp Bizkit, or the trailer-park pimp-strut of Kid Rock. Eminem's macho bravado is often as ironic as it is idiotic, belying an intelligence utterly absent from the stance of the white aggro-rock acts. In addition, Eminem's self-dissection, within or without the Slim Shady persona, conveniently distances the man from his statements, and proves yet again that there are brains behind the bravado.

Whereas bands like Korn and the crop of new metal bands that have sprung up in their wake express their rage and childhood hurt more through sound and veiled lyrics, Eminem relates his story in details that at the least allow the listener to decide if he is or is not a misogynist.

"I used to really hate Eminem, for two reasons," says author and journalist Farai Chideya. "One is that he's a total misogynist and two is that he's gotten a free ride for a lot of things from the press. Now I've taken a step back from my initial reaction to him. I do think he's an incredible artist who has developed a unique style. And I still think he's a misogynist who gets a free ride from the press."

Eminem's ubiquitous love for his daughter and efforts to be a good father flesh out his persona, and complicate the issue by enabling the public to very easily access through his lyrics a more rounded portrait of a hardcore rapper. In the fundamental message of his art, Eminem sketches himself from all sides: as an angry white man, as the product of a damaged home and a dysfunctional romance, and as a doting, protective, sensitive father. There is enough humanity in Eminem's work to balance his harshest statements, to lend credibility to the belief that it is only a pose. His detractors would say, of course, that the same sensitivity is also a pose.

"I loved people like Dr. Dre and Snoop, and they had a whole school of lyrics where bitches ain't nothing but 'hos and tricks,'" says Sia Michel, editor-in-chief of *Spin* magazine, the first woman to helm a national rock publication. "That school of lyrics had been going since the late eighties, even with 2 Live Crew. So by the time Eminem came around, to a certain point, you were desensitized towards it if you had been listening to hip-hop for a while. What I think happens with women is that you listen to the lyrics and you look at the person as a whole and try to decide for yourself if the person is really, really sexist or not. I think with Eminem, women look at him and say, 'OK, he raps about Kim rotting in pieces but he's an adoring father to a little girl.' He had what to most people would look like a pretty bad childhood, and that evokes sympathy in women, that sort of, whatever, feeling about taking care of them and mothering them. And I think he works that very strongly on women as well. He makes anyone think that if he loves his daughter that much, he can't really be that bad, which is what a lot of young women think."

Further to that point, Richard Goldstein feels that Eminem's praise in the mainstream media in 2003 was not analyzed along gender lines and thus represents a dangerous evolution in the resurgence of male domination in American culture.

"The primary subject of Eminem's music until recently was the restoration of male authority and macho," Goldstein says. "When he did his famous performance at the MTV Awards and he marched down the aisle with a regiment of men who looked exactly like him, he sort of seized the stage and the crowd was on its feet, roaring. It was this image of a phalanx of males marching, in uniform, seizing the center of attention—it was a very powerful image of male restoration. That is the idea in Eminem's music that people don't see that is very frightening to me. I'm not saying he's responsible for violence against women or that there's a problem with enjoying his music. The problem is enjoying it without examining it. Once we stop discussing what it means, this stuff will begin to assert itself as a social value. It seeps in, and because it's so popular and profitable, many other people do the same thing and eventually it's a ruthless message with this ideology in it. And that is what is damaging to women. I'm not saying that people hear his music and will go out and kill women, though I do know a woman who was raped by a guy who was reciting Eminem lyrics. It does happen, there are enforcers for every ideology, a certain number of people who will hear stuff and act it out. But you can't regulate culture on the basis that somebody will actually perform a fantasy, otherwise there would be no erotica. But I do regard Eminem as a pornographic artist—his ideology is similar to porn in many ways. I would never say that he isn't talented, he certainly is, but the reason why he is where he is is not his talent—it is his ideology. His ideology made him stick out from the pack. He was a white boy dissing women and gay people, though it is primarily about women. From a social perspective this is really dangerous because when a generation grows up under these values they become sexualized and normal, and people really do begin to live their lives by them. You will find women picking guys like this, getting into relationships with damaged guys. The real character Eminem portrays is very damaged. A simple question to ask is why has the greatest artist of his generation never written a love song to an adult woman?"

Eminem is like a million others just like him. For better or worse, he embodies modern male machismo and a new paradigm of the young American male. He is opinionated, uncompromising in his values, devoted to his daughter, untrusting of women and any authority but his own, and, above all, very, very angry. But his younger fans, as well as his older ones, do not see Eminem's view of the world or his influence as the role model he purports not to be as problematic, or even worth mentioning, judging by the unwavering positive public opinion. Male dominance in popular music has a long history, from blues to rock and roll to rap, and contemporary permutations of it have grown more raw with time. It is seen, it seems, as ritualistic, primal, and central to some music, just as the mating dance is to some male animals. In the context of Eminem's genre, male dominance and competition is certainly a cornerstone of hip-hop, in which the primary goal is to emasculate your enemy.

As a result, homosexuality is a top-tier insult in rap. In the same light, if women and feminine characteristics are seen as weakness, so men displaying the same are equally weak. In lyrics, rappers order foes to "suck their dicks," call them "bitches," and tell peers they feel are copying their style to "stay off their dicks." In this hierarchy, the least feminine man rises to the top as the alpha male. That might be why Eminem has never written a love song: in a game in which he's already under the microscope, he can't afford to reveal sentimental feelings (i.e., a weakness for the "lesser" sex). Of course the answer could be as simple as the fact that Eminem's longest romantic attachment has been complicated, to say the least. Eminem does reveal his weakness, constantly—it is at the heart of some of his best work. As he said in "Hailie's Song" on *The Eminem Show*, "My insecurities could eat me alive." He is an artist in touch with his Achilles heel, but he compensates for his sensitivity with the best defense: a good offense.

"It's been so important to harder rap and for black males to be as male as you can be for a lot of interesting reasons going back hundreds of years," says Sia Michel. "Sometimes that means talking about bitches and other times it's talking about fags and other times it's talking about violent imagery and guns. Hard music in general has so often been misogynistic, whether it was metal or hard-core rap, that as a woman, if you want to listen to that music at all, you have to start picking through the code and trying to figure out what is truly offensive to you and what you think is antiwoman for some kind of cheap cosmetic reasons."

With exceptions like LL Cool J and Common or Jay-Z's "Bonnie and Clyde '03," love in rap today is most often synonymous with sex as an expression of submission or power. As Ja Rule has emblazoned on his chest, "Pain is love": the existence of feeling is damaging. There is no innocence in hip-hop, as there is little left in American youth today. The sexual promiscuity of teens and preteens in all economic spheres is proof positive of that. It is a time when twelve-year-old girls and boys are contracting sexually transmitted diseases, and when in Boston in December 2002 neither police nor school officials had a legal or administrative precedent for disciplining a fifteen-year-old girl who was caught fellating a sixteen-year-old boy on her school bus while three of his friends cheered her on. The very adult imagery of hip-hop and pop music is adopted by teens and preteens at progressively earlier ages.

"The question to me is not is Eminem good or bad," says Farai Chideya. "It is, what is his place in society? Here's this guy with this very adult content and it's not friendly to girls but I've seen him on many teen magazines targeting girls. Would a black rapper who was on some pimp trip end up on the cover of a girls' magazine? I don't think so. And I don't necessarily think it's a good thing. It's great that people are acknowledging Eminem's artistry, but celebrity in America puts people in privileged positions where they're lauded in ways that don't even make sense. It's one thing for me as a thirty-three-year-old woman to listen to his album, it's another for a twelve-year-old girl to listen to it. It's hard because kids are much more worldly than anybody wants to admit, but at the same time, when I've had conversations with girls, mostly black girls, about these issues, they'll say 'He's not calling me a bitch, he's talking about those other bitches.' When you talk about hip-hop lyrics, you never want to think you are the one that's getting called out, but the reality is that when somebody is talking about women, you're all getting called out. You're a bitch, I'm a ho, my mom's a bitch. There's a consciousness gap in the way people process these lyrics."

Eminem has said from the start that his music is for adults. He plays only clean versions of his music around his daughter, and does not grant interviews to the teen press. Those magazines that feature him on their covers do so without his consent. Regardless, younger fans who are coming of age in an era of harsh entertainment and male-dominant music, unless they care to research the past, have no other norm; that worldview is what they dance to. While other generations worry about the implications of this imagery, males and females alike shrug it off as another aggressive expression. It would seem that an antifeminist age is certainly upon us when anti-Kim Mathers websites and endless anti-Kim messages are posted on the Internet by Eminem's young female fans.

"Gay liberation and women's liberation threatened the hierarchy of male dominance," Richard Goldstein says. "There is a hierarchy that figures like Eminem stand for, which is heterosexual males, with white males at the top. It still really is, for all the ideology of racial harmony, a hierarchy based on race. It is a hierarchy based on maleness, so the person with the least femininity rises to the top. When Eminem says he is indifferent to women and hates them and ejects any sign of femininity from his personality and projects everything he hates about himself onto women, that is a macho value, which makes him an alpha male. They have to be homophobic because any man identified with the feminine must be on the bottom; otherwise, the hierarchy is threatened. When gay liberation and women's liberation threatened those roles, you had a state of terror among men and women. What happens when the order isn't there? What happens to desire? What is heterosexuality like without the hierarchy? These are major questions."

If a greater equality between men and women has caused a backlash in gender perception, Eminem has become the poster child for female-backlash fans, whether they are old enough to remember the sixties feminists, have just finished reading *Men Are from Mars, Women Are from Venus*, or don't remember a time when girls weren't shown on MTV in bikini tops in sunny climes and seated on the shoulders of boys they've just met. Eminem has fans in suburbia with children of their own, who should in no way support songs about spousal homicide, mother-hating, and free use of the word *bitch*. But Eminem embodies the handsome bad-boy fantasy that women love, the one that—

despite the equality and capability they have to fend for themselves—they desire, whether it is for protection, for the eroticism of being dominated, or to have a focus for an object of maternal nurturing. The generation of young women who are now in their teens may have been attracted to nice guys in boy bands when they were younger, but the complexities of adolescence are the terrain Eminem speaks to. Boy bands don't. Celebrations of maleness are nothing without female cheerleaders, even those who are conscious of their subordinate role, from girls flashing their breasts at Guns N' Roses, concerts in the eighties to those grinding onstage with R. Kelly, even after recent lurid sexual allegations. To women in our anti-feminist-backlash culture, Eminem elicits empathy, eros, and respect. The interesting questions were how and why.

"I think Eminem truly is rebellious," Sia Michel says. "He really does do exactly what he wants to do and for the most part says what he wants to say, as long as it is not racially insensitive. But you can use antifemale feelings as a cheap form of rebellion—and, if anything, that's the conflict some women have, though mainstream culture is so misogynistic that the only way to avoid it would be to live completely apart from it. I think that is why some women are fine with it, but also because they grant Eminem a distance from his lyrics. Most people have violent fantasies or anger directed toward the opposite sex. They see him using them and shaping a story as a narrator, apart from the actual person. The era of women universally disliking anyone who says something that seems antifemale is very much early-nineties identity-politics-driven. I don't see that very much anymore. I'm not saying it's better this way, it's just generally the tenor of the times right now. Misogyny in lyrics was written about until it got boring. It doesn't mean it's not an issue anymore. In the same way, the racial diversity of bands used to be mentioned in a very positive way, how they were 'multicultural.' Now it's just an accepted norm: D12 has a white guy, and Linkin Park has a Japanese-American rapper, and the best rock guitar player is Tom Morello [Rage Against the Machine], a black guy."

"What a terrible time to be a young woman," says critic Sasha Frere-Jones. "Who would you possibly look up to? Who would you possibly be inspired by? I want the female Eminem. We need the kind of woman who can create that kind of excitement."

It is impossible not to see Eminem and his views, as well as the manner in which they are expressed, as the product of a single-parent, matriarchal home. If the antifeminist backlash is the result of men asserting their power, among them are a significant number of young men who probably spent their childhood answering to their mothers, the only obstacle to the top of the power pyramid. If society, particularly the hip-hop circles that Eminem aspired to, espoused a macho-male hierarchy, Eminem's stormy days with his mother and his struggle for financial independence took on epic proportions to him, the very real depth of which can be heard in the music. In his most trying times, Eminem was emasculated by society, the hip-hop community that did not support him, his mother's inconsistent behavior, the contempt of his girlfriend's family, and his own self-loathing for being unable to properly provide for his daughter. The rage and tension in great Eminem songs such as "The Way I

Am" or "Lose Yourself" or "8 Mile" are a palpable clench and release, a siphon to the frustration and ache of those days. "If I hadn't've made it in rap," he says, "I'd've worked at Gilbert's Lodge. Probably gone postal at Gilbert's Lodge." Though Eminem was unlike many of the white kids he grew up around, in many ways he was just like them: a product of an unhealthy single-parent home, and a young man who became a parent too young.

Eminem's history with Kim and his mother reads like a Sigmund Freud parable. Eminem is the son of a willful, perhaps delusional mother and he married a willful, possibly deceitful woman. He fights with both and makes his revenge a reality—in song and in fantasies. He has used these women as the inspiration for some of his canon's most distraught and improperly funny episodes. They are, Kim particularly, the key to understanding Eminem. Like a two-sided muse, Kim brings out his extremes: loyalty and revenge, maturity and primal rage.

Marshall and Kim met when she was thirteen and he was fifteen. They were dating by the time he was sixteen and Kim lived with Marshall and his mother on and off for years, before and after Hailie was born.

"She lied to us from the beginning," Debbie says. "She moved in with us when she was twelve and said she was fourteen. She used to sleep downstairs on a couch and told me a few years later she always snuck upstairs to Marshall's room. She told me just to hurt me. Kim is a very jealous person. She doesn't want him talking to anybody or to have any friends. And he has a lot of friends, just like me."

All of the eleven years that Eminem and Kim have been

together in some form or another have been tumultuous.

"We've just broken up and made up so many times, man," he said in 1999, before fame made matters worse. "We've got issues, issues. It was fucked way before. We just don't get along."

"Once me and Eminem and Bizzare all went fishing," Proof told me that same year. "Then we went to this club 1212 to perform. We come back and Kim's thrown all of Em's clothes out, which was about two pairs of pants and some gym shoes. He spent the night at my grandmother's with me. This is what I love about Em. He's like, 'I'm leaving her, I ain't never going back, fuck it, I'm leaving her.' Next day, he's right back with her. The love they got, man, it's so genuine, it's ridiculous. He gonna end up marrying her."

In 1999, he did, in a private ceremony in his mother's native St. Joseph, Missouri. In July of 2000, when the Anger Management Tour, that summer's most lucrative outing, came to Detroit's Auburn Hills arena, Kim was at home with her mother, Kathleen Sluck, who was watching a video with Hailie when she wandered upstairs in search of her daughter. According to an interview Sluck granted *People* magazine, Kim's mother discovered her in the bathroom, ready to cut her wrists. Her mother couldn't restrain her daughter, so she called 9-1-1. According to the article, the tape of the call captures her mother's imploring Kim to put down the razor and Kim's reply that she doesn't want to be here anymore. The hospital reported five lacerations requiring stitches. Soon after, the couple began proceedings to divorce.

In 2002, while Marshall was linked, both falsely and kinda not so falsely, to a variety of film and music talent (Mariah Carey, Brittany Murphy, Kim Basinger, porn star Gina Lynn), Kim became pregnant by another man, Eric Harter, whom she allegedly began dating in 2001.

"She's due any day," Eminem told me in April of 2002. "It's not mine. But Hailie's going to have a baby sister. It's going to be tough to deal with, the day she comes to me and says, 'Why can't my baby sister come over, Daddy?' Those are issues I've tried to keep her sheltered from. Of course she's going to find out shit about her mom and me as she goes through life, but I really don't want her to learn all the fucked-up shit on my shift. I have no idea who the father is, what that is about or anything, I just know she's due any day."

After delivering her second daughter, Whitney, Kim recovered at the house that Eminem bought after their divorce. By early 2003, speculation held that they might remarry.

"Oh, no, no more marriage," Eminem also said in April 2002. "I would rather fucking be on a coach flight with *NSYNC at the back of the plane—the last row in them seats that don't go back. I'd rather be stuck there with the bathroom out of order. I would rather have a baby through my penis than get married again. I'm chillin' on marriage. Girlfriends, maybe, here or there. But no more marriage, dog. I don't ever want to go through what I went through last year again."

He went through a divorce, a countersuit, a settlement, a battle for joint custody of his daughter and, soon after, an appeal of the child support settlement, which allowed Kim $142,000 a year. It seemed to be, given her coming child, an appeal with ulterior motives, particularly in light of the fact that Harter is wanted by the city of Detroit on a felony warrant for possession with intent to distribute drugs and several other offenses—jail time would clearly hinder his ability to provide child support. "I can't say too much about my family for legal reasons and what happens when I say too much," Eminem says. "But about that, I really can't say anything. I just try to keep Hailie sheltered from these things."

Eminem and Kim shared the kind of first love that is etched in high-school desks; one that can be as intoxicating and unstable as a crack habit. It is a love—hate bind on a par with Eminem and his mother—it makes for tragic, tormented art and great newsprint, and it isn't a joyride. Little is known of Kim's point of view outside of what can be gleaned from her actions. She refuses to be interviewed. I met her circumstantially when Eminem's fame was still a whiff on the air. I doubt she wanted to meet anyone new, especially a writer, late that night on Eminem's first night home, just a few nights before he would leave again, this time for a performance at MTV's Spring Break. She was civil, but hardly friendly; her raised guard was a sensate force-field.

Kim's comments in the press, mostly the Detroit press, have been few. She maintains that she and Eminem do not care to live a flamboyant life; that Eminem's anger toward his mother in song is very real; that since most of his fans are women, they don't want to know that he's married; and that nobody "in their right mind would cheat on their millionaire husband—especially with a nobody at a neighborhood bar."

"Kim is the person I want to know about," says Sasha Frere-Jones. "She is the one I feel bad for. I might do those things if I were Eminem's wife, if my husband had people chanting 'Kill Kim.' My heart goes out to her. I'd like to read her autobiography. It just seems like their whole thing is nothing but bad. And she's been sacrificed by her husband. It would be one thing if Eminem were married to Jay-Z, then they could do diss records back and forth. But this poor woman doesn't get to respond. Jesus, do you imagine it's easy to live with Eminem? What could she possibly have done?"

The few signs there are point to a woman unprepared for the chaos and distance of a famous partner. One side of her portrait is of a regular girl who wants a life and family. "It's hard for Kim being the only parent," her mother told *People* magazine in 2000, "and handling all the [media] outside her house. She can't even go in the backyard."

"This is a lady who prefers to wear jeans and gym shoes as opposed to Versace and Armani," said Kim's lawyer, Neil Rocking, in the same article. "A small-town girl who wants to be a mom."

Whatever the reality, Eminem's relationship with Kim is a recurring theme in his music; his love for her, his hatred. "If I was her, I woulda ran when I heard some of those songs," Dr. Dre says. "That shit is out there. She gives him a concept, though, and that's cool shit, no doubt." For all the ups and downs that Kim and Marshall Mathers have had—as kids, as young parents, as husband and wife, as litigants in court— one truth remains: Eminem needs the mania of their relationship to create his music, but Marshall, the man, has a place in his heart for Kim that will probably never be filled by another woman. But that, like everything in this man's life, is anyone's guess.

"Divorce is probably the hardest thing that I've ever worked through," Eminem says. "I feel like I'm a better person because I went through it, I feel stronger now, but you know, it was hard at first. I've known this chick all my life; she's the first real true girl-friend that I ever had. I grew up with this person, and then they want to leave you. At first you don't know what to do. I put the blame on everything. I put the blame on myself, I put the blame on the business, my career. I put the blame on everything except—I don't know if I should say that—I took a lot of the heat for that. I blame myself for a lot of that shit. But it's like, as it pro-gressed and I got through it and everything like that, I step back and I look at the whole picture, I realize that it wasn't my fault and there's nothing I coulda did. It was inevitable anyways. Which is cool, because me and Kim, we're on speaking terms, we can communicate, no hard feelings, fuck it. Didn't work, you know; after eleven years, it ended up not working."

This troubled relationship did, however, yield the one constant source of joy for Eminem's life: his daughter. He will truly do any-thing for Hailie. All he has achieved is for her, the one person who inspired responsibility in an artist who channels excess. For all the antiauthority, hardcore traits in his art, Eminem's views on parenting are midlevel conservative. When we first met, Eminem was more worried by the fact Hailie had asked to wear makeup than he was by the pressure of his escalating career. He has said repeatedly that he wouldn't let his seven-year-old listen to his albums and pointed to the necessity of a parental advisory sticker on his music.

"People don't know this about me, but in everyday life, being a father, I limit the swear words," he says. "I don't cuss around my daughter. If someone else is around and they say the F-word, she's heard it before; I don't say, 'Hey, watch your mouth around my daughter.' That would be ridiculous. After all, I'm Eminem, Mr. Potty-Mouth King. To me it's different when it's in a song because it's music and it's entertainment. Hailie hears it, but you can't avoid that, it's just part of life—you're going to hear swear words and you're going to hear what they mean; it's up to you if you want to repeat them or not. I'd rather have her do that than running around beating people up."

When Eminem isn't on tour—especially in 2001, when he was in Detroit making *The Eminem Show* and *8 Mile*—he spends as much time as possible with his daughter. "When I'm home, I wake her up in the morning, feed her cereal, watch a little TV, take her to school, pick her up," he says. "We watch a lot of movies—typical shit." In the Eminem canon, his daughter is the only woman who receives his undying love, the only one to be the object of his devotion.

Eminem is characteristically clear-eyed about the themes of his songs and how his daughter may feel about it. "When I was six years old, music flew by my head, but I caught it if there was a swear word in it," he says. "Kids nowadays are a lot smarter than we were growing up, but if there's a song that I have that has a lot of swear words in a row, I make her clean versions and I play those in the car. At the end of the day, I would give my life for my little girl. If there's something that I believe in my heart is going to affect her, then I won't say it, that's where I draw the line. There's a couple of things I said on *The Eminem Show* that I ended up spinning back because I didn't want her to go to school and have people say, 'Oh, your mom did this.'"

Eminem knows he will have some explaining to do, as surely as he fears Hailie's teens will bring out the Slim Shady in him. "I'm sure Hailie is going to come to me and ask me about all of it when it's all said and done," he says. "I'm sure she'll come to me, probably when she's a teenager—which I dread. I have no fucking idea what I'm going to do when she starts dating. I'm gonna kill boys. It's gonna drive me crazy. It's the greatest feeling in the world to watch your seed grow, to watch a life that you created look at the world through another set of your eyes. It also hurts to know that one day she's going to grow up and be out of the house. But that's what we're here for—to create more life, I guess."

The white rapper with a story to tell has piqued the interest of sectors of the media and populace that had hitherto ignored this thing called hip-hop. They finally had a reason to learn about it, whether it was to discover how or why or if it was dangerous that this blond white kid was a hardcore rapper, or to better comprehend American youth, most of whom had something to say about Eminem. In 2002, Eminem explained himself and his roots more clearly than he ever had through two accessible, engaging, masterful pieces of art, *8 Mile* and *The Eminem Show*. Those Americans that hadn't before, listened, and though they hadn't shown the same courtesy to generations of black rappers, mainstream America wanted to understand Eminem, to relate to him, to take care of him.

America has adopted Eminem like a troubled foster child whose problems could no longer be ignored. An unlikely cross-section of Americans also wanted to define themselves in his image, to embrace him, to find similarities between their lives and his, no matter how tenuous. It was more than celebrity worship, it was the casting of a white male icon, one who could only become so because the values of the times made his harshest moments acceptable, virtually unnoticeable. He was also acknowledged because he spoke from, to, and about the moral heart of main-stream America. Eminem's values were not learned through a life on the streets; they were learned as the oldest child of a single mother who was struggling to get by.

"People now understand that this is a pained guy," says Shelby Steele. "He didn't have the best, most classic American childhood. And he's obviously singing about it. America gives people like that a chance. I think at the beginning they thought he was another Vanilla Ice, a kind of fraudulent figure who was stealing the thunder of rap music, who was being really extreme just for its own sake. Now people sense that there's something more to it, that it has its own authenticity. He won a point there, won a battle. How long he'll keep going, I don't know. But people have given him a chance."

People had given Eminem and, by extension, what he meant to them, a chance. Maybe in Eminem mainstream America sees what their kids could have been. Positive or negative, there is something about Eminem that reflects our culture back to us. To some, it isn't a pretty picture. "Eminem is a paranoid male person-ality with a sense of aggrievement that is out of proportion to reality, which is then projected through his music so that millions of people sign on to the paranoia," says Richard Goldstein.

The contradictory values embodied in Eminem's lyrics meet subtly and uncomfortably, titillating, taunting, and aggravating, sometimes all at once. He explores the depth of his most violent fantasies, lampoons every norm and authority, and in his merciless dissection of his own white American family unit, he exposes conditions common to many. Eminem was shunned and embraced for the same act, meaning that America not only has changed its mind since he arrived on the pop-culture scene, America, too, has changed. He is the voice of a generation who loves no one truly (but his daughter). Maybe that fact alone is the reason why America fell in love with him. Perhaps not. As Richard Goldstein says, "You find women picking guys who are like Eminem and getting into relationships with damaged guys. The real character Eminem portrays is very, very damaged. A guy who wants to be at the top of a male pecking order is not going to be able to be intimate with you. Is that what young women need in a guy? Will they find him attractive if he doesn't act like this? It is a danger for young girls who can't play with these roles."

Anyone who doesn't think that media of all kinds affects us is naive. At the same time, anyone who thinks the media directs us is equally naive. In his monthly column "Terrordome" on the Public Enemy website, Chuck D addressed the same issue in regard to the negative image of African-Americans presented in the persistently thuggish imagery of mainstream rap videos. "When I was a kid, watching a great football game would send us in the streets afterwards trying to replay what we just saw. Bruce Lee movies had us kids kicking Coke machines in the theater afterwards. A love song made you call your girl. Now, how the hell can a negative image not do the same, especially when that adult stereotype looks so familiar?" Of course, only the truly disenfranchised will make art imitate life, like the fictitious stalker "Stan" on *The Marshall Mathers LP*. Eminem, of course, said it all in his song "Role Model," from *The Slim Shady LP*, warning the world not to follow Shady's lead. But he's also told the world that there are a million kids who act, dress, and feel just like him—and there are. His avowal of all things he is and is not is the stance of a deft battle MC, making him untouchable.

"Eminem is a cultural phenomenon," says Shelby Steele. "That's why we like him. So much of rap is cover-up, cover up all that pain, and here's a guy—he's sort of marching through it. It's very much, in a larger sense, like the blues. The blues are when the singer fingers the jagged grain of his worst pain. The singer came home and the house was completely empty. So he makes a kind of clown of himself, and you identify with him. And, looking at the pain, there's a certain transcendence. He's a compelling figure. The vulgarity and the homophobia and the sexism and so forth, I see those in a context of his life. In black culture—and he was very close to that—there was a lot of homophobia. With a mother like that, you might be a little sexist. Shrinks would say he's working something out there."

Watch me, 'cause you thinkin' you got me in this hot seat

Conclusion. From a sinner to a saint

I decided to write this book because of a dinner I had in Connecticut three summers ago (2000). We sat outside, on the porch, not many of us. I was the stranger among two families who shared a long history. One of the critics interviewed in this book was there, and as the night grew later, we occupied an end of the table and spoke furiously about music, agreeing to interrupt Van Morrison's stately tenor to play "Stan" for the others, who were predominantly unversed in hip-hop and Eminem, outside of knowing his infamy. They needed to hear it.

Listening to the song, twice, with them, sitting in the near-dark, I watched the curious, engaged, rapt faces, taking in this night's camp-fire folk tale, though differently than they enjoyed the troubadours in their record collections. Eminem's literary storytelling impressed me anew; it was universal enough to capture the interest of a very discerning musically savvy, test group of the populace. I saw the future that night, a microcosm of the generation gap that Eminem would soon hop.

I did not foresee the degree of admiration from unlikely sources awaiting Eminem in 2003. As *8 Mile* fever infected the country, a motley crew of new fans gathered around Eminem, singing his praises from the *Today* show to *TRL*. Daniel Day-Lewis reported that he blasted Eminem in his trailer to rev himself up for his scenes in *Gangs of New York*, and even Queen Barbra Streisand "saw herself" in Eminem, one of the many hip-hop-illiterate adults who found hope and heroism amid the remains of the American dream in Eminem's film debut. Eminem's new audience became the focus of his story, as he once again uncannily predicted in the art and music of his album. The new fans related to the elements of Eminem that suited them and held him up as their own multipurpose emblem. I was amazed again at what I'd already admired: Eminem's well-crafted vision, devotion to his work, and a talent that communicates emotion as only true artists can. In 2003, Eminem outdid Slim Shady, transcending his own celebrated bad reputation and succeeding without his trademark avenger. As Eminem he achieved the ultimate revenge and validation; he truly had, as he claimed in "Without Me," everyone kissing his ass.

"Now people have begun to see what they couldn't see before, which is a complicated character," Dave Marsh says. "How he pulled that one off is the measure of what a great artist he is, and he truly is a great artist. He was able to take himself from a position where he was totally despised by everybody and flipped it, hard. To me, it's just, 'wow.' I don't know what it does to him. Obviously he has some of the issues worked out better in the script than he has in real life."

As I began to speak to people about this book, casually and during the interviews, I heard an array of opinions on every level, from the microscopic view of the psychological issues and rhythmic meter at play in the music, to the macrofocus of Eminem's effect on the near future, when a new generation grows into young adults. Whatever the opinion, there always was one; no one I spoke with was indifferent to Eminem. Neither were any of the strangers I eavesdropped upon. Everywhere I went at the end of 2002, I found it was only a matter of time before I heard someone discussing him.

For my own part, I found myself thinking, writing, and talking more about American society than I was about Eminem, and the thematic segues were natural. He was a symbol to that representative American cross-section that was holding him so high in 2003; but he was a mirror, too, one I wasn't sure all of his new fans had peered into.

"There's a certain sophistication involved with Eminem, because he is literary in a certain way," Shelby Steele says. "Even his imagery is, in this self-report, the openness of his life with him as a character; there is vulnerability. There's self-examination, and boy, that has a lot more power than the tough-guy thing. He has the bravery of the real artist to put himself out there. That's the secret that's distinguished him from the others."

America likes a hero, and in *8 Mile* Eminem fit the bill. It mattered as little that he was playing a character in the film as it did when he offended so many playing a character on his records—fiction and reality, entertainment and real life, it seems, are almost interchangeable. When I told Eminem's manager, Paul

Rosenberg, about the kind of book I intended to write, he said that he expected someone to do so now that Eminem's public image had changed and his fan base had expanded. The time was certainly now, for the reason of new mass Eminem awareness, as much as for the issues Eminem brings to light.

"The thing about Eminem, whether it's real or not, that people have bought into is his life," says writer Soren Baker. "I think a lot of people, especially the under-thirty crowd, can identify with not getting along with their mom or being in a single-parent home and trying drugs, maybe not selling them but trying them. And having a problem with their girlfriend or mother of their child but feeling like they love their daughter—everybody can identify, especially the younger people, the people under thirty. That's something that he's done that really no other rapper that is as popular as he is has done. He's made his life entertainment like the title *The Eminem Show* would suggest, but he's also made his life matter to people."

Eminem embodies the mind-set of our current America in so many ways, from the nearly invisible boundary between his art and his life to the nuances of his character to the elements of our culture that he brings together as much as those he drives apart. Eminem is an artist of contradiction: doting father, gun-toting probationer, innovative performer, anti-celebrity celebrity, potty-mouthed rapper, conscientious producer-CEO in the making, rebel against authority, a good neighbor. He is an oxymoron: the controversial family man. The same attraction of opposites is in his music: undeniably clever humor, base violence, innovative twists of language, disturbing misogyny, singsong refrains, themes of alienation. It should be no wonder, then, that the mainstream public's reaction has been a contradiction: complete disapproval, utter praise, talk of censure, votes for an Oscar.

Maybe this contradiction more than anything is at the heart of America's love for Eminem. We're a country heading toward a greater division between rich and poor, where race politics is unpopular and racial identity is as mutable and multifaceted as the stew of influences informing popular music. We are a country in which youth culture is consumed by parents, adolescence extends into adulthood, and upper-middle-class kids speak the slang of the inner cities. Alienation cuts across all sets of our society, and hip-hop speaks to kids of all ages and circumstances. Whether this is the dawn of the kind of understanding and unity that can change the fabric of society or an extension of post-9/11 nationalism is not yet clear, but America desperately wants to celebrate our commonalities, disallow our differences, and move forward.

"So much stuff is getting dragged into this phenomenon surrounding Eminem," says Sasha Frere-Jones. "You have to step way back and remove him, even take him out of it. Obviously, this is a huge moment for race relations, but it's kind of hard to see how. I also think that everyone who feels like they're losing their edge, like a lot of the older people who are into Eminem, think it is their one surefire way to not be wack."

It certainly is a moment for race relations; and there, too, Eminem represents a unification that may also cause division—a troubling contradiction. He is an unassailable talent and an anomaly, the one white rapper who both got it right and did it his way;

309

the first to eclipse or equal all of the MCs of his day. Eminem is, like Tiger Woods and Venus and Serena Williams, a brilliant, gifted exception who is making history. His wit, rhyme style, and lyrical skill are a contribution to hip-hop culture, a cinematic, narrative voice in that canon. But unlike Tiger Woods and the Williams sisters, three minority players in games that have traditionally been dominated by whites, Eminem is a white person who is dominating a traditionally black game and garnering praise from those who most likely wouldn't want to hear the same from a blond man. Though he's clearly no friend to the system and has lived and identified with a life more black than white, Eminem's achievement is a bittersweet victory to some. Whereas Woods and the Williams sisters represent a rebel victory, a toppling of the traditional power structure, and a reversal of race roles, Eminem represents a reversal of race roles and a toppling of one of the only visible power structures (along with professional sports) that is dominated by black men, at a time when more black men than anyone else are in prison. Ours is an era in which racial-identity politics has fallen out of favor, while most of the social conditions that birthed those issues remain. Eminem's gifts as a rapper, his album sales, the critical praise he's received, and his portrayal of the hip-hop world in *8 Mile* inspire mixed feelings, begrudging acceptance, and anxiety about his influence on the culture among some black hip-hop fans. Celebrating Eminem, for some, is not simple. Perhaps it is for this reason that only four of the sixteen African-American critics, academics, and artists whom I approached for interviews for this book agreed to talk to me. Many did not respond at all to requests made over a period of months. Others enthusiastically consented to the interview but did not respond to any further and persistent efforts to arrange it. "That's not surprising," says Farai Chideya. "I think that black people who consistently write about this stuff get tired of nobody listening to them, because mainstream audiences don't read it. There is this tendency to only value the voice of the white critic, no matter what the situation. I'm happy to talk because I'm just one person and I'm not speaking for black America; I'm speaking for myself."

One thing is certain: Eminem is going to be willfully unavailable for a while, in light of his banner year, 2003. He'll be sorting out, in his way, what Eminem means. He is beloved by the mainstream, but Eminem has made it clear already that he has no desire to join it any more than he has; and, by all indications, no one minds. He turned down the opportunity to perform at America's most coveted mainstream gathering, the Academy Awards. He did not attend, yet he won Best Original Song from a soundtrack for "Lose Yourself"; the statuette was picked up by Luis Resto, his keyboard player and musical collaborator. Eminem similarly declined a performance slot and ticket to the American Music Awards. He won four awards that night, all accepted by Mekhi Phifer, his costar in *8 Mile*, who at one point showed the audience his cell phone, said Eminem was on it, and thanked them for him.

A retreat is in order for Eminem, whose sense of timing and image management are nothing short of exceptional. He will not be taking a vacation; his year is already full of production work for D12 and Obie Trice, whose projects are the next two albums slated for his label Shady Records. Eminem hasn't had more than a few days off in four years; his downtime before his latest record, *The Eminem Show*, was spent in court and making *8 Mile*. "I haven't had any long breaks or solid rest really since this started," Eminem says. "When I do get a few days, sometimes I take the family up north, like my aunt and uncle and Hailie. There's cottages and stuff that we rent, but what happens is that I'll start writing and I can't control the thoughts, so even when I'm not writing I'm working."

Eminem lives in the world he dreamed of, the one he threatened to create when he gave up on fitting in back in Detroit, when he birthed Slim Shady. He is a producer, one of the top rappers making music, the head of a record label, a burgeoning actor, and the owner of a clothing line. He is a perfectionist, as critical of himself as the hip-hop purists waiting for him to make a mistake.

"He's got to be under so much pressure now," says photographer Jonathan Mannion, who has shot Eminem for his last two album covers. "He's got more responsibility and so many more people interested in him and everything he does at every second of the day. That's got to wear on you, harden you a bit. You know, the Grammys was the first time that I saw him where he just didn't even seem like he wanted to be around. It was the first time I didn't see him, like, trying to hide a smile after winning an award."

"I've always felt, since my first day of rapping, that my time is ticking," Eminem told me in 2002. "The day that I made it, I felt that my time was ticking. I always feel that my next album could be my last, so I have to give it everything that I've got. And that's how I've set the standards for myself and that's how I've based my whole career, that this chance may never happen again. I invest my money, and you know, I treat every dollar like it could be my last, every album like it could be my last, every song like it could be my last. That's how I make my music."

When Eminem resurfaces, all eyes will be on him. In his absence, he leaves the legacy he longed for, the days of "wilding out and being violent" reminiscent of N.W.A and 2Pac, that was nonexistent in the hip-hop mainstream of 1999. Hip-hop tastes in 2003 are leaning again toward thug-life stylings not seen in years, indicated by the record-breaking debut sales (1.5 million copies in a week and a half) and utter industry dominance of Eminem and Dr. Dre's Shady Records artist 50 Cent. Inter-artist conflicts are starting up again, as are incidents of violence, from the tragic death of Jam Master Jay of Run-D.M.C to drive-by shootings at the offices of Violator Management (who handle 50 Cent and Busta Rhymes among others), Murder Inc. (Ja Rule), and one that nearly injured Snoop Dogg in April 2003. 50 Cent is the ultimate thug, but others are coming, like Freeway, a rough-hewn Philadelphia rapper who is signed to Jay-Z's Roc-a-Fella Records.

Even if American entertainment and morals take a turn for the puritanical, Eminem, by revealing his humanity and sharing his life, has been accepted by those he lives to bait. He may choose to lose his new fans by extreme acts of impropriety, but given the content that's already been presented, he will be hard-pressed to top himself. "Short of killing his own daughter," Sasha Frere-Jones says, "it doesn't seem like he could do anything that would repel people. He might be such a genius, though, that he is one of those people like Madonna, who have their shit so worked out and are so strong that he could become basically institutionalized in mass culture and still be transgressive and powerful enough that he will still be interesting. He probably isn't going to be like Bob Dylan, have a motorcycle accident and decide he wants to do thrash, or become Christian, which I think could be totally interesting."

A listen to the singles Eminem has recorded or rapped on between his studio albums provides some clues to the stylistic changes he is pursuing. Judging by the Benzino response tracks that Eminem recorded at the end of 2002 and his verse on "Go to Sleep" performed with DMX and Obie Trice for the *Cradle 2 the Grave* soundtrack, Eminem may continue the hardcore style of songs like "Till I Collapse" and "Soldier" from *The Eminem Show* or "The Way I Am" from *The Marshall Mathers LP.* If so, gone will be the characteristic humor, perhaps for good, leaving only the limits of Eminem's intensity.

Whether Eminem will deliver another episode of his life for us to devour, inhabited by Kim Scott, his mother, those who oppose him, or the light of his life, Hailie, is unclear. It is improbable that Eminem's private and public life will simultaneously reach the feverish peak of 2001, though the Brady / Shady Bunch conditions of Eminem's new home life could prove to be interesting fodder. An older Eminem may begin to look outward and comment on society at large more than he has in the past. A political Eminem, as moments of "Square Dance" from *The Eminem Show* indicate, would really be something. One thing Eminem has made clear is that when he has nothing left to say, he will put down the mike.

"All that Eminem has to do is just be a great rapper," says André of OutKast. "What's happened with his career, it really is a phenomenon. Him being white definitely helped a lot, but really it is a phenomenon. Just like his rapping, I listen to him rap, this white dude, and he's got perfect timing. He listened; he paid attention. He's proved that, so now he can do anything. As far as his music, he's done his work, so he can play now. I don't mean he can go and not give a fuck about music anymore, I mean he can do whatever he wants. He can change the backdrop, the musical style, the tempo, the delivery—anything."

"I think Eminem is going to have a really long, amazing career," Sia Michel says. "In terms of how many more albums he's going to make, I don't know if he'll make that many more. But the way he's dealt with something like 50 Cent and his label and the film role, I think he's going to be the white equivalent of some of the black stars who are diversified, like a Queen Latifah or an LL Cool J. He'll be someone who acts, produces, and performs."

If Eminem retired today, he would retire as a legend. He has changed hip-hop and pop culture forever, not just with his talent, but by personifying true cultural cross-pollination and the new racial paradigm in America. He honed his craft in an underground culture in which race is an issue to some, but authenticity, talent, and innovation rule all, and he brought those values to the mainstream. It is the hip-hop code by which so many live their lives in this country and around the world, as the culture's influence continues to spread.

"Hip-hop is so multicultural," Eminem said in 1999. "There's gonna be Korean rappers, Lebanese, Japanese—every culture. People are gonna start coming out of the woodwork. When you start seeing Japanese rappers coming up and you find one that's dope, it's gonna be the same thing—you're gonna be like, 'Damn, where did this motherfucker come from?'"

Eminem's creative output, at least in its most recent incarnations, is appreciated for its sophistication and technique, even by those who don't enjoy it. That is the greatest testament to Eminem's gifts. But the reaction to Eminem's evolution was truly amazing. It was an astonishing, unprecedented redefinition of an artist's public perception. There really isn't an appropriate vanguard to judge him by, no comparable context, no similar instance that is quite the same. No one can deny Eminem's talent, but his ascension in American culture in 2003 is only partly about that. The truth of it lies more in how and why the American people and the American media machine sought him out, an artist who hasn't done much to court anyone other than the hip-hop nation, and why they did so now. I'd like to think that mainstream media and mainstream America, through Eminem, is trying to understand, reach out, and learn about the predominant cultural force and minority voice that, for all of its influence, is still marginalized. Time will tell if the embrace of Eminem is an awkward first step by the middle of the road to delve deeper, perhaps even to understand the roots, the ills, and the conditions reflected in hip-hop, circumstances that are very real. If such is the case, I wonder, would a more thorough mainstream, white comprehension of hip-hop culture do more harm than good? Would it change anything in our society? Would mass awareness be limited only to entertainment, an industry controlled and regulated by far-reaching corporate conglomerates? It is a tricky road but the most prominent signpost, a starting point perhaps, is one seen clearly by all: he's blond, blue-eyed, and planted at the cross-roads. Phenomena are like hurricanes, confluences of atmospheric conditions, and so, too, is Eminem, as a person and a persona, a gathering of the forces at play in American society. Eminem emerged at exactly the right moment in exactly the right way. And he delivered. Using the expansive, universal language of hip-hop, inadvertently or not, Eminem has expressed something beyond his music, maybe just by being the most true, complete example we have in the public eye of what American society is and what it is becoming. By defining himself on his own terms and following his own lead, even when the world around him doubted, Eminem achieved the goal he set for himself: a career in rap lucrative enough to support himself and his daughter. He achieved it, and then some.

When I first spoke to Dr. Dre about Eminem, just as *The Slim Shady LP* was topping the charts in 1999 and Eminem was flying to Mexico for MTV's *Spring Break*, I asked him what he saw in Eminem's future.

"It's happening so fast that some people are saying he's going to be a fad like so many other white rappers," I said. "Do you think he is going to get the credit he deserves?"

"Yeah," Dre answered slowly in his rich baritone. "If he remains that same person he was the first day we went in the studio, in five years, he'll be as big as Michael Jackson. I'm almost positive he will, but there are those 'buts,' and those 'ifs.' But my man, he's dope and he's very humble. If that's the man he remains, he'll be fuck-ing *bigger* than Michael Jackson."

Anthony Bozza worked as a writer and editor at *Rolling Stone* from 1995 to 2002. His writing has also appeared in *Maxim*, *Elle*, *Arena* and *The Fact*. He lives in New York.

Bibliography

Aaron, Charles, "Chocolate on the Inside," *Spin*, May 1999.

Allen, Harry, "The Unbearable Whiteness of Emceeing," *The Source*, February 2003.

Baker, Soren, "Eminem, *The Slim Shady LP*," *Los Angeles Times*, 21 February 1999.

Bessman, Jim, " 'Respond' Offers Antidote to Music Hateful to Women," *Billboard*, 27 March 1999.

Bever-Callahan, Noah, "Triple Threat," *XXL*, March 2003.

Blomquist, Brian, "Chesney Wife Does a Rip-Hop Number on Eminem," *New York Post*, 14 September 2002.

Bodipo-Memba, Alejandro. "Uncle Sells a Piece of Eminem's Past," *Detroit Free Press*, 8 November 2002.

Boehlert, Eric, "Helping Eminem Sell Records," Salon.com, 14 September 2000.

——, "Slim Shady Takes a Hit from the FCC," Salon.com, 13 June 2001.

Boyd, Herb, "Rap under Attack," The Black World Today.com, 28 February 2003.

Bozza, Anthony, "Eminem Blows Up," *Rolling Stone*, 29 April 1999.

——, "Eminem: The *Rolling Stone* Interview," *Rolling Stone*, 4–11 July 2002.

Brown, Ethan, "Classless Clown," *New York Magazine*, 26 June 2000.

Browne, David, "The Eminem Show," 3 June 2002.

——, "Shock Jams, Vol. 1: *The Slim Shady LP*," *Entertainment Weekly*, 12 March 1999.

Bryant-Poulson, Scott, "Fear of a White Rapper," *The Source*, June 1999.

Campbell, Matthew, "Election No Big Deal for Tipper Gore," *Calgary Herald*, 24 September 2000.

Carioli, Carly, "Dirty Dozens: The Blackface Metal of Korn and Family," *Boston Phoenix*, 21 September 1998.

Christgau, Robert, "Consumer Guide," *Village Voice*, 17–23 March 1999.

——, "Getting Them Straight," *Village Voice*, 16–22 August 2000.

——, "Pazz & Jop Preview," *Village Voice*, 7–13 February 2000.

——, "Rap," *Playboy*, 1 July 1999.

——, "What Eminem Means—and Doesn't," *Los Angeles Times*, 18 February 2001.

——, "White American," *Village Voice*, 5–11 June 2002.

Clark, Antoine, "True Redemption," *The Source*, February 2003.

Clifton, Hugh, "*8 Mile* Goes Long Way to Changing Media's Tune about Eminem," *PR Weekly*, 2 December 2002.

Cohen, Jonathan, "Florida Mayor Prevents Eminem Appearance," Associated Press, 3 April 2002.

Considine, J. D., "An Original Hip-Hop Sound," *Baltimore Sun*, 18 March 1999.

Croal, N'Gai, "Slim Shady Sounds Off," *Newsweek*, 29 May 2000.

D, Chuck, "State of the Art 2003 . . . Hip-Hop . . . Watering the Seeds with Gasoline?," PublicEnemy.com, 1 December 2002.

——, "The War of Art," PublicEnemy.com, 3 February 2003.

Dade, Corey, "Rapper Sues Detroit over Video," *Detroit Free Press*, 15 July 2002.

Davis, Johnny, "Trouble Loves Me," *The Face*, May 2002.

DeRogatis, Jim, "Eminem, *The Eminem Show*," Salon.com, 30 May 2002.

Dowd, Maureen, "The Boomers' Crooner," *New York Times*, 24 November 2002.

Dretzka, Gary, "Red Carpet Rollout for *8 Mile* Debut," *Detroit News*, 8 November 2002.

Dukes, Rahman, Minya Oh, and Shaheem Reid, "Benzino Ignites Beef by Calling Eminem '2003 Vanilla Ice,'" MTVNews.com, 22 November 2002.

Durade, Alonso, "The Trouble with Eminem," *The Advocate*, 27 February 2001.

Dyson, Eric Michael, "Niggas Gotta Stop," *The Source*, June 1999.

Eddy, Chuck, "The Daddy Shady Show," *Village Voice*, 25–31 December 2002.

Ehrlich, Dimitri, "Eminem, *The Eminem Show*," *Vibe*, August 2002.

Elrick, M. L., "Eminem's Dirty Secrets," Salon.com, 25 July 2000.

——, "Eminem's Wife Pleads Guilty to Disorderly Conduct in Club Incident," *Detroit Free Press*, 25 October 2000.

——, "The Hometown: Eminem Driven on the Hard Streets," *Detroit Free Press*, 30 June 2000.

——, "Mathers Stressed, Her Attorney Says," *Detroit Free Press*, 12 July 2000.

"Eminem and Marilyn Manson Come under Fresh Attack ffrom the Senate; Their Name is . . . Mud," *New Musical Express*, 14 September 2000.

"Eminem's Ex in Baby Battle," *Celebrity Justice* (www.celebrityjustice.com), 10 April 2003.

"Eminem: *The Marshall Mathers LP*," *New Musical Express*, June 2001.

"Eminem vs. Benzino on Hot 97", DaveyD.com, 16 December 2002.

"Eminem's Mom Speaks," *The Pulse*, Fox News, 27 February 2003.

Ex, Kris, "*The Eminem Show*, Eminem," *Rolling Stone*, 4 July 2002.

Farber, Jim, "Once Thriving Female Musicians See Decline in Album Sales," *New York Daily News*, 14 September 2000.

——, "Shock Rapper," *New York Daily News*, 25 March 1999.

Farley, Reynolds, Sheldon Danziger, and Harry J. Holzer, *Detroit Divided*, New York: Russell Sage Foundation, 2000.

Farley, John Christopher, "Motown Motormouths," *Time*, 21 June 1999.

——, "White-Out Alert," *The Source*, June 1999.

——, "A Whiter Shade of Pale," *Time*, 29 May 2000.

Fouratt, Jim, "When Hate's the Message, Industry Is Responsible," *Billboard*, 10 June 2000.

Frere-Jones, Sasha, "Haiku for Eminem," *Da Capo Best Music Writing 2002*, New York: Da Capo Press, 2002.

Fuchs, Cynthia, "With or Without You," PopPolitics.com, June 2002.

Gabler, Neal, "For Eminem, Art Is Hype and Vice Versa," *New York Times*, 17 November 2002.

——, *Life the Movie: How Entertainment Conquered Reality*, New York: Knopf, 1998.

Gannon, Louise, "Scary? No, Eminem Is a Sweetheart," *The Express on Sunday*, 4 March 2001.

Gay and Lesbian Alliance Against Defamation, "GLAAD, Eminem, and the Grammy Nomination," *GLAAD Alert* (www.glaad.org), 2 January 2001.

——, "GLAAD to Protest Eminem Appearance at MTV Music Awards," *GLAAD Alert* (www.glaad.org), 6 September 2000.

——, "Moby Takes a Stand," *GLAAD Alert* (www.glaad.org), 22 February 2001.

——, "Musical Gay Bashing Doesn't Sound So Good," *GLAAD Alert* (www.glaad.org), 25 May 2000.

——, "Rally and Write Against Hate Lyrics," *GLAAD Alert* (www.glaad.org), 25 January 2001.

——, "Statement by the Gay and Lesbian Alliance Against Defamation Regarding Eminem," *GLAAD Alert* (www.glaad.org), 30 May 2000.

——, "Statement Regarding Elton John's Decision to Perform with Eminem at the Grammy Awards," *GLAAD Alert* (www.glaad.org), 10 February 2001.

——, "Statement Regarding Eminem's Performance at the Grammy Awards," *GLAAD Alert* (www.glaad.org), 9 February 2001.

George, Lynell, "Groping to Find a Voice for a Lost Generation," *Los Angeles Times*, 30 June 2002.

George, Nelson, *Hip Hop America*, New York: Viking Penguin, 1998.

Gilatto, Tom, Amy Mindell, Mary Green, Pam Grout, K. C. Baker, Alexandra Hardy, Ken Brailsford, "Sugarless Eminem," *People*, 24 July 2000.

Goldstein, Richard, "Celebrity Bigots," *Village Voice*, 12–18 July 2000.

——, "The Eminem Consensus," *Village Voice*, 13–19 November 2002.

——, "The Eminem Shtick," *Village Voice*, 12–18 June 2002.

Gundersen, Edna, "Eminem, We've Seen the Likes of You Before," *USA Today*, 3 June 2002.

Hall, Chris, "The Eminem Debate Part 1: Why Should Color Matter?," DaveyD.com

Hall, Jermaine, "*The Source* Hip-Hop Power 30," *The Source*, January 2003.

Hermes, Will, "Eminem Domain," *Entertainment Weekly*, 2 June 2000.

Herszenhorn, David M., "Rich States, Poor Cities, and Mighty Suburbs," *New York Times*, 19 August 2001.

Hood, John, "End Games," ReasonOnline.com.

Ingraham, Laura, "Eminem a Rebel? You Gotta Be Kidding!" MichNews.com, 13 November 2002.

Johnson Jr., Billy, "Back to the Lab: Eminem," *The Source*, May 2000.

Kenner, Rob, "13 Ways of Looking at a Whiteboy," *Vibe*, June–July 1999.

"Kimberly Mathers' Side of the Story," *Detroit Free Press*, 7 June 2000.

Klein, Amy, "Palace Cited for Allowing Risqué Video," *Detroit Free Press*, 15 August 2000.

325

Kloer, Phil, "Marketing Makeover of Eminem," Cox News Service, 13 November 2002.

Kot, Greg, "Eminem, *The Slim Shady LP*," *Chicago Tribune*, 21 March 1999.

——, "Feeding the Frenzy," *Chicago Tribune*, 9 April 1999.

Light, Alan (ed.), *The Vibe History of Hip Hop*, New York: Crown, 1999.

Lynch, Jason, Karen Brailsford, Pamela Warrick, and Amy Mindell, "Boy Next Door," *People*, 8 July 2002.

Madonna, "In Defense of a Fellow Artist," *Los Angeles Times*, February 2001.

Manolatos, Tony, "Eminem Doubles as Rap Icon, Doting Dad," *Detroit News*, November 2002.

Marcus, Greil, "Days Between Stations," *Interview*, 1 August 2000.

Mays, David, "The Front Lines," *The Source*, March 2003.

McCollum, Brian, "Anger's There, but Artistry Is the Draw," *Detroit Free Press*, 26 May 2002.

——, "*8 Mile*: Film Exaggerates the Support Early Hip-Hop Had," *Detroit Free Press*, 10 November 2002.

——, "*8 Mile* Style," *Detroit Free Press*, 11 August 2002.

——, "Eminem on Top: 2002 Brought Giant Success, Steely Focus," *Detroit Free Press*, 28 December 2002.

——, "To Hometown Roar, Eminem Goes Straight for the Gut," *Detroit Free Press*, 7 July 2000.

McCollum, Brian and John-John Williams IV, "Double Trouble for Rappers: Banned in Detroit, Busted in the Palace," *Detroit Free Press*, 8 July 2000.

McGraw, Bill, "Motor City Journal," *Detroit Free Press*, 29 October 2002.

Mecca, "Playing the Dozens," *The Source*, April 2001.

Moser, Whet, "Why Eminem Should Get the Grammy," Salon.com, 21 February 2001.

Munson, Kyle, "Reviews," *Des Moines Register*, 18 March 1999.

Murphy, Keith, "Eminem, *The Eminem Show*," *XXL*, August 2002.

Needham, Alex, "Review: *The Eminem Show*, Eminem," *New Musical Express*, 26 May 2002.

Osorio, Kim, "Eminem, *The Eminem Show*," *The Source*, August 2002.

Parales, Jon, "Pop Music's War of Words; While Eminem Is Attacked, Steely Dan Gets a Free Pass," *New York Times*, 18 February 2001.

——, "A Rapper More Gauche Than Gangsta," *New York Times*, 17 April 1999.

——, "Slim, What if You Win?" *New York Times*, 19 February 2001.

Parker, Erik, "World War of Words," *Village Voice*, 20–26 November 2002.

Passey, Charles, "Rap's Appeal Not Lost on 'Older' Critic," *Washington Times*, 19 August 2000.

"Perspectives," *Newsweek*, 16 December 2002.

Pinkser, Beth, "Eminem: Albums Not Action Figures," *New York Post*, 10 November 2002.

Powers, Ann, "Art Can Be Transporting, Even in Songs of Murder," *New York Times*, 8 July 2000.

Powers, John, "I'm Sorry Mama," *Los Angeles Weekly*, 27 December 2002.

Q, "Chicago's J.U.I.C.E. Comes '100%,'" SOHH.com, 16 February 2001.

"The Real Slim Shady Interview with Eminem's Mother," *ABC News* transcripts, 21 November 2002.

Reid, Shaheem, Minya Oh, and Sway Calloway, "Benzino Calls Eminem 'the Rap Hitler,' Says There's No Beef," MYVNews.com, 5 December 2002.

Roff, Peter, "Eminem and Lynne Cheney, "United Press International, 21 February 2001.

"Roundtable Discussion: Hip-Hop Under Attack," *The Source*, March 2003.

Saladana, Hector, "Eminem Brands His Own Rap Style," *San Antonio Express-News*, 30 June 1999.

Samuel, Anslem, "Eminem, *The Marshall Mathers LP*," *The Source*, August 2000.

Samuels, Allison, N'Gai Croal, and David Gates, "Battle for the Soul of Hip-Hop," *Newsweek*, 9 October 2000.

Sanneh, Kelefa, "Sympathy for the Devil: Eminem Pleads His Case," *The New Yorker*, 24 June 2002.

Schloss, Joe, "The Joke's on Us," *Seattle Weekly*, 15 April 1999.

Schmitt, Ben, "Counterclaim Is Filed by Eminem in Divorce," *Detroit Free Press*, 29 March 2001.

——, "Eminem Divorce Case Is under a Gag Order," *Detroit Free Press*, 13 June 2001.

——, "Eminem's Wife Tries to Take Own Life," *Detroit Free Press*, 10 July 2000.

——, "Mr and Mrs. Slim Shady Call Off Divorce," *Detroit Free Press*, 15 December 2000.

Selvin, Joel and David Marsh (eds.), *Sky and the Family Stone: An Oral History*, New York: Avon Books, 1998.

Serpick, Evan, " 'Show' Business," *Entertainment Weekly*, 20 May 2002.

Shine North, Kim, "Eminem to Share Custody of Child," *Detroit Free Press*, 30 August 2000.

Simmons, Russell with Nelson George, *Life and Def: Sex, Drugs, Money and God*, New York: Crown, 2001.

Smith, R. J., "Trailer Park White Boy Crossover Dreams," *Village Voice*, 6–12 November 2002.

Steele, Shelby, "The Age of White Guilt," *Harper's Magazine*, November 2002.

——, *A Dream Deferred: The Second Betrayal of Black Freedom in America*, New York: HarperCollins, 1998.

——, "Notes from the Hip-Hop Underground," *Wall Street Journal*, 31 March 2001.

Strauss, Neil, "Eminem Grabs Spotlight, but Steely Dan Wins Best Album," *New York Times*, 22 February 2001.

——, New Eminem Walks Right out of Stores," *New York Times*, 28 May 2002.

——, "A New Look at Eminem," *New York Times*, 26 December 2001.

——, "Seeking Truth about Eminem," *New York Times*, 21 December 2000.

——, "Will the Real Voters Please Stand Up?" *New York Times*, 14 February 2001.

Strong, Nolan, "Benzino Associates Convicted in Assault of NBA Player," AllHipHop.com, 8 November 2002.

Takahashi, Corey, "Rap Sheet," *Entertainment Weekly*, 16 June 2000.

Thigpen, David E., "Raps, in Blue," *Time*, 5 April 1999.

Tindal, K. B., "Ray Benzino: Interesting Conflicts," HipHopDX.com, 21 November 2002.

Toré, "Review: *The Marshall Mathers LP*, Eminem," *Rolling Stone*, June–July 2000.

"Vice President's Wife Continues to Speak Out against Eminem," Associated Press, 20 February 2001.

Vineyard, Jennifer, "Did Eminem Bite French Composer's Beat?" MTVNews.com, 4 April 2002.

White, Timothy, "Music to My Ears, Eminem: The Best Way to 'Respond,'" *Billboard*, 6 March 1999.

Williams, Kevin, M., "Eminem at the House of Blues," *Chicago Sun-Times*, 8 April 1999.

Index